P9-CEF-650

2/25/14

MORRIS AREA PUBLIC LIBRARY
604 Liberty St.
Morris, IL 60450
(815) 942-6880

Where Nobody
Knows Your Name

ALSO BY JOHN FEINSTEIN

One on One: Behind the Scenes with the Greats in the Game

Moment of Glory: The Year Underdogs Ruled Golf

Living on the Black: Two Pitchers, Two Teams, One Season to Remember

Tales from Q School: Inside Golf's Fifth Major

Last Dance: Behind the Scenes at the Final Four

Next Man Up: A Year Behind the Lines in Today's NFL

Let Me Tell You a Story: A Lifetime in the Game

Caddy for Life: The Bruce Edwards Story

Open: Inside the Ropes at Bethpage Black

The Punch: One Night, Two Lives, and the Fight That
Changed Basketball Forever

The Last Amateurs: Playing for Glory and Honor in
Division I College Basketball

The Majors: In Pursuit of Golf's Holy Grail

The First Coming: Tiger Woods, Master or Martyr?

A March to Madness: The View from the Floor in
the Atlantic Coast Conference

A Civil War: Army vs. Navy

Winter Games

A Good Walk Spoiled: Days and Nights on the PGA Tour

Play Ball: The Life and Troubled Times of Major League Baseball

Running Mates

Hard Courts

Forever's Team

A Season Inside: One Year in College Basketball

A Season on the Brink: A Year with Bob Knight and the Indiana Hoosiers

Doubleday

NEW YORK LONDON TORONTO SYDNEY AUCKLAND

Where Nobody Knows Your Name

◆

LIFE IN THE
MINOR LEAGUES OF BASEBALL

◆

John Feinstein

MORRIS AREA LIBRARY

Copyright © 2014 by John Feinstein

All rights reserved. Published in the United States by Doubleday, a division of Random House LLC, New York, and in Canada by Random House of Canada Limited, Toronto, Penguin Random House companies.

www.doubleday.com

DOUBLEDAY and the portrayal of an anchor with a dolphin are registered trademarks of Random House LLC.

Book design by Maria Carella
Jacket design by John Fontana
Jacket illustration © Mike Janes / Four Seam Images

Library of Congress Cataloging-in-Publication Data
Feinstein, John.
Where nobody knows your name : life in the minor leagues of baseball /
John Feinstein.
pages cm
1. Minor league baseball—United States—History.   I. Title.
GV875.A1F37   2014
796.357'64—dc23   2013030645

ISBN 978-0-385-53593-9 (hardcover)
ISBN 978-0-385-53594-6 (eBook)

MANUFACTURED IN THE UNITED STATES OF AMERICA

1 3 5 7 9 10 8 6 4 2

First Edition

3 9957 00181 2730

This book is dedicated
to the memory of Rob Ades.

A friend in deed.

CONTENTS

CAST OF CHARACTERS

SCOTT ELARTON—Pitcher. A one-time first round draft pick who won seventeen games for the Houston Astros at the age of twenty-four, his career was brought to a halt in 2008 by injuries and drinking issues. In August 2011, Elarton realized he wasn't finished with baseball, and he talked himself into a tryout with the Philadelphia Phillies . . . that ended up exceeding his wildest expectations.

RON JOHNSON—Manager, Norfolk Tides (Triple-A team of the Baltimore Orioles). Johnson is fifty-seven and has spent most of his adult life in the minor leagues. He played in twenty-two major-league games and likes to say, "I'm in the twilight of a mediocre career." It is that approach that makes him a perfect Triple-A manager, because he loves coming to the ballparks—any ballpark—every day. Johnson's other saying about Triple-A life is very direct: "If you don't like it here, do a better job."

JON LINDSEY—Designated hitter. Lindsey is a footnote in baseball history: He had played more minor-league games without a major-league call-up than any player in history. In 2010, his unwanted streak came to an end. Lindsey liked to say he was "an accident away," from a return to the major leagues. "Not rooting for anybody to get hurt," he would say. "But people *do* get hurt. It's just a fact."

MARK LOLLO—Umpire. At thirty years old, Lollo had finally made it to the major-league "call-up list" in 2011, meaning he got to work a handful of games at the big-league level and was in line to move up to the majors in the near future. But 2012 was more difficult: there were fewer call-ups and there were questions about his umpiring future.

NATE McLOUTH—Outfielder, Baltimore Orioles. A perfect example of the vagaries of baseball life, McLouth went from being an All-Star in Pittsburgh in 2008 to Atlanta to Pittsburgh, where in 2012 he was released while hitting .140. He wondered if his career might be over before he got a chance in Triple-A Norfolk and made the most of it, ending up as the Orioles starting left fielder in the 2012 playoffs. In a five-month period he went from out of baseball to signing a $2 million contract to play in Baltimore in 2013.

CHARLIE MONTOYO—Manager, Durham Bulls (Triple-A team of the Tampa Bay Rays). At forty-seven, Montoyo is considered one of Triple-A's best managers—his team has reached the postseason six times in seven seasons in Durham, and the Rays loved the way he develops players. But he hasn't been able to get a serious sniff for a major-league job, even though he's been successful and is highly respected.

SCOTT PODSEDNIK—Outfielder. A World Series hero in 2005, hitting a walk-off home run in game 2 for the Chicago White Sox, helping lead to their four-game sweep of the Houston Astros. Two years later he was looking for a job. He became a baseball wanderer, going from Kansas City to Chicago to Philadelphia to Boston—getting hurt and dropping back to Triple-A along the way. He began 2012 in Lehigh Valley, Triple-A team of the Philadelphia Phillies, thinking he should retire, and ending up on a head-spinning baseball odyssey.

CHRIS SCHWINDEN—Pitcher. He lived through one of the most remarkable seasons in baseball history in 2012, but not for the reasons a player would want his season to be considered remarkable. In a five-week period he was released and then picked up by four different organizations. In thirty-seven days he went from New York to Buffalo to Las Vegas to Columbus to Scranton Wilkes-Barre and—at last—back to Buffalo, where he finally found a home that wasn't a hotel room.

BRETT TOMKO—Pitcher. A one-hundred-game winner in the major leagues. Tomko came all the way back from a serious shoulder injury suffered while he was winning his one-hundredth game in 2009. He started over in rookie league ball where he was—his words—"absolutely terrible"—but pitched his way back to the major leagues in Texas two years later. He started the 2012 season in Louisville, Triple-A team of the Cincinnati Reds.

Where Nobody
Knows Your Name

Introduction

JUNE 2, 2012

On a spectacular late spring evening in Allentown, Pennsylvania, a sellout crowd of 10,100 people packed Coca-Cola Park, the five-year-old stadium that has served as the home for the Lehigh Valley Iron-Pigs since 2008. Dusk was rapidly approaching. The temperature was seventy degrees with just a hint of breeze. It was a Saturday night, and clearly the ballpark was the place to be in the town of just under 120,000 that was made famous by Billy Joel's 1982 ballad.

Sellouts, or near sellouts, have become commonplace since the franchise that once resided in Ottawa as the Lynx moved to Allentown and became the Lehigh Valley IronPigs. And with the Pawtucket Red Sox in town for a twi-night doubleheader, the park was jumping with noise as the second game began.

The IronPigs had just, thirty minutes earlier, come from behind for a 5–4 win in game one, and game two had also started promisingly for the home team. The PawSox had been forced to start Tony Peña Jr.—normally a reliever—because the scheduled starter, Ross Ohlendorf, had opted out of his contract a day earlier to sign with the San Diego Padres.

Such is life in the minor leagues: today's starter for Pawtucket could become tomorrow's starter for Arizona. Or, just as often, it happens the other way around.

Peña had lasted three innings. Arnie Beyeler, the Pawtucket manager, would have taken Peña out at that point even if he hadn't given up six runs. He had thrown fifty-four pitches, well beyond the number a manager normally wants to see a reliever throw. And so, when the IronPigs came to the plate in the bottom of the fourth leading 6–4, Beyeler went to his bullpen.

———

In every minor-league ballpark, there is no such thing as nothing going on between innings. Fans expect entertainment that goes beyond hits, runs, and errors, and they get it.

There are all sorts of contests for fans to participate in, and there is always some kind of entertainment going on to distract those in the stands. To put it in perspective, one of the biggest disappointments of the 2012 season in Durham was when George Jetson Night was rained out.

In Allentown, one of the more popular fan-participation contests is called Whack an Intern. And yes, it is family entertainment . . . not what you might otherwise think. A large box with four holes cut in the top is brought out to the third-base line. Four of the Pigs' summer interns crawl beneath the box. Two fans are selected and handed plastic bats. Each time an intern pops his head out of one of the four holes, the fans attempt to whack him. The fan who connects most is the winner.

While almost everyone in the ballpark was paying rapt attention to Whack an Intern, the reliever called into the game by manager Beyeler jogged in from the left-field bullpen. When the public address announcer introduced him, there wasn't a hint of a reaction from the crowd. The plastic bats ruled at that moment.

The relief pitcher was Mark Prior, who had last pitched in a major-league baseball game on August 10, 2006. In the almost six years since then, he had pitched a total of forty-eight innings (an average of just eight innings per season) in the minor leagues, for three different organizations—San Diego, Texas, and the New York Yankees. He was thirty-one years old, and there was no way his presence on the mound, throwing his warm-up pitches, was going to distract anyone from the announcement of who had won Whack an Intern.

This was remarkable only if you happened to remember who Mark Prior had once been. In 2001, coming out of USC, he had been the No. 2 pick in the amateur draft in all of baseball. The only reason he wasn't No. 1 was that he had notified the Minnesota Twins—who owned the No. 1 pick—that he didn't want to play for them. The Twins drafted local hero Joe Mauer instead . . . a pick that ended up working out just fine for them.

Prior signed with the Cubs for a $10.5 million bonus, a record for a first contract that wasn't broken until 2009, when Stephen Strasburg signed with the Washington Nationals for $15 million. Prior was in the majors by 2002, and a year later, at the age of twenty-two, he won eighteen games for the Chicago Cubs and finished third in the Cy Young Award voting in the National League. He and Kerry Wood had led the Cubs to the National League Central title, and to within one win of the team's first World Series appearance since 1945.

Prior was the pitcher on the mound during one of the more infamous moments in Cubs history—when Steve Bartman made his grab at Luis Castillo's foul ball in the eighth inning of game six of the League Championship Series that year. If Moises Alou had caught the ball, the Cubs, leading 3–0 behind Prior's pitching, would have been four outs from the World Series.

The Cubs never got there, though, and Prior never became the star he was universally expected to become in the eyes of those who knew baseball. In 2003, Prior was to the game what Stephen Strasburg was to baseball in 2012—except that he'd never had Tommy John surgery on his pitching elbow.

For Prior, the injuries began a year later; a torn Achilles started it, and then they came one after another. He stayed healthy enough to win eleven games with the Cubs in 2005 but went on the disabled list with a strained shoulder in August 2006, after having been on the DL for two months earlier in the season. When he did get on the mound that year, he was as miserable as he had been brilliant three years earlier: a 1-6 record with a 7.21 ERA.

After deciding against surgery in the off-season, he pitched one inning in the minor leagues the next year before being forced to undergo surgery. The Cubs released him at the end of 2007, which started his minor-league odyssey: San Diego for two injury-plagued seasons, during which he never pitched; Texas for one; the Yankees for one. He pitched a total of twenty-one times in those four seasons, never staying healthy long enough to make a serious run at getting back to the majors.

He had signed with the Red Sox in May 2012 and had been working in extended spring training in Florida to get his arm in shape. Now, exactly one month after his signing, the Red Sox had sent him to Allentown to join the PawSox. His hope was to get to Boston as a middle reliever. That would be a victory—even if it was a long, long way from the days when he had been called "the future of pitching."

On this evening in Allentown, Prior's reality was Whack an Intern.

———

The names are there every single day in the newspapers, listed under the heading "Transactions." The type size for the list of transactions is a small font used for statistical data, commonly known as agate. On almost any given day of the year in baseball, lives change . . . and those changes are recorded in the agate.

Scott Elarton. Brett Tomko. Chris Schwinden. Scott Podsednik. Nate McLouth. John Lindsey. Charlie Montoyo. Ron Johnson. Mark Lollo.

Nine names that serious baseball fans might—or might not—recognize. Three pitchers, two outfielders, a designated hitter, two managers, and an umpire. Each spent all, or most, of the 2012 baseball season playing in the International League at the Triple-A level, with the exception of McLouth, who went from the majors to "released" to Triple-A and back to the majors again.

All, with the exception of Lollo—umpires don't rate making the agate when their lives change—have appeared in the agate multiple times during their careers. Schwinden appeared eleven times . . . during 2012 alone. Their stories are symbolic of what life is like for *most* baseball players. Only the most gifted and fortunate make it to the major leagues and then stay there until the day they retire.

Jeff Torborg, who spent most of his playing career as a backup catcher and then went on to manage the Cleveland Indians, Chicago White Sox, New York Mets, Montreal Expos, and Florida Marlins, was asked once during the winter meetings if a trade about to be announced by the Mets was the "big one" (there had been rumors about a major trade throughout the week).

"To the guys involved it is," Torborg answered.

Mark Prior appeared in agate type three times during 2012: "Signed to a minor league contract by the Boston Red Sox"; "Called up to Triple-A Pawtucket from extended spring training"; and, finally, in August, "Released by the Boston Red Sox."

In every baseball season, there are thousands of these "transactions" that go virtually unnoticed. Every once in a while someone will glance at the agate section and see a name like Prior's—or Miguel Tejada or Dontrelle Willis—and think, "So that's what happened to him," and then move on with his daily routine.

But every single one of those transactions is life changing for those involved. It can be the zenith or the nadir for a baseball player: a moment of overwhelming joy or gut-wrenching disappointment. It means families being uprooted—sometimes for no apparent reason—and it always has repercussions that go beyond the player himself. When someone gets called up, it means someone gets sent down, and three or four guys who *think* they should be called up are left to deal with yet another letdown and to ask the most ever-present question that floats through Triple-A clubhouses: "Why not me?"

A season of Triple-A baseball is filled with hundreds of stories. Some are more compelling—or surprising, poignant, funny, or remarkable—than most. This book is about a handful of men who run the gamut of life in Triple-A; men who have been stars and have fallen; men who have been rich and then far from rich; men who have aspired to those heights and never quite reached them.

Elarton. Tomko. Schwinden. Podsednik. McLouth. Lindsey. Montoyo. Johnson. Lollo.

Scott Elarton was a first-round draft pick coming out of high school—someone who won seventeen games for the Houston Astros at the age of twenty-four and then crashed to earth, brought down by injuries and by, as he puts it, "living the major-league life."

Brett Tomko was good enough to win a remarkable hundred major-league games, but in 2012, at the age of thirty-nine, he found himself looking for work at the Triple-A level because he wasn't ready to give the ball up just yet.

Chris Schwinden started 2013 with exactly a hundred wins fewer than Tomko . . . but his odyssey in 2012 was one matched by few players *ever* in baseball history.

Even those who have had success—great success—can find themselves wondering what they have done to deserve the karma that seems to chase them. In 2005, Scott Podsednik experienced a moment only a handful of players have ever gotten to experience: he hit a walk-off home run in a World Series game and sprinted in from center field to join one of sport's most joyous celebrations after the final out in the Chicago White Sox' four-game sweep of the Houston Astros. Seven years later, during 2012, he walked away from the game twice—only to return twice, believing if he could just stay healthy he could still contribute on the major-league level.

Nate McLouth believed the same thing, even after he was released in May 2012 by the Pittsburgh Pirates. His journey took him from the top to the bottom and back again, all in a season. His was one of the stories that keep minor leaguers going.

Players aren't the only ones who live the minor-league life dreaming of the majors. Charlie Montoyo, the Durham Bulls' manager, has spent most of his twenty-six professional baseball years in the minors—interrupted only by a one-month stint in Montreal, during which he got to the plate five times.

Ron Johnson also played in the major leagues: for twenty-two games on three different occasions. Then he worked his way through the minor leagues to make it to Boston as a first-base coach in 2010, only to find himself victimized by the post-collapse purge of 2011. He returned to Triple-A, in Norfolk, where he cheerfully tells those who complain about life at that level, "If you don't like it here, do a better job."

Both Montoyo and Johnson know firsthand that traveling on Triple-A buses or staying in three-star motels is far from the worst thing that can happen to someone, which is why you aren't likely to hear either one of them complain . . . ever.

Umpires live the same life—except that they don't have any home games. Like players and managers and coaches, they have beaten the odds by getting to Triple-A, but they are still not where they want to be. The big money and the luxurious life for them also exist only at the big-league level. Mark Lollo was generally considered the top umpire in the International League in 2012. He had worked major-league games and felt he was on the cusp of achieving that goal. But he still wasn't there, and whether he would get there was not something he could control. Which made for a lot of tossing and turning at night.

Each, in his own way, defines the struggle of people who are extremely good at what they do—but *not* as good as they want to be at given moments. Often, when Triple-A players do finally get to the majors—or back to the majors—it is so overwhelmingly meaningful that tears, not words, explain how they feel.

And on some occasions, it takes only a few choice words to explain what it means to a player to climb that mountain. As Nate McLouth stood in left field at Camden Yards on a brisk October night, just months after being released by the Pittsburgh Pirates, tossing a ball with center fielder Adam Jones as the Orioles prepared to play the Yankees in game one of the 2012 American League Division Series, his thoughts were very simple.

"This," he thought, "is pretty cool."

————

It is stories like the one McLouth wrote in 2012 that keep baseball players grinding through those moments when they see their names not in lights but in agate. The grind is different for everyone, and it is almost always agonizing for one reason or another.

Pitching for the Oakland Athletics, Brett Tomko won his hundredth game as a major leaguer in September 2009 and walked off the mound in Texas thinking he had blown out his shoulder and would never pitch again. Trying to throw a fastball past Chris Davis, he had felt something pop in his shoulder at the start of the ninth inning and had finished the game throwing strictly breaking pitches because he thought his arm might fall off if he tried to throw a fastball.

Tomko was right about his shoulder—he had blown it out. Not wanting his last baseball memory to be walking off a mound with his arm hanging limp, he came back after the surgery and dropped all the way back to rookie-league ball briefly, and then to Class A, pitching in Stockton, California, against a bunch of kids who seemed to hit rockets off every pitch he threw. In six starts he pitched to an ERA of 7.52.

"I couldn't get anyone out," he said. "It was embarrassing. There was almost no one watching, but a lot of those who were kept screaming at me, 'Go home, old man. You're done.'"

Tomko knew their reaction to the pitcher they were seeing at that moment was understandable. But he still believed that locked inside somewhere was the pitcher who had not only won a hundred games in the major leagues but also pitched there for fourteen seasons, been given the ball as a starter 266 times, and struck out 1,209 batters in 1,816 major-league innings.

"The doctors had told me it would take a while to feel healthy again," he said. "Of course I'm like everyone else who has ever been any good: I thought once the pain was gone, I'd be who I was before the injury. It's never that simple. I still thought I could make it back. But I also thought maybe I owed it to my wife and kids to just face the reality of it all and go home."

His wife talked him into not coming home. Slowly, Brett Tomko began to become again the pitcher who had spent all those years getting big-league hitters out. He worked his way back up the minor-league ladder, reaching Triple-A Sacramento by the end of the season. And yet he still wasn't back. The best offer he could get for 2011 was a minor-league contract from the Texas Rangers. He took it, even though he knew he had no chance to make the team out of training camp; he hadn't even been invited to major-league camp.

"I can't tell you how many times I was ready to hang it up," he said. "We'd had twins four days after I hurt my shoulder in '09, and I missed them every day I was away. But I couldn't walk away."

On April 20, with the season barely under way, the Rangers called Tomko up, needing some middle-relief help. As luck would have it, his first appearance in the majors was on the same mound where he had hurt himself nineteen months earlier.

"I came into the game and got through the inning, got the side one-two-three," he said. "It felt like it was supposed to feel, like I was a major-league pitcher again.

"After I got the third out, I started to walk to the dugout, and it hit me that I had made it all the way back—that I hadn't let the day I got hurt be the end. I got two steps into the dugout and lost it—I mean completely lost it. I didn't want everyone to see me crying like that, so I went straight into the runway where there's a small bathroom, went inside, and locked the door.

"It took me a while to get my act together. After a couple minutes [manager] Ron Washington came and knocked on the door. 'Big guy, you okay in there?' he said. 'You all right?'

"I told him I was fine. When I came out, he was smiling because he knew what had happened. He didn't say another word. He didn't have to. I knew he got it."

Tomko smiled at the memory. "Sometimes going full circle in life isn't a good thing. In this case, it was as satisfying as anything I've ever done."

———

The most poignant stories in sports are never about the multimillionaires who make their games look easy but about the guys who love their games, even though they often fail while playing them.

The exploits of LeBron James or Tiger Woods or Roger Federer or Miguel Cabrera may awe us, but they hardly produce a lump in the throat. But when Adam Greenberg gets a second at-bat in the major leagues, seven years after being hit in the head during his first at-bat, we all stop and watch and smile and get a chill. When Jimmy Morris makes it to the major leagues at the age of thirty-five—after blowing out his arm and leaving baseball entirely to become a high school coach—and then pitches a total of fifteen innings over two years, it not only becomes a Disney movie; it becomes one that leaves us wiping tears away during the final scene.

What made *The Rookie* special was that it was real—you couldn't make it up. There isn't a baseball player alive, especially among those who have had to fight to get to the major leagues, who hasn't seen the movie at some point. Without fail, when Morris's story comes up, they shake their heads in amazement because they all understand how remarkable it is that he pitched those fifteen innings in the majors.

"Fifteen minutes in the majors means you're a great baseball player," said Detroit Tigers manager Jim Leyland—who never got his fifteen minutes above the Triple-A level. "People just can't understand how good you have to be to get there at all."

Those who have been there and come back, and those who have gotten only as far as Leyland got, know what it means to get that call, to get called in to the manager's office and to hear those three simple words: "You're going up."

"No one grows up playing baseball pretending that they're pitching or hitting in Triple-A," said Chris Schwinden, who in 2012 pitched for five different teams in a period of five weeks. "No one goes into his backyard and says to himself, 'Here's Schwinden on the mound for the Buffalo Bisons.'"

He smiled. "No one dreams of pitching in a minor-league park when it's forty degrees at first pitch and there are two thousand people in the stands. And yet almost all of us do it—some for a little while, some for a long while. The reality is almost always different than the dream."

Schwinden is in many ways symbolic of the reality. In 2012 he was called up to the major leagues on three different occasions. He was also released by four different teams. While his case may be extreme, being moved from team to team and level to level is something many—if not most—baseball players go through. Almost without exception they all spend time in the minor leagues. All of them—even those who go on to be multimillion-dollar-a-year stars—can remember that first call-up. For others, who dance with stardom and then return to the minors, getting called back up may be even more gratifying because the first time around they take it for granted. For some, a brief trip to the majors, even if it lasts only a few days, is the highlight they carry with them long after they have retired. And there are others who never get that call even once.

As Schwinden points out, they all grow up dreaming of playing in the big leagues—in the massive ballparks with forty thousand or more fans screaming their names as they make a heroic play on the mound, at the plate, or in the field. No one dreams about playing in Triple-A.

Charlie Montoyo has managed the Durham Bulls since 2007. He has spent most of his life in the minors and still hopes his chance to prove himself in the majors will come someday soon. Ron Johnson, who returned to the minors as Norfolk's manager in 2012, hopes for the same chance.

"The good news is we've got a great bus," Johnson said one night prior to a nine-hour trip to Gwinnett. "Nobody beats our bus."

Both men love their game and are devoted to it but have seen firsthand how unimportant it can feel when real life—in the form of crises involving their children—has intervened. Montoyo keeps a photograph of his two children inside his cap at all times as a reminder to himself that a missed umpire's call isn't *that* important.

"Doesn't mean I don't argue," he said, smiling. "But I try to remember that the ump has a family too, and he's probably trying just as hard as I am."

There are so many stories about minor-league life that telling even a handful of them in one book is virtually impossible. But some stand out because they are about persevering. A lot of baseball is about persevering.

"It's very easy to say, 'Wait a minute, I'm a big leaguer, I don't belong here,'" Scott Elarton said of minor-league life. "But the game usually gives you what you deserve—good or bad. And you realize, especially when you get away from it, that you're going to live a lot of your life as an ex-ballplayer. That's why a lot of us figure out that hanging on for as long as you can possibly play the game is a good thing. It really isn't hanging on—it's savoring what you've got."

Of course *that* is easier said than done.

————

Every player knows how much the first call-up means. Which is why there is almost always a celebration of some kind in a Triple-A clubhouse when someone gets the call for the first time. Everyone understands what an extraordinary moment it is in a player's life. Those who have been called up remember what it meant to them; those who have not know how much they want it to happen.

J. C. Boscan's story isn't quite the same as Jimmy Morris's, because he never stopped playing. He signed with the Atlanta Braves in the summer of 1996 at the age of sixteen and spent the next fourteen seasons bouncing around the minor leagues. He first reached Triple-A in 2002 but couldn't take the next step, because, even though he was a solid catcher, he just couldn't hit well enough to be regarded as a serious big-league prospect.

He left the Braves for a couple of years to play in Double-A and Triple-A for the Milwaukee Brewers and the Cincinnati Reds. He signed back with the Braves in 2008, because the people running the organization had so much respect for him as a clubhouse leader and someone who would set a good example for younger players that they were willing to bring him back—knowing he was unlikely ever to play in Atlanta.

Two years later, playing in Gwinnett, he had his best offensive season. Nothing spectacular, but a career-high five home runs and a batting average of .250—higher than his lifetime average of .222. Late in August, Boscan began to hear that he might be on the September call-up list.

Every year on September 1, major-league teams can expand their rosters to as many as forty players (the regular roster size is twenty-five). Rarely do they bring up more than five or six players. Those who are brought up usually provide depth in the bullpen or on the bench or are young players being given a taste of the major leagues. Every once in a while, a team will give a player a "good-guy promotion"—bring him up so he can make major-league pay for a month as a reward for being a good guy and not complaining about being stuck in the minor leagues.

Boscan had been in the minors for fourteen years and had never seen the inside of a big-league clubhouse except during spring training. At thirty, he was a long way from being the bright-eyed teenage prospect the Braves had brought to the United States from Venezuela in 1997.

On August 31, the word in the Gwinnett clubhouse was that the Braves were going to make their call-ups after the game. Boscan remembers being more nervous that night than at any other time in his career.

"I walked on the field that night, and all I could think was, 'If I don't get the call tonight, it's never going to come,'" he remembered. "I honestly thought this was my last shot and my best shot to ever get to the majors. I could barely keep my mind on the game. All I could think about was what was going to happen after it was over. I was praying to God to let this be my time."

When the game ended, Boscan sat in front of his locker and picked at the postgame meal. Hitting coach Jamie Dismuke had been designated by manager Dave Brundage to bring players into his office so they could be told they were going to make the thirty-seven-mile trip down I-85 to Turner Field. As Dismuke worked his way around the clubhouse, that thirty-seven miles felt more like a million to Boscan.

The first player called in was Freddie Freeman, the twenty-year-old phenom, who was hitting .319 and was considered a lock call-up. He came out of Brundage's office with a huge smile on his face and was engulfed in congratulations.

Dismuke continued his rounds. One player after another walked around the corner to Brundage's office and came out wearing the giveaway grin. The congratulations continued. No one had made a move to leave because this was a happy night—for those going up.

Six players had gone in to see Brundage—entering as Gwinnett Braves and coming out as Atlanta Braves—and there was no sign of Dismuke for a couple of minutes. Boscan's heart sank. That was it—six guys. His dream had died.

Dismuke appeared again, this time walking directly toward Boscan.

"Skip wants to see you, JC," he said. He wasn't smiling. Boscan panicked. Maybe Brundage had gotten the good news out of the way first, and now he was going to let Boscan know that the team needed him in Double-A to work with a young catcher. Or, maybe he was being released.

Brundage was, in fact, preparing that kind of speech for Boscan. "I was going to look very sad and tell him that sometimes things don't turn out the way you want them to in baseball," he said. "But when he walked in here, he was shaking. I couldn't go through with it."

The entire Gwinnett staff was in the room when Boscan walked in.

"Have a seat, JC," Brundage said, trying to look grim.

Boscan sat on the couch across from Brundage's desk.

"You ever been to the big leagues?" he asked—knowing the answer.

"No," Boscan said, shaking his head.

Brundage couldn't keep up the charade.

"I was going to mess with you, JC, but I can't do it," he said, feeling himself start to choke up. "This is your day. You're going up."

Boscan burst into tears. Everyone else in the room was fighting to hold tears back.

"I've been a minor-league manager a long time," Brundage said. "I can honestly say that was the best moment I've ever had."

After Boscan had thanked everyone and shaken everyone's hand and been hugged all around, he walked out of the office. Brundage's office is in a hallway that leads to the clubhouse area where the players' lockers are located. When Boscan turned the corner to reenter the locker area, the entire team was waiting for him.

"It was like the last scene in *The Rookie*," he said. "The whole team was in on it. They all knew and they were all waiting there for me. The feeling I had when I saw them all and they all started clapping and then cheering and hugging me is something I'll never forget for as long as I live."

Boscan was in the agate the next day around the country, one of seven players mentioned in the same paragraph, amid the call-ups made by all thirty major-league teams.

"ATLANTA BRAVES—CALLED UP CATCHER J. C. BOSCAN FROM TRIPLE-A GWINNETT."

This book is about J. C. Boscan.

And all those like him.

1

Scott Elarton

STARTING OVER

There is no aspect of baseball that has changed more in recent years than spring training. Or, more specifically, spring training facilities.

Once, the winter homes of most baseball teams were old, dank, and cramped—minor-league facilities that served for six weeks each year as the headquarters for an entire baseball organization. The ballparks were older too, havens for fans who wanted to get close to players, but often creaking from age with outfield fences that looked as if they had been constructed shortly after Abner Doubleday invented the game.

Even in Vero Beach, where in 1947 the Brooklyn Dodgers set up what was then the model for a spring training facility—Holman Stadium and the facilities around it became known as Dodgertown— there was the feeling of being in a time warp. The dugouts never even had roofs. They were just open-air cutouts along the baselines where players either sunbathed or baked—depending on one's point of view—during games.

Through the years, almost all the older facilities have disappeared. Dodgertown sits empty now during the spring, used on occasion by local high school teams while the Dodgers train in a brand-new multimillion-dollar headquarters built for them in Arizona. Because spring training has become a big business, local governments in both Florida and Arizona have lined up to build modern baseball palaces for teams, complete with every possible amenity players could ask for—from massive weight-training areas to sparkling training fields to sun-drenched stadiums that look like miniature versions of the big-league parks the teams play in once the season begins.

There is no better example of the modern spring training facility than Bright House Field, which has been the spring home of the Philadelphia Phillies since 2004, when it was built for $28 million to replace Jack Russell Memorial Stadium, which had been the Phillies winter home since 1955. Jack Russell, as it was known in the Clearwater area, was the classic old spring training spot: the stadium was made of wood, and the paint was peeling in every corner of the old place when the Phillies moved out.

The old spring training clubhouses—in baseball no one talks about locker rooms, they are clubhouses—were cramped and crowded with players practically on top of one another, especially at the start of camp, when between fifty and sixty players might be in a room designed to hold no more than thirty to thirty-five lockers.

Jack Russell was one of those dingy old clubhouses. The Phillies' clubhouse at Bright House Field could not be more different. It is spread out and spacious with room—easily—for fifty lockers. There are several rooms off the main area that are strictly off-limits to anyone but Phillies personnel, meaning players can rest or eat their post-workout or postgame meals in complete privacy without tripping over unwanted media members or anyone else who might have access to the main clubhouse area.

Even though he had been out of baseball for most of four years, Scott Elarton felt completely comfortable walking into the Phillies' clubhouse in February 2012. Many of the players had no idea who he was because professional athletes' memories rarely extend back more than about fifteen minutes. In baseball world 2012, Cal Ripken Jr.—who retired in 2001—was an old-timer who played in a lot of games, Willie Mays is a distant memory, and Babe Ruth is the name of a league for teenage players.

Elarton had won fifty-six games as a major-league pitcher in spite of numerous injuries, including seventeen for a bad Houston Astros team in 2000. But he hadn't been in a major-league baseball clubhouse since 2008 and even though he stood out at six feet seven, a lot of players had no idea who he was.

"It's not like anybody looked at me and thought I was some hotshot prospect," he said with a laugh. "I probably look every bit of thirty-six."

Seven months earlier, even Rubén Amaro Jr., the Phillies' general manager, hadn't recognized Elarton. That was in August, when Elarton had called to him while standing on the field during batting practice prior to a game between the Phillies and the Colorado Rockies. Elarton was watching BP with his seven-year-old son when he noticed Amaro standing a few yards away and, on a complete whim, decided to try to talk to him.

"I had taken my son to the game because I was friends with several guys on the Phillies: Raúl Ibañez, Roy Oswalt, Cliff Lee," Elarton said. "They set us up with tickets. The town we live in is about an hour from Denver, so we drove over. They'd also arranged for us to have field passes, which I knew would be cool for Jake. We went onto the field, and we were standing with all the other people with field passes behind this barrier they set up so that you don't get too close to the players or bother them while they're hitting.

"I'd seen that barrier a couple thousand times in ballparks—but always from the other side. I had never even thought about what it might be like to be on the field like that in street clothes and *not* be a player. I felt completely humiliated. I just hated being there.

"Then I saw Rubén standing nearby. I'd never met him, but I certainly knew him. So I called his name. He looked over at me, and I could tell right away that he had no idea who I was. But he's a polite guy, so he walked over to where we were standing."

Elarton was right; Amaro hadn't recognized him. "I knew who Scott Elarton was," Amaro said. "He'd pitched too long for me not to know who he was. But he had lost some weight since I'd last seen him pitch, and it had been a few years. But when he said, 'Rubén, I'm Scott Elarton,' it came right back to me."

Elarton had lost weight—a lot of weight. After he had stopped playing in 2008, he had ballooned from 260 pounds to just under 300 pounds after having surgery on his foot. "I didn't exercise at all for a while after the surgery," he said. "I wasn't doing anything at all to stay in shape. On the day I got on the scale and weighed 299, I knew I had to stop. I didn't want to see 300. So I started working out. I started throwing batting practice to the high school team in my hometown. By the time we went to Denver that day, I was probably down to 225."

After Elarton had introduced himself and introduced his son, he said something to Amaro that surprised him—even as he spoke. To this day, he isn't quite certain why the words came out of his mouth.

"Rubén, do you think there's any chance I could make a comeback in baseball?" he said. "Do you think I could pitch again?"

Amaro was, to say the least, surprised by Elarton's question. Perhaps the only person more surprised was Elarton. "I'm still not honestly sure what possessed me," he said, shaking his head. "The thought never crossed my mind until the question came out of my mouth. Maybe it was standing behind the barrier that way. Something clicked in my brain that said, 'I don't like the view from here.' Or the feeling I had standing there."

To Elarton's further surprise, Amaro didn't answer him with a response along the lines of "Are you insane?" or even a polite blow-off. Instead, he shrugged his shoulders and said, "If you'd like, I'll send someone to watch you throw once the season's over."

Elarton couldn't ask for more than that. "Great," he said. "How should I get in touch with you?"

Amaro gave him his card, and they shook hands again, leaving Elarton standing there wondering what in the world he had just gotten himself into.

———

As it turned out, Amaro was as good as his word—better than that, in fact.

Elarton had gone home to Lamar, the town of just under eight thousand where he had grown up, and had begun throwing on a regular basis with Josh Bard, a former major-league catcher who lived nearby. He wasn't counting on a call from Amaro—or even 100 percent certain he wanted one—but he wanted to be ready just in case. He could feel the adrenaline each time he threw to Bard, and as the season wound down, he began to believe—"maybe just a little bit"—that he wasn't entirely crazy.

Shortly after the World Series ended, Amaro called. He was going to be in Denver for a banquet in which Shane Victorino, then with the Phillies, was scheduled to receive an award. If Elarton was still interested and could make the drive to Denver, he would watch him throw the morning after the banquet.

Elarton and Bard made the drive early on a November morning, and Amaro met them at a local school. Amaro stood and watched as Elarton began to throw. After about five minutes he asked him to stop.

"I remember thinking, 'Am I really that bad?'" Elarton said. "I had kind of talked myself into believing I was throwing pretty well, and when Rubén told me to stop after five minutes, my heart sank. I thought I had wasted my time, his time, and Josh's time."

Not exactly.

"I don't know what you've been doing, but you look completely different than I remember from the last time you were pitching," Amaro said. "You look comfortable, your ball has movement—I really like what you're doing. If it's okay with you, I'd like to shoot some video while you keep throwing."

It was more than okay with Elarton. Amaro had him throw about fifty pitches in all. Encouraged by what Amaro had said early on, Elarton thought Amaro would tell him that he'd be in touch. That would leave him with some hope.

Amaro didn't do that. "I'd like to sign you," he said. "If you give me your agent's information, I'll get in touch and we'll work out a deal."

Elarton was almost dazed. If nothing else, he had gotten himself out from behind the barrier.

Four months after that meeting, Elarton walked into the spacious clubhouse at Bright House Field and found a crisp, clean uniform with the number 59 on it hanging in a locker that had his name on it. A number of veteran players, guys he had pitched against in his first baseball incarnation, came by to say hello and welcome him.

"If you've been a player, a baseball clubhouse is a very comfortable place to be if you're in uniform," he said. "Even if you haven't been around for a while, if you're in uniform, then you feel like you belong. If you're not in uniform, then you don't. It really doesn't matter who you are or who you've been, that's the way it is."

Players talk often about the fear of someday not having a uniform or a locker anymore. Elarton had taken that a step further when he had shown up in Denver as a "civilian," as players call anyone not in uniform. Putting on a uniform again, even surrounded by so many unfamiliar faces, was comforting.

His negotiations with the Phillies after Amaro's visit had gone smoothly except for one small glitch: performance incentives. Elarton didn't want any. The Phillies were offering a fairly typical two-way contract: If he was on the major-league roster, he would be paid $600,000—which was $120,000 over the major-league minimum because it included bonuses for making the team. If he was in the minors, he would be paid a very high Triple-A rate: $15,000 a month.

"Take the incentives for making the major-league team out," Elarton told Michael Moss, partner of his long-time agent Ron Shapiro, who had also represented Cal Ripken Jr. and Kirby Puckett in the past.

"You want them *out?*" Moss said, stunned for obvious reasons.

"Out," Elarton answered. "I don't want money getting in the way of me making it back to the majors. If it's a close call and it's me or another guy and they have to pay me extra if I make it up, they may call the other guy up. I don't want to take a chance on that happening."

Moss called Amaro back to tell him he had an unusual request. Amaro had never in his life had a player ask for *less* money potentially, but he laughed when he heard what Elarton was thinking.

"Tell Scott that, being honest, the amount of money we're talking here will have *no* influence on whether he gets called up or not," he said. "If he pitches well enough to earn the bonuses, he should get them. But if we need him in Philadelphia, this money isn't going to get in the way. I promise."

Elarton was still a tad doubtful when Moss told him what Amaro had said but finally agreed.

He arrived in Clearwater with a simple goal: pitch so well during spring training that it would be impossible for the Phillies to send him down.

"Realistically, there weren't any spots open—especially for a starter," he said. "All you had to do was look at the rotation and you knew there wasn't any chance. They had stars and veterans. I hadn't pitched, except for three starts in Charlotte in 2010, since 2008. Intellectually, I knew the deal. But as a competitor I was going there to show them I was still a major-league pitcher. If I didn't think I was good enough, there wasn't much point in my being there."

The first three times Elarton got into games, he showed them. When he was on the mound facing real hitters, it all came back like riding a bike. His unorthodox delivery, all arms and legs coming at the batter from his six-foot-seven-inch frame, had hitters who hadn't seen him before way off balance.

"First three times I pitched I didn't have to pitch from the stretch once," he said, smiling at the memory. "It almost felt like I was back in Houston and it was 2000 again."

That was the year Elarton won seventeen games pitching for the Astros before injuries and a taste for the nightlife sent his promising career off the rails. Twelve years later, back in the March heat of Florida's west coast, he was twenty-five again. He could tell by the looks he was getting from his teammates in the clubhouse that they were noticing.

And then, not surprisingly, he came back to earth. It wasn't as if he crashed; he descended more slowly than that, pitching reasonably well but not lights out the way it had been at the start of camp. As

March came to a close, he knew the numbers he had been concerned about in February were clearly stacked against him. Nevertheless, with a week left before the team broke camp, he was still on the roster.

"I was in early one morning to work out before I was supposed to throw a bullpen," he said. (When pitchers throw on their days off, they do so in the bullpen, thus everyone in baseball refers to those workouts as "throwing a bullpen." Many pitchers shorten the phrase to "My bullpens have been good lately.") "I was on a bike when [pitching coach] Rich Dubee came in. I said, 'Hey, Rich, what time am I supposed to throw this morning?' He just looked at me and said, 'Need to talk to you in Charlie's office.'"

Charlie Manuel was the Phillies' manager. Elarton knew he wasn't being invited in for breakfast. "In baseball there are two reasons you get called into a major-league manager's office and both are bad," Elarton said. "The first one is if you're being taken out of the rotation—or benched. That's not good. The second one is a lot worse."

This was the second one. Rubén Amaro was sitting with Manuel when Elarton walked in, a clear sign of what was to come—if Elarton had needed one. Both men were very complimentary about Elarton's spring: He had worked hard, done everything they had asked. They believed he was capable of pitching in the big leagues again if he could improve his command. (Another pitching term, which, in English, means being able to throw pitches to the exact spot where a pitcher wants them. Missing by an inch can be the difference between a swing and a miss and a line drive.) But as he knew, the team was blessed with starters like Roy Halladay, Cliff Lee, and Cole Hamels—not to mention guys like Joe Blanton and Vance Worley who weren't stars but had solid big-league résumés.

Manuel finished with the inevitable line ballplayers have been hearing for as long as the minor leagues have existed. "Go down and keep working hard and there's a good chance you'll be back up here. It's a long season."

Elarton was disappointed, though not surprised, yet also elated. He had gone from standing behind a barrier trying to wave Amaro down the previous August to being on the cusp of making a big-league roster seven months later. He knew Manuel's words—although clichéd—were true: it *was* a long season, and if he pitched well in Triple-A, there was a chance he would make it to Philadelphia. He believed he was good enough.

He thanked Amaro and Manuel for the chance they had given him and packed up his locker to move across the complex to the minor-league camp. The walk from the big-league clubhouse to the minor-league clubhouse took only a few minutes, but it was as if Elarton had traveled through time and space to another dimension.

"The minute I opened the door all the memories flooded back," he said, a smile crossing his face. "It was as if I was a kid pitcher on my way up again except that I was thirty-six years old. I took one step inside and there it was again, the smell."

Athletes talk often about the smell of failure, of disappointment, of fear. This smell was different.

"This was the *smell*," Elarton said. "The minor-league clubhouses in Florida are usually built for about fifty guys, and at that time of year there are two hundred guys trying to figure a way to move around in there. It smells—big-time."

Baseball players understand that no one goes straight to the big leagues. Once upon a time, an occasional player might bypass the minor leagues either because of extraordinary talent or because a team needed instant publicity. Nowadays, no one does that—even phenoms like Stephen Strasburg, Bryce Harper, and Mike Trout spend *some* time in the minor leagues.

But they all assume that their journey will go in only one direction—up. They all believe that once they walk out of a minor-league clubhouse heading for the big leagues, they aren't coming back. Of course many do come back. Some end up on an escalator that takes them up and down to the point where they feel dizzy.

Danny Worth, who made the Detroit Tigers' postseason roster in 2012, had been sent back down to the minor leagues eleven times in four years before making it back to Detroit late in the 2012 season.

"Every time you get sent down it hurts," he said. "It doesn't matter if you know it's coming or not. You can do one of two things: you can sulk and say you got screwed, or you can be honest with yourself and say, 'I haven't played well enough to stay up there.' It's really pretty simple."

Scott Elarton had ridden the escalator, particularly near the end of his first baseball incarnation—even dropping briefly back to Double-A at one point. "You rationalize it by saying it wouldn't have happened if you hadn't been hurt," he said. "But after a while it doesn't matter. You look around and there are plenty of guys who have been hurt, plenty of pitchers who have had shoulder surgery more than once.

"You want to think you're going to wake up one morning and you're going to be twenty-five and your shoulder is going to be completely healthy. Then you wake up and realize that's never going to be the case again. One morning I woke up and decided it was time to go home."

That is ... until that summer afternoon in Denver, standing behind a barrier with his son, when he decided it was time to try again—one more time.

And so, on this late March morning in Clearwater, Elarton stood for a long moment and looked around the packed minor-league clubhouse. Then he took a deep breath and went to find his locker. No one even looked up at him. He was another face in the crowd. He was back where nobody knows your name.

2

Podsednik and Montoyo

THE WALK-OFF HERO AND THE .400 HITTER

Scott Elarton's story was different from most because he had decided to start over again after almost three years away from baseball. But the call into the manager's office, and the speech ("work hard and you'll be back"), and the long walk from the major-league clubhouse to the minor-league clubhouse, was a scene being repeated throughout March in thirty spring training camps.

For some, it was more difficult than others. When Scott Podsednik, who had been in the Phillies' camp at the same time as Elarton, got the call into Charlie Manuel's office, he wasn't completely shocked. But Podsednik was so horrified by the thought of playing in Triple-A again that his first thought, as Manuel told him how well he had performed in March (he had hit .343 for the spring), was, "I don't know if I can do this again."

Podsednik had just turned thirty-six. He was seven years removed from a moment about which baseball players literally fantasize from the time they first pick up a bat and glove: on a cold October night in Chicago he had hit a home run in the bottom of the ninth inning of game two of the World Series. Podsednik was a leadoff hitter, someone who specialized in getting to first base and then stealing second (he'd stolen 120 bases in the previous two seasons), and he hadn't hit a single home run during the 2005 regular season. But he turned on a

2-1 pitch and watched it sail through the air into the right-field seats as if, in that instant, he had somehow become "the Natural."

The term in baseball nowadays is a "walk-off home run." It didn't exist until Kirk Gibson hit his famous pinch-hit home run off Dennis Eckersley in game one of the 1988 World Series and Eckersley referred to it as "a walk-off," meaning, quite simply, that when someone does what Gibson did to him in that game, there's nothing left to do except walk off the mound into the dugout and then into the clubhouse.

Referring to a game-winning home run in a World Series game as a "walk-off" doesn't quite capture the drama of it. The stadium explodes with noise, and the hero is mobbed at home plate in a manner he has never experienced before—regardless of how long he has played the game.

"I'm a much better hitter when I don't try to hit for power, because that's not what I do," Podsednik said on a warm March morning just before the Phillies' exhibition season was to begin. He had worked out for an extra hour following the team's morning workout. "I wasn't trying to hit a home run when I went up there. But I managed to turn on the ball and it just took off. When I realized it was going out, I had to pinch myself for a minute to be absolutely sure I was awake.

"It's almost hard to come down from that kind of thing. After we ended up winning that Series [in a four-game sweep], it seemed as if we were back in spring training talking about trying to do it again about an hour later. It just happened *so* fast."

Everything happens fast at the elite levels of sports. If you get hurt and don't produce, having been a hero doesn't mean much.

Podsednik's road to that moment in 2005 hadn't been an easy one. He had dealt with injuries for what felt like his entire career and had played most of eight and a half seasons in the minor leagues before finally making it to the majors on a full-time basis in 2003, at the age of twenty-seven.

"There had been times when the thought that 'this just wasn't meant to be for me' had crossed my mind," he said. "For a lot of years, every light at the end of every tunnel was a train."

Following his World Series walk-off, Podsednik played very well again in 2006, but the injury bug bit him again in 2007. He played in only sixty-two games and hit just .243 in those games. Rather than go to arbitration with him for a third time after paying him $2.9 million that season, the White Sox released him.

Like so many players who are past their thirtieth birthday and have had good moments and bad, Podsednik became a baseball drifter. He had a good year in Kansas City in 2010, but injuries again sent him back to the minors in 2011. That was why he was in the Phillies' camp on a minor-league contract a year later hoping to prove himself valuable enough to make the major-league team.

He had come close, but that was no consolation when the difference was being in the major leagues with a minimum salary of $482,000 a year and the planes are chartered versus the minors, where the maximum salary is under $100,000 a year—and the only charters are the ones that travel on interstates.

Podsednik had two young children at home in Texas. He knew that Lehigh Valley, the Phillies' Triple-A team, played in an almost new stadium with facilities that were as good as one could find in Triple-A. But that just didn't seem like enough. Not when you were thirty-six. Not when you could still feel the ground shaking under you as you circled the bases after a World Series walk-off, even if almost seven years had passed since that moment.

"I just couldn't face it again," he said. "I thought I was good enough to help the Phillies, certainly help a major-league team. If I was going to be away from my family, I wanted it to be in the major leagues. That would make it worth doing."

With the Phillies' permission, he went home to his wife, Lisa, and their two boys. The team wasn't prepared to release him, but there was an understanding that Podsednik was trying to decide whether he was willing to go back to Triple-A or just call it a career.

He stared at the phone for ten days, hoping the Phillies would call to say he'd been traded or called up. Nothing happened. He talked it over with Lisa. They both agreed that if he continued to play well, he would almost certainly get another chance. And so, on April 8, he took a deep breath, packed his bags, and got on a flight to Allentown.

When he walked into the Lehigh Valley clubhouse, he felt himself sag. He had first reported to a minor-league team in 1994 at the age of eighteen. Now he was back again. And although he was in a very nice minor-league clubhouse that was spacious and comfortable and *not* filled with two hundred players in an area that could comfortably fit fifty, this was still the minor leagues. He looked around the room and saw a lot of players who reminded him of him—fifteen to twenty years earlier.

"I really wasn't sure I could do it," he said. "I told myself I had to have a good attitude, not sulk."

He smiled. "Sometimes in life things are easier said than done."

———

For many players, spring training is the best six weeks of the year. The Florida and Arizona clubhouses feel like summer camp, especially the first few days, when players begin arriving and friendships that have been dormant for four months are renewed.

For the established veteran with a long-term contract, mid-February to the end of March is a time to slowly work yourself into baseball shape. Pitchers need a little more time—which is why they report earlier than position players; catchers report early because pitchers need someone to throw to—but even they have plenty of time to play golf or just relax in the sun.

Before exhibition games begin, most spring training days are over before noon. Once the games begin, veterans play only two or three days a week, and when they do, they're rarely still in the game after the fifth inning.

For the veteran trying to make a team on a minor-league contract—players like Scott Elarton, Scott Podsednik, J. C. Boscan, and Brett Tomko (to name a few)—every day is tension filled. Anytime a coach walks near you in the clubhouse, you wonder if he's coming to get you so the manager can tell you that you're going down. For young players who know they aren't going to make the big-league ball club, spring training is exciting, a chance to show your bosses what you've got.

And then there are the bosses. Most managers arrive in camp knowing whom they want on their team in April. Injuries can force changes, and a superb spring might bring about another change or two. But managers have a plan that they lay out for their coaches in February. Every day has a purpose, even though it doesn't always appear that way.

It can be argued that no one enjoys spring training more than minor-league managers and coaches. Many have lived the big-league life, some for extended periods of time, some only briefly. Some have never been there and can only dream about what it must be like.

They all get to live The Life in the spring—especially the Triple-A staff because they work side by side with the major-league staff until the very end of spring, when players are sent down to play for them and they have to start dealing with the disappointed looks on the faces of those who won't be starting the season in the majors.

"The first thing I say to my team, once I have a team, is, 'I know you guys don't want to be here,'" said Charlie Montoyo, who in 2012 began his sixth season as manager of the Durham Bulls, the Triple-A farm team of the Tampa Bay Rays. "I tell them if they sulk about it, they'll probably be with me all season. But if they put it behind them and work hard, there's a good chance they'll be in the majors at some point soon. I can say that because, a lot of the time, it turns out to be true."

Montoyo was forty-six and had grown up in the town of Florida in Puerto Rico, about an hour's drive from San Juan. He was a very good hitter and infielder as a kid, good enough to draw attention from scouts, although he was never offered a contract by a major-league team.

At the age of eighteen, he had been given the chance to go to De Anza College in California to play baseball, and he had jumped at it. He spoke no English but learned the language hanging around his friends and teammates and from watching television. "Atlanta Braves baseball on TBS and *Bewitched*," he said. "I liked Elizabeth Montgomery."

He transferred to Louisiana Tech after two years and, two years later, was drafted in the sixth round of the 1987 draft by the Milwaukee Brewers. He spent most of the next ten years in the minor leagues, making it to the majors in 1993 with the Montreal Expos. He got to bat five times that September and went two for five.

"Forget Ted Williams," he likes to say. "I'm baseball's last .400 hitter."

When he retired in 1996, he got a job in the Rays' minor-league system thanks to a former teammate, Tom Foley, who had just been hired by the team to put together a minor-league staff for 1997. The major-league team wouldn't begin play until a year later, but they were building the organization from scratch. He'd been with the Rays ever since, reaching Durham in 2007. He had won five straight division titles and one International League championship. In 2009, he had been voted Manager of the Year for the entire minor-league system at all levels.

"Which just means we've had a lot of good young players coming up through the system," he said. "If I've done something well, I hope it's that I've helped get them ready for the major leagues. That's what they pay me to do."

Like almost everyone in Triple-A, Montoyo had thought about the day he might manage in the major leagues. He believed he was good enough to make the jump, but it wasn't what drove him and it certainly didn't consume him, as it did many of his peers.

"Anyone who has managed at the Triple-A level, anyone who has worked at that level, has moments when he thinks, 'I wonder how I would do up in the big leagues.' Human nature. It isn't really about the money that much"—he paused and smiled—"although you're certainly aware of it. What it's really about is believing you're good enough to do it, to compete against the best at what you do.

"Players feel it when they're playing, and when you've managed awhile, you feel the same way.

"But at this point in my life, what's most important to me is that I have a job. I have the first two-year contract of my life—which is nice. I have a 401(k) and I have insurance. I can take care of my family. It isn't that I love baseball any less now than I did when I was a kid. When I retired"—another smile—"I should say, *got* retired, I knew I wanted to stay in the game. I got the chance to do that, and I'm making a living doing it. That's what I focus on."

Montoyo, who makes about $80,000 a year working for the Rays, has good reason to focus on being able to take care of his family. He met his wife, Samantha, when he was playing in Charleston, and they have two boys: Tyson, who turned nine during the 2012 season, and Alexander, who turned five in October 2012, shortly after the season ended.

Montoyo vividly remembers his second son's birth.

Alexander Montoyo was born on October 17, 2007. The doctors told his parents right away that he had been born with a heart defect called Ebstein's anomaly. It is extremely rare, a defect that forms in the womb and affects the flow of blood from the right ventricle in the lower part of the heart to the right atrium in the upper part of the heart.

"In a way, we were very lucky," Montoyo said. "The doctors told me that ten years earlier there probably would have been nothing they could do for him. Now it's treatable."

Treatable—but terrifying. Within hours of his birth, Alexander had been taken by helicopter to a hospital in Phoenix. He had to have open-heart surgery a month later and a second surgery when he was four months old. Doctors told the Montoyos he might need a transplant—very dicey surgery, to put it mildly, for one so young.

Alexander fought through it all after being taken to UCLA hospital, where there were specialists who worked on children with the anomaly. Montoyo spent the 2008 season commuting to both Los Angeles and Phoenix—where he and his family live during the off-season—frequently leaving his team when it had a day off to fly round-trip out west so he could spend a few hours with his son.

Alexander had a third surgery two years later and faced a fourth—one that doctors hoped would be the last—in April 2013.

"All my life, I've been a competitor," Montoyo said softly, smiling.

"I've loved to play and compete for as long as I remember. I'm like everyone else in that I've never liked losing. But since Alexander was born, it feels a little different."

He took off the Bulls cap he was wearing and looked inside it. "Whenever I feel myself starting to get frustrated or angry about something during a game, or before or after a game, I take my cap off and look inside it."

He held it out. Inside was a photograph of Tyson and Alexander, both with big smiles on their faces. "I look at this and I know that losing a game isn't that important. Given a choice, I'd much rather win than lose. But it isn't important the way it used to be for me."

The 2012 season would turn out to be the most difficult Montoyo had experienced as a manager. But when June came around and school was out in Arizona, he could look into the stands at Durham Bulls Athletic Park on most nights and find Samantha, Tyson, and Alexander sitting there watching the game.

Which meant that he didn't need to look inside his cap to know what was truly important in his life.

3

Lindsey, Schwinden, and Lollo

THE MAYOR, THE TRAVELER, AND THE UMP

At the moment that Scott Podsednik arrived in Allentown, John Lindsey would have been thrilled to swap places with him. Lindsey was essentially the same age as Podsednik (he was ten months younger) and had been drafted out of high school by the Colorado Rockies in the thirteenth round in 1995, a year after Podsednik.

Lindsey's dreams were like those of anyone who is ever drafted by a major-league team. "I figured I'd be in the majors in about two years," he said, smiling. "I remember my dad telling me back then that everyone else was thinking the same thing but I was like, 'Yeah, I know, but I'm right.'"

He was off by fourteen years. On September 8, 2010—more than *sixteen* years after his draft day—Lindsey made it to the majors. In doing so, he set a record for the longest minor-league apprenticeship that eventually led to the big leagues in baseball history.

"Not a record I was trying to set," he said with a laugh. "By the time it happened, I had pretty much given up. It was the second-to-last day of the season and I was packing up so I'd be ready to go home right after we played the next day, when I got called into the manager's office."

The Albuquerque Isotopes were in Round Rock, Texas, finishing their season when manager Tim Wallach called Lindsey in to tell him he was going to the Dodgers. Lindsey still remembers Wallach's words. "He said, 'John, I'm honored to be the one to tell you that you're going to the major leagues. I know you've waited a long time.'"

Lindsey was so stunned by Wallach's words that his first thought wasn't, *"Oh my God!"* but rather, "I have to call my wife."

Christa Lindsey was making the six-hundred-mile drive from Hattiesburg, Mississippi, to Round Rock to pick her husband up the next day. She was already en route. "I had to get her turned around," he said. "At first she didn't answer. Finally, I got her. It was one of those funny phone calls. 'Honey, I'm sorry you've driven three hundred miles for nothing, but here's why . . .'"

Lindsey is a quiet and thoughtful man, very religious and extremely considerate of others' feelings. Which may explain why he didn't tell any of his teammates what had happened when he walked out of Wallach's office that day. "I just thought it wouldn't look very good if I was jumping up and down and screaming, 'I'm going to the majors,' when the rest of them were all going home the next day," he said. "I guess I must have had some kind of smile on my face, though, because Iván DeJesús, who lockered right next to me, noticed.

"He said to me, 'What's going on, why'd Skip call you in?' I said, 'Nothing, man, no big deal.'

"And then he started screaming, 'You're going up! You're going up! I know it, I can tell by the look on your face!'"

When Lindsey confessed, a clubhouse celebration in the J. C. Boscan mode ensued. When a player has been around baseball for as many years as Boscan or Lindsey without making the majors, it is, at least in part, because he is looked to by younger teammates as a mentor. If not, teams wouldn't keep him around. That's why the joy is so genuine when one of them makes it.

Lindsey managed to get to bat twelve times in Los Angeles before he broke a hand when he was hit by a pitch, ending his season. His first time up, he was almost shaking when he stepped into the batter's box. Then he looked out to the mound and saw Wandy Rodríguez pitching for the Houston Astros.

"I just told myself that I'd faced Wandy lots of times before in the minors—which I had—and this was no different," he said. "I tried to make myself think it was just another at-bat, no different than all the at-bats in the minors. Of course it wasn't."

Lindsey got one hit—in his tenth at-bat—a sinking line drive to left field that fell just in front of the Astros' Carlos Lee. The pitcher was Nelson Figueroa, whom he had also faced often in the minors. He is grateful to this day that the less-than-graceful Lee was the left fielder that night. "Someone with a little more speed gets to the ball," he said. "Not Carlos. That was the hit I waited to get all my life."

When Lee tossed the ball back to the infield and play was stopped, the Astros' Reed Johnson picked it up, looked at Lindsey, and made a motion as if he were going to throw it to a fan in the stands.

"I panicked for a second," Lindsey said. "He just smiled at me and rolled it into our dugout. He knew."

Players always know. The ball sits today in the room of John Lindsey III—Lindsey's son, who was born a year before his dad reached the majors.

In the spring of 2011, Lindsey was back in the minor leagues. Dodger injuries had gotten him to the majors in September. Good healing in the L.A. outfield sent him back to Triple-A in Albuquerque. At the end of that season no one offered him a contract—even a minor-league contract. He was about to turn thirty-four, and he wondered if it wasn't time for him to finish college and move on with his life. He had been taking online classes at the University of Phoenix. It was his father, who had told him as a teenager that life in baseball might not be quite as easy as it looked, who told him he might not want to walk away just yet.

"You don't quit until there's nothing left," John Lindsey Sr. told his son. "I have a feeling you still have something left. Once you stop, it's over; you aren't starting again. Don't stop until you have to stop."

Lindsey decided his father was right. He went on an intense diet, thinking he had gotten a step slow with the passing years. He ate only healthy foods, mostly vegetables and chicken, and at times fasted for several days. He lost thirty-five pounds, dropping from a slightly fleshy 260 to a rock-hard 225. Still, there was no major-league team willing to even bring him to spring training on a minor-league deal. It seemed as if his time had passed.

But then his agent came to him with an offer to play in Laguna, Mexico. The Mexican League is roughly the equivalent of Triple-A baseball, although the pay isn't as good. Lindsey decided to take a chance. Off he went to Laguna, where he was fortunate to share an apartment with a teammate who was bilingual.

It wasn't exactly Dodger Stadium. It wasn't even Albuquerque. But it was baseball.

———

Chris Schwinden was very happy to be where he was in the spring of 2012. Sort of. A year earlier, he had been facing a return to Double-A ball as a relief pitcher. He was twenty-five, and four years removed from being drafted in the twenty-second round by the New York Mets out of Fresno Pacific University.

As soon as he signed, the Mets sent him to play for their short-season A-league team in Brooklyn—which was usually a sign that they considered a player a prospect. The Mets' majority owner, Fred Wilpon, had grown up in Brooklyn worshipping the Brooklyn Dodgers, and he had built a ballpark for the minor-league team in order to bring baseball back to Brooklyn in some form.

"Pitching there wasn't the typical rookie-ball experience," Schwinden said. "You were playing in front of eight thousand or nine thousand people every night. You knew everyone in the organization paid attention to how the team was doing and to the players on that team. It was fun for me. I liked the crowds and the buzz and the attention."

He pitched well in the summer of 2008—his ERA was 2.01—and began a steady climb up the Mets ladder. He had made it to Double-A Binghamton two years later and had been used primarily as a starter the second half of the season. But he hadn't pitched especially well in that role, and the following season began with him headed back to Binghamton—as a reliever.

"It was discouraging," he said. "My entire baseball career had always been about moving forward. This didn't even feel like a lateral move. It felt like a demotion."

Baseball luck—bad for Boof Bonser, who was in Triple-A Buffalo's starting rotation, good for Schwinden—intervened. Bonser hurt his elbow in his first start of the season, and because he had starting experience, Schwinden was called up from Double-A Binghamton to Triple-A Buffalo on April 17 for a spot start. He pitched well enough to earn a second start. He pitched well again. That earned him a spot in Buffalo in a starting role after Bonser had to undergo Tommy John surgery. Schwinden's second go-round as a minor-league starter went much better than the first one had. In 2010, as a starter in Binghamton, his ERA had been 5.56. This time, in a league where any ERA under 4.00 was considered good (small ballparks, wide strike zones, generally speaking), his ERA was 3.87.

He knew his pitching had been solid throughout the 2011 season and was thinking he might have earned himself an invitation to the Mets' major-league camp in the spring of 2012. On the final weekend of the season, soon after he had made his last start of the year, he was getting dressed when Ricky Bones, the pitching coach, walked over to his locker and said, "Skip needs to see you for a minute."

Schwinden was baffled for a moment, wondering if perhaps Tim Teufel wanted to see if he might be able to come in out of the bullpen on the last day of the season.

"I really was clueless," he said. "But then, as we were walking into Tim's office, Ricky said to me, 'You're going to need some better clothes.' I sat down and Tim said to me, 'Well, Chris, you've had quite a year. You started it pitching relief in Double-A. You're going to finish it starting in the majors.'

"It's one of those things where at first you think you misheard or something. But you know your manager would never kid you about something like that. I think I just stared at him for a second. Finally, he said, 'You better get going, you're starting in New York tomorrow.'"

And so it was, twenty-four hours later on a chilly September evening, he found himself on the mound at Citi Field pitching the first game of a twi-night doubleheader against the Atlanta Braves, who were fighting for a playoff spot. "The whole thing was surreal," Schwinden said. "One minute I'm wrapping up the season in Buffalo; the next I'm on the mound in New York pitching to Chipper Jones. It was pretty amazing."

As Teufel had predicted, he finished the season as a starter in the majors. He started four games and didn't pitch horribly or wonderfully—his ERA was 4.71—and went 0-2. That was good enough to put him in contention for a spot on the team in the spring of 2012.

By then, the Mets' rotation was healthy again. Johan Santana and Mike Pelfrey were both back from injuries, and Schwinden's best chance to make the team was going to be coming out of the bullpen. Even that was a long shot, because the Mets had several veteran relievers in camp. Schwinden thought he had pitched well enough to make the team, but the Mets decided to go with more experience (and then some) in forty-one-year-old Miguel Batista. Three days before the regular season was scheduled to start, Schwinden was sent back to Triple-A Buffalo.

"It was disappointing but not that surprising," he said. "Terry [Collins] gave me the usual talk—stay ready, keep working. I felt good that at least I'd come close. And I knew it was a long season."

He couldn't possibly imagine just how long it was going to be.

———

Who enjoys spring training the most? It might be the media, which has access to players and managers both before and after morning workouts and before and after—occasionally during—exhibition games, very few of which are played at night.

Or it might be the umpires—especially those who are accustomed to the minor leagues but find themselves living the big-league life for the month of March.

Mark Lollo was starting his eleventh season as an umpire—his fourth in the International League. The previous season, he had made the call-up list of Triple-A umpires and had worked six games in the major leagues.

The call-up list consisted of eighteen Triple-A umpires who, like Lollo, had worked their way from the low minor leagues to one step from the majors—taking much the same route most players took. The call-ups were the guys who were brought to the majors periodically during the season to fill in for umpires who were on vacation or injured or sick. They were divided, informally at least, into four different categories: the top five on the list were likely to spend as much as a month in the majors during a season. They were umpires who major-league baseball had pretty much decided were ready for the majors and were just waiting for openings to occur—which they did every year as older umpires retired—so they could make the move to the majors.

The next five were a step behind, umps who had proven themselves to the point where they were likely to find themselves in the majors at some point in the near future unless something went wrong: they got injured, got out of shape, or for some reason, in the eyes of their evaluators, failed to progress the way they had on their way up the ladder.

The last eight were the ones who were still question marks. They were being tested. Five of them were guaranteed some major-league work during the season, and the last three knew their work would almost certainly be dependent on the unexpected happening: injury, illness, the birth of a child, or, on a very rare occasion, an umpire being suspended.

Most of the time the last eight were where they were because they weren't as experienced as the top ten. Lollo knew, based on the fact that he'd gotten only six games in 2011, that he had been in that group, but that didn't bother him. "First year on the list that's what you expect," he said. "It really isn't until the third year in most cases that you start to be concerned."

Lollo was in his second year on the list and was hoping for more major-league work in 2012. He knew that Randy Mobley, the president of the International League, was a fan of his work because Mobley had told him so. Mobley was a good advocate to have, but it was still the major-league evaluators and those who were in charge of umpiring in the offices of Major League Baseball who made the final decisions.

"More often than not, it's three years up or out," Lollo said. "If you're on the call-up list for three years and they don't believe you're major league ready, they're probably going to move on. It's not a choice for the umpire. Players can say, 'I'll deal with life in the minors.' A Triple-A player can keep his job or go back to Double-A if necessary if he wants to keep playing. Not an umpire. If they don't think you're going to make it to the majors, you're gone."

Lollo knew he had already beaten long odds getting to where he was. About 1 percent of umpires who come out of umpiring school and are hired at the rookie-league level get to the major leagues. Almost one-third of those who get to Triple-A get there. And if you make the call-up list, your chances increase exponentially.

He had reached the doorstep. The last two falls he had been assigned to work in the Arizona Fall League, which was extra money and extra experience and meant he was being watched by a lot of major-league personnel because the league is full of top prospects on their way up to the majors.

In the spring of 2012 he found out that he was going to work major-league games in spring training. This was a big step. It was also a financial windfall. Like players, umpires make a lot less money in the minors than in the majors. A major-league umpire makes a minimum salary of $90,000 a year plus $420 a day in per diem. A top minor-league umpire—like Lollo—makes $3,200 a month in addition to a $48-a-day per diem. Major-league umpires pay for their own hotels out of their per diem and tip the clubhouse guys who take care of them in the ballparks about $40 a day, compared with about $10 a day in Triple-A. Even so, there's a wide gap.

By working twenty-five major-league games in March at $175 a game while being able to stay in his grandparents' home north of Sarasota most of the month, Lollo would increase his income for 2012 by close to 40 percent. Which meant he might not have to work quite as hard the following winter back home in New Lexington, Ohio, where he lived with his wife and two sons—the second of whom had arrived the previous December. He had done some substitute teaching in the past and had also done snow removal. The extra money from spring training meant he could cut back his hours and spend more of his off-season with his family.

"Which is a big deal," he said. "Because during the season this isn't a lifestyle conducive to family life."

Umpires never have home games. The closest Lollo came was when he did games in Columbus—about fifty-five miles from home.

March, though, was a fun month, one of the most enjoyable Lollo had experienced since he had gone straight from high school to umpiring school eleven years earlier. The sun was warm, the games were relaxed, the facilities were comfortable, and the drives—compared with the regular season—were short.

He was looking forward to the season—to working in real big-league games again and to proving he was ready for the next and most important step of his career.

"The toughest steps you take are usually the first one and the last one," he said with a smile. "I got through the first one okay. But we all know that the last one can be rough because a lot of it is out of your control. Players have numbers that don't lie. Umpires don't have that. We have to have good eyes to do our jobs well. You have to hope the guys evaluating you see things as clearly as they want you to see things."

Unlike players such as Elarton, Podsednik, and Schwinden, who spent spring training hoping to begin the season in the major leagues, Lollo knew he would be heading back to Triple-A after he made the drive back north. That was fine with him.

For this year. He turned thirty at the end of March, just as spring training was winding up.

He was ready, he believed, to take that last long step.

4

Slice of Life

ROLLING WITH THE PUNCHES IN . . . ALLENTOWN . . .
PAWTUCKET . . . NORFOLK

On the first Saturday of June—June 2 to be exact—the Pawtucket Red Sox were in Allentown, Pennsylvania, preparing to play a twi-night doubleheader against the Lehigh Valley IronPigs. The teams had been rained out the previous night, and because there are so few scheduled off days (eight) during a minor-league season, the game was rescheduled for the next evening as part of a doubleheader.

That afternoon, a couple of hours before first pitch, Pawtucket manager Arnie Beyeler sat in his small office a few yards from where his players were dressing in the visiting clubhouse. Beyeler had a problem: Ross Ohlendorf had been scheduled to pitch the second game of the doubleheader. That wasn't going to work, though, because Ohlendorf was no longer on the team.

Like a lot of veteran Triple-A players, Ohlendorf had a clause in the free-agent contract he had signed prior to the season that gave him an "opt-out" date. Almost everyone with an opt-out is someone who has pitched or played in the major leagues in the past who doesn't want to commit himself to one team for an entire season if that means he won't get a crack at returning to the majors.

"It gives a guy a chance to hook on with another club if it looks like there's no chance for him to make it back to the big leagues where he is," Beyeler said. "Sometimes it means a guy gets a specific offer to go. Sometimes they just want a change of scenery."

Ohlendorf had a specific offer. His opt-out was June 1, and his agent had gotten a call earlier that week from the San Diego Padres, who were interested in signing him on his opt-out date and promoting him to the major-league team. Naturally, with no sign that the Red Sox were going to call him up, Ohlendorf let the team know that he was planning to opt out and head west and—more important—up and out of Triple-A.

Because of the way the calendar fell, the Red Sox didn't have to release Ohlendorf until Monday the fourth, meaning he could pitch on Saturday night in Allentown if they so desired. But Ben Crockett, the Red Sox' farm director, had called Beyeler that morning to tell him the team was going to release Ohlendorf right away. The thinking was twofold: why pitch someone who isn't part of our future, and, as a courtesy, let him go to his new team fresh and ready to pitch.

Beyeler hung up the phone with Crockett and walked into the cramped clubhouse to find Ohlendorf and give him the news. He stopped at Tony Peña Jr.'s locker to let him know he would be pressed into duty that night as an emergency starter. Peña, who had played in the major leagues as a starting shortstop for the Kansas City Royals before becoming a pitcher, wasn't shocked by the news.

"He's been my most versatile pitcher for two years," Beyeler said. "Anything I ask him to do, he does it. Down here, guys know things change every day—sometimes every hour. Nothing surprises him."

As Beyeler talked to Peña, he glanced up at one of the clubhouse TV sets. Every Triple-A clubhouse has at least one TV set in it, and most—if not all—are wired for the Major League Baseball package. That means when a Triple-A team's big-league squad is playing, that game is on the clubhouse TV.

At that moment, down the hall in the home clubhouse, the Phillies game was on in the IronPigs' clubhouse. In Beyeler's visiting Pawtucket clubhouse, the Red Sox game was on all the screens.

Most of the time, players just glance at the televised game or pay no attention to it at all as they get ready to play. Beyeler kept an eye on the Red Sox games because—as always—he knew that if one of the Red Sox got hurt or if a pitcher had a bad day, his phone might ring and Crockett would be on the other end asking him who would be the best fit for whatever hole he needed to fill in Boston.

As Beyeler was finishing his talk with Peña and was about to go and find Ohlendorf, he noticed a commotion. "About ten guys had jumped up and were crowding around the set," he said later, smiling. "It usually doesn't take a genius to figure out why that happens."

This time, it didn't take Beyeler long to confirm that his instinct was right. Red Sox shortstop Mike Avilés had closed on a ground ball just before it took a wicked hop and ricocheted off his wrist. He had come up in pain, grabbing the wrist right away, and trainer Rick Jameyson and manager Bobby Valentine had come out of the dugout to see how badly Avilés was hurt.

"If he's down, someone's going up," Beyeler said. "If someone goes up, other guys' playing time and their place in the lineup is affected. I've seen it hundreds of times. It isn't as if any of those guys are sitting there waiting for someone to get hurt, but the minute they see Avilés come up holding the wrist, their first thought is, 'Could I get the call?'"

As it turned out, Avilés hadn't broken any bones and was able to shake off the injury. Everyone returned to what they were doing.

"You never know, though," Beyeler said. "It could swell, or they could find something wrong with it after the game. They're all thinking the same thing.

"The good news in a situation like that is you get to call someone in and say, 'Pack your bags, you're going to the major leagues.' Those moments are the best part of this job—by far." He smiled. "Of course, once that guy leaves with a big grin on his face, you have to deal with the five who didn't get called up. *That's* the hardest part of the job."

Or, as Baltimore Orioles manager Buck Showalter, who spent his playing career waiting for the call-up that never came and then managed in Triple-A for four years, puts it: "Managing at that level is the worst job there is in baseball. Why? Because *no one* wants to be there."

Baseball's minor leagues have a long and storied history, at least in part because almost every great player in the game has played in them at some point in time.

Years ago, baseball had so many minor leagues and minor-league teams it was almost impossible to track them all. Leagues were classified from Triple-A down through Class D. More often than not, the minor-league teams were completely independent from the major-league teams they did business with, their affiliations being informal as often as they were formal.

Minor-league teams are still owned independently nowadays, but with the exception of a handful of teams that play in what are called—cleverly enough—independent leagues, they all have formal ties to major-league teams.

The major-league teams control the baseball operations: they assign the manager and the coaches and provide the players to each team. The owners take care of everything non-baseball, from owning (or leasing) their stadium, to tickets sales and marketing, concessions, licensing, and parking.

There are now six levels of minor-league baseball: rookie-league; short-season A (the teams begin play in June since most of the players are high school and college draftees); low-A; high-A; Double-A; and Triple-A.

Players in Triple-A like to say that they are "one accident away" from the big leagues—an approach that might sound a bit ghoulish but is quite real.

Echoing the words of Arnie Beyeler, John Lindsey put it bluntly one night: "It isn't as if you sit around hoping for someone to get hurt, but you know that it's a fact of life that people *do* get hurt. The phone is going to ring. The manager is going to call someone in to his office. You just hope when that happens it will be you. When you're in Triple-A, you're 'this close,' but you can also be a million miles away."

There are two leagues at the Triple-A level: the Pacific Coast

League, which has sixteen teams, and the International League, which has fourteen teams. Although the tie-ins change frequently, each team has a working agreement with one of the thirty major-league teams. The minor-league ownership stays the same; those on the field switch uniforms.

The oldest of the minor leagues is the International League, which has existed in one form or another since 1884. Once, the league truly was international: there were teams from Canada, Puerto Rico, and, for six years in the 1950s, Cuba. The Cuban team had to move in 1960, two years after the noted baseball fan Fidel Castro took over the country. The team ended up in that most international of cities, Jersey City, New Jersey.

There are no longer any international teams in the International League. The last one disappeared in 2008, when the Ottawa Lynx, who were an affiliate of the Philadelphia Phillies, moved to Allentown, Pennsylvania—which is a lot closer to Philadelphia than Ottawa— and became the Lehigh Valley IronPigs.

The I-League, as it is commonly called, has three divisions: North, South, and West. The North Division has six teams: Pawtucket, Rochester, Syracuse, Buffalo, Lehigh Valley, and Scranton/Wilkes-Barre. The South and West have four teams each: Norfolk, Durham, Charlotte, and Gwinnett play in the South; and Columbus, Toledo, Indianapolis, and Louisville play in the West.

The playoff system is a simple one: The three division winners qualify, and there is one wild card team. The four teams play best-of-five semifinals and then a best-of-five championship series. In 2012, Pawtucket, the wild card team, won the Governors' Cup that is given to the league champion. The Governors' Cup was first presented in 1933 when the I-League became the first league at any level of baseball to expand its playoffs to include four teams. Major League Baseball didn't follow suit until 1969.

The original Governors' Cup, which was worth $3,000 and was sponsored by the governors of New York, New Jersey, and Maryland and the lieutenant governors of Quebec and Ontario, was donated to the Hall of Fame in 1988. The new cup, which is a replica, was actually smashed by a drunken fan at a Scranton/Wilkes-Barre game in 2009 and had to be extensively repaired. The Pacific Coast League uses an identical playoff system.

Among the managers who have hoisted the Governors' Cup in the past are men like Walter Alston, Dick Williams, Bobby Cox, Davey Johnson, Hank Bauer, Joe Altobelli, and Charlie Manuel—all of whom went on to manage World Series winners. And yet every manager in the I-League says the same thing about winning the championship: it's nice, but it isn't what you are paid to do.

"You try to win every night, but you know you aren't ultimately judged on wins and losses," said Durham manager Charlie Montoyo, whose team made the playoffs five straight seasons prior to 2012 and won the Governors' Cup in 2009. "My job is to develop players, help them be ready for the big leagues, keep their attitudes in the right place, and be ready to do whatever the big club needs at a moment's notice—no matter what it does to my team. Some nights, all I'm looking for is a way to have enough pitchers to get through nine innings. If I do that, then I've probably done my job."

On a July night in 2012, Montoyo's phone rang shortly after midnight. The Bulls had managed to pull out a 7–4 victory earlier that evening against Rochester, but Montoyo had noticed after arriving home that the Tampa Bay Rays game against the Seattle Mariners had gone fourteen innings. When he heard farm director Chaim Bloom's voice on the other end of the line, he laughed.

"What took you so long to call?" he asked.

Bloom laughed too. The two men had done this drill before. The fourteen-inning game meant that the Rays had gone deep into their bullpen. They would need to have another pitcher available the next night. César Ramos was the choice. He would be on a plane to Tampa the next morning. How long he would stay in Tampa was hard to say, but for the moment, since it might be only a few days, the Rays were not going to send anyone up to Durham from their Double-A team in Montgomery, Alabama.

"Oh, one more thing," Bloom added. "Don't use [Brandon] Gomes tomorrow. We may need him Sunday if we have to use Ramos right away."

Montoyo sighed. That meant he would be two pitchers down for the rest of the weekend. It also meant the first person he would need to talk to when he got to the ballpark the next day would be backup catcher Craig Albernaz—who was also his emergency pitcher.

"We've already had to use him a couple of times to finish games this year," Montoyo said. "You don't like to put a position player in to pitch, but sometimes you have no choice." He smiled. "Actually the first couple of times he came in he did pretty well. Then I let [pitching coach] Neil Allen work with him in the bullpen a little bit, and the next time out he got lit up.

"Fortunately, he has a great attitude about it. That makes it a little easier for me."

In a small twist of irony, Albernaz and Gomes had grown up in the same town—Fall River, Massachusetts. Albernaz has such a thick New England accent it almost sounds as if he's exaggerating for effect. He has the classic catcher's body—five feet eight and 195 pounds—and, at the age of twenty-nine, was happy to do whatever his manager wanted him to do.

"Anything to get between the white lines," he said that afternoon after Montoyo had put him on pitching standby. "The only reason I'd prefer not to get in to pitch is it probably means we're in bad shape in the game. But I'm ready if he needs me."

Baseball people talk often about how bitter a Triple-A clubhouse can feel. Many of those playing in Triple-A have played in the major leagues, and most of them believe they should still be there. Some are back because they've gotten hurt. Others have had short stints and are convinced they should be back—and will be back—in the near future. Others have had lengthy major-league careers and believe that their presence in Triple-A at that moment is an anomaly, that they will be back where they really belong very soon.

"What's amazing is how quickly guys develop a major-league attitude," said Tony La Russa, who managed in the major leagues in Chicago, Oakland, and St. Louis for thirty-three years but spent most of his playing career in the minors. "What I mean by that is a guy can spend ten years in the minors carrying his own bags, staying in roadside motels, and riding buses and then goes up to the majors for two weeks and comes back thinking he should never carry his own bag again."

He smiled. "Usually those are the guys who don't go back. The guys who understand that they're back in the minors because they need to play better are the ones who end up being major leaguers again."

Albernaz had never been to the big leagues. He had spent more time in Double-A than in Triple-A but had seen enough teammates get the call through the years, even for short stints, that he hadn't ruled out the possibility.

"If it never happens, well, I've come pretty close by getting this far," he said. "I'm one of those guys who has to do the little things to succeed. I understand that. If Charlie tells me he needs me to pitch, I'm happy to pitch."

So, as it turns out, Buck Showalter was wrong: there are guys who are happy to be in Triple-A.

But they are few and far between.

————

Chris Dickerson is far more typical of those playing in Triple-A than Albernaz. He had played in the major leagues for parts of four seasons when he arrived in Tampa for training camp in February 2012. He was six weeks shy of thirty, and as loaded as the Yankees usually are, he knew they liked experienced players on the bench. That was why he thought he had a chance to make the team. He had played in sixty games for the Yankees in 2011, most as a defensive replacement. That was fine with him—the majors were the majors.

Dickerson was a classic example of what scouts call a 4-A player. He was probably a little too good to be playing Triple-A but not quite good enough to play regularly in the major leagues. In 2008, the last season in which he had spent most of his time in Triple-A, he had hit .287 with eleven homers, fifty-three RBIs, and twenty-six steals in ninety-seven games. He had speed, he could play defense, and he could hit the occasional home run. He just couldn't hit quite well enough at the major-league level.

Still, Dickerson wasn't prepared when the Yankees told him early in training camp that he was being outrighted to Triple-A. There are several ways to be sent to the minors. The best way is to be optioned. That means you are still on a team's forty-man roster, which makes it easy to be brought back to the majors. If you are outrighted, you are off the forty-man roster, and if you are called back up before September 1, you have to go through waivers—meaning another team can grab you.

"I was stunned," Dickerson said. "It wasn't as if I thought I was a lock to make the team, but I thought I'd get a chance. I was hurt and I was angry. I just think I'm a better player than that."

He shook his head at the thought of spending an entire season in the minor leagues. "When you go home for the winter after being on the big-league ball club, it means something," he said. "People look at you a certain way. You go home after being in the minors, and people say to you, 'So, do you think you'll make it back to the pros?'

"*That* is the most annoying thing anyone can say. What do people think I've been doing since college, playing for fun? People don't understand—Triple-A baseball is very real and very good. The guys playing Triple-A are really, really good baseball players."

He smiled and shook his head. "Of course no one wants to be one of them," he said. "Including me."

5

Johnson and Montoyo

MANAGING EXPECTATIONS

If there was anyone working in the International League in 2012 who had a right to feel he deserved better, it was Ron Johnson.

The thought never crossed his mind.

Johnson, known to one and all in the Norfolk Tides' clubhouse as RJ (pronounced as a name—Arejay—not as two letters), was an old-time baseball guy who believed in old-time baseball rules—written and, mostly, unwritten. He had worked in the minor leagues for most of his adult life, signing with the Kansas City Royals in 1978 as a twenty-fourth-round draft pick after graduating from Fresno State.

He had played for eight full seasons and had three brief stints in the majors with the Royals and the Montreal Expos, playing in a total of twenty-two games. He'd been to bat forty-six times in the majors and had hit .261 without a homer and with two RBIs.

"To be honest, I'm pretty proud of the fact that I got there at all," he said, smiling. "I was a long shot when I signed, a long shot when I was playing, and a long shot after I stopped playing. I guess I've always been a long shot. Maybe that's why it doesn't bother me to be back in the minors. It's the life I've known for thirty-five years.

"Of course anyone who tells you they don't want to be in the majors is either lying or crazy. Especially once you've been there."

He looked around his small office for a moment. "This is real life. There's nothing real about that life."

Johnson had coached and managed in the minors for twenty-four years after retiring as a player. Then, in the fall of 2009, the call had finally come: the Red Sox were promoting him from the managing job he had held for five years in Pawtucket to be Terry Francona's first-base coach.

"Dream come true," Johnson said. "It took me a while, but I was finally there. And, I wasn't going to be sent down after a week or a month. I was in the major leagues."

If there was any manager in baseball whose job appeared to be secure at that moment in time, it was Francona. At the age of fifty-four, Johnson was in the majors, and he hoped it was for a long ride.

Little did he know that the ride would be the bumpiest of his life, filled with a personal tragedy when one of his daughters was in a catastrophic accident and a stunning ending when the Red Sox collapsed in the final month of the 2011 season, costing Francona his job.

"You have an eight-game lead with a month to go and you don't make the playoffs, people are going to lose their jobs—especially in Boston," Johnson said. "As soon as Tito [Francona] was gone, I knew I wouldn't be far behind."

The Red Sox had been good to Johnson, especially following his daughter's accident. They had given him all the time he needed away from the team and helped with the family's expenses. Everyone in baseball had come to the family's aid during that time.

But wins and losses on the field have very little to do with family issues off the field—at least in the minds of those in charge. You win, you get a raise. You lose, sooner or later, you get fired.

"I figured I would take a year off and relax," Johnson said. "I've been on the road my entire adult life. It actually sounded pretty good to me."

A month after he was fired in Boston, Dan Duquette, the new general manager in Baltimore, called Johnson. The two men had worked together when Duquette had been the Red Sox' GM. He needed a manager in Norfolk. Was Johnson interested?

Johnson thought about it briefly, discussed it with his wife, and made a quick decision. "I'll take it," he told Duquette. "I'm not sure why I'll take it, but I'll take it."

Actually, he knew exactly why he was taking it: it was baseball and he was a baseball guy.

"I get paid to go to the ballpark and put on a uniform every day," he said. "How can I possibly complain?"

It was after midnight as he spoke, a half-eaten plate of food in front of him. He was about to go home for a few hours of sleep. There was another game the next day.

Johnson would be there, in uniform—six hours before first pitch—to get ready for another day in baseball.

———

No sport is more wedded to ritual than baseball. The day after the World Series ends each year, the question "When do pitchers and catchers report?" is asked as part of the ritual of the off-season. Of course most baseball people don't acknowledge that there is an off-season. They refer to the winter months as "the hot stove league"— a nickname for yet another baseball ritual that dates to the days when people literally sat around their stoves to keep warm and talk about the trades their team might make while the snow was still falling outside.

Ritual.

For established major leaguers, the ritual of spring training is often a family affair. Cars are packed up for long drives to Florida or Arizona. Kids get their homework assignments for several weeks, or, these days, parents hire tutors to work with them while they miss school for a month to spend time in the sun as their classmates shiver in colder climates in late February and through spring break into March.

It is different for those who have spent all or most of their careers in the minor leagues. Their February ritual almost always involves saying good-bye to their families for six weeks. Maybe they can steal a week away during spring break, but often as not the work involved— not to mention the money involved—in the travel isn't worth it.

For baseball teams, spring training is an all-hands-on-deck affair. Nowadays, they all have massive, modern complexes that have enough fields to accommodate everyone under contract—the fifty or sixty players who are invited to major-league camp and about two hundred more who report to the minor-league facility.

The players invited to the major-league camp work with the major-league manager and his coaches and with a number of people who will be working in the minor leagues once the season begins: the Triple-A manager and his coaches (most teams have two, some three) and various instructors who rove the minor leagues at all levels during the season, not only working with players, but also reporting to the major-league front office on their progress.

For those who know they will begin the season in the minor leagues, spring training is a time to savor, not just because everything is fresh and the weather is warm, but because you live the life of a big leaguer for six weeks.

"Lots more room in the clubhouse, and the food is a lot better," Durham manager Charlie Montoyo said on a bright February Sunday, sitting inside the Tampa Bay Rays' clubhouse in Port Charlotte, Florida.

Montoyo had just been through the good-bye ritual with his family, which was never easy. It was easier this time because his four-year-old son, Alexander, who had already been through three heart surgeries and was facing a fourth in the future, was healthy and doing well. It didn't make leaving easy; it just made it a little less worrisome.

"I miss them [his wife and two sons] a lot," he said. "But I remind myself I'm not the only one dealing with missing my family. It's part of the deal when you do this for a living."

Montoyo was about to start his sixth season as the manager of the Durham Bulls—arguably the most famous minor-league baseball team in history. The Bulls were immortalized in Ron Shelton's 1988 movie, *Bull Durham,* and remain the one minor-league team even casual baseball fans can name off the tops of their heads.

Much has changed in Durham in the quarter century since the

movie was filmed there. For one thing, the Bulls no longer play in the Class A Carolina League, several long steps from the majors. (Nuke LaLoosh being called up to "The Show" direct from the Bulls was one aspect of the movie that is extremely unlikely to ever happen.) Since 1998, the Bulls have been the Rays' No. 1 farm team, which means that most of the Rays' current stars have passed through Durham at some point.

The Bulls no longer play in Durham Athletic Park, although it still exists and hosts high school, college, and American Legion games. Their new park, which is a mile down the road from the old place, is called Durham Bulls Athletic Park. In Durham, most people just refer to it as the Dee-BAP. It opened in 1995 and is a modern, redbrick facility that seats ten thousand people. The famous snorting bull— "Hit Bull Win Steak"—was moved to the new ballpark, where it now sits atop and behind the left-field wall, known as the Blue Monster, because it is a blue copy of Fenway Park's Green Monster. In tribute to twenty-first-century diets, the grass that the bull is standing on reads, "Hit Grass Win Salad." About one or two players a year hit the bull and collect their steak. To the best of everyone's recollection, no one has cashed in on a salad yet.

The Bulls have retired two numbers in their history, which dates to 1902: One is the number 18 worn by the Hall of Famer Joe Morgan when he played for the team in 1963 on his way to starring first in Houston and then as a two-time MVP in Cincinnati. The other is the number 8 worn by Crash Davis.

Davis did, in fact, play for the Bulls in the 1940s and spent three years in the major leagues prior to that, playing for the Philadelphia Athletics. That's not why his number is retired, though; it's retired because Shelton and Kevin Costner made it—and him—famous.

Montoyo has seen *Bull Durham* and appreciates the unique history of the team he manages. Most days, though, he drives to the ballpark from his two-bedroom apartment, sits in his small office under the first-base stands, and makes out a lineup—knowing that the players available to him that day may not be available the next day.

"I've loved baseball since I was a kid, and I still love it," he said. "But at this point in my life, I'm forty-six and I have two kids to raise. Baseball's my job. The best thing I have going for me this year is that I have a two-year contract. That's the first time since I got drafted out of college that I've had that kind of security. That's important to me."

Montoyo has coached and managed in the Rays' farm system since he "got retired" as a player in 1996. He was talented enough as a kid growing up in Puerto Rico that he was offered the chance to move to California to play junior college baseball by a man named Don Odderman.

"He was Puerto Rican and he looked for kids he thought had a chance to make it in baseball in the U.S. and he financed them," Montoyo said. "It was kind of a scholarship program. A number of good players came to the U.S. because of him."

Odderman set Montoyo up to play at De Anza College in Cupertino, California. His coach picked him up at the airport and drove him to the house of a local family that hosted some of De Anza's players. Montoyo was eighteen and spoke no English. The family he was staying with spoke no Spanish.

After two years at De Anza, he was recruited to play at Louisiana Tech. "I felt like I had to learn a third language when I went down there," he said. "Southern. People would say to me, 'Well, I'm fixing to go now,' and I'd say, 'What is it you're going to fix?'"

He majored in business at Louisiana Tech but didn't stick around long enough to get a degree. The Milwaukee Brewers drafted him in the sixth round in 1987, and since playing baseball was his goal, he left school to play rookie ball in Helena, Montana. From there he moved up the minor-league ladder from Beloit to Stockton to El Paso to Denver. Prior to the 1993 season the Brewers traded him to the Expos, which made sense for Montoyo because the Brewers had Pat Listach, who had been the American League's Rookie of the Year in 1992, playing second base, meaning Montoyo was more likely to get a shot in the majors with another team.

Sure enough, his shot came late in the 1993 season. On September 7, Montoyo arrived at the ballpark in Ottawa, which was then the

Expos' Triple-A team, at about two o'clock in the afternoon and was called into manager Mike Quade's office.

"You want to play tonight?" Quade asked him.

Montoyo was surprised by the question. "Of course I do," he answered.

"Well, then you better get going," Quade said. "The game in Montreal starts at seven-thirty."

It took Montoyo a split second to understand what Quade was saying.

"Seriously?" he asked.

Quade just nodded.

"Naturally, I got lost on the way," he said. "There was no GPS or anything other than a map or asking directions. I pulled in to a gas station looking for help. I spoke Spanish and English, and they spoke French. It didn't work so well."

Montoyo finally got to Olympic Stadium at about seven o'clock. He got into uniform and sat on the bench—"pretty much in awe"—as the game against the Colorado Rockies moved along. In the eighth inning, with the game tied, manager Felipe Alou turned and pointed at Montoyo.

"Grab a bat," he said, which is baseball for "you're pinch-hitting."

Montoyo is fluent in three languages: Spanish, English, and baseball. He grabbed the first bat he could find.

Montoyo came up against the Rockies' reliever Gary Wayne with the go-ahead run on second base and two men out. He promptly singled up the middle, driving in what proved to be the winning run. "The best thing was Felipe sent me up there so quickly I had no chance to think about how scared I was," Montoyo said. "If I'd thought about it, I probably wouldn't have been able to get the bat off my shoulder."

Montoyo spent the rest of the season with the Expos—twenty-two days in all. He had five at-bats and two hits—the second one driving in two runs, meaning he had three RBIs in five at-bats. As it turned out, that was the beginning and the end of his career as a big-league ballplayer.

He played in the minors for three more seasons. He was a player-coach at the Double-A level in 1996 and was fairly certain he wasn't going to be offered any kind of playing contract for the next season. "I actually thought I might get cut in spring training in '96, but they sent me to Double-A," he said. "I hit behind Vlad Guerrero [who would go on to hit 449 major-league home runs] for a lot of that season in Harrisburg and got back to Triple-A for a little while before the end of the season.

"But the Expos had some young guys coming along, so I knew I was probably done," he said. "I knew I wanted to stay in baseball. The question was, how?"

The answer was the Rays. Tom Foley, whom Montoyo knew from his time in the Expos' organization, had been hired as a field coordinator by the Rays and was looking for someone to manage the Rays' Class A team in Princeton, West Virginia, during the 1997 season. The Rays would not start playing in the American League until 1998, but they had minor-league teams playing a year earlier. Montoyo had just turned thirty-one. He had played for ten years, including his stint in Montreal in 1993. As a minor leaguer, including six seasons in Triple-A, he had hit .266. Only as a major leaguer did he hit .400—leading to his oft-repeated line about being the game's "last .400 hitter."

"I knew another chance might not come down the pike to make the switch," he said. "So I told Tom I'd love to come and work for him."

He has been with the Rays' organization ever since, moving steadily up the minor-league chain from Princeton to Hudson Valley (upstate New York); Charleston, South Carolina (where he met his wife, Samantha); Bakersfield, California; Orlando; Montgomery, Alabama; and finally Durham in 2007. He had just won the Double-A title in Montgomery in his third year managing the Biscuits in 2006 when he got the Triple-A job in Durham. He was an instant success there, winning the division title in 2007 while continuing to receive rave reviews from his players and those running the Rays' organization.

By then he was a father, his son Tyson having been born in 2003.

Shortly after the end of his first season in Durham, Alexander was born with the heart issues that made hospitals a too-familiar place for the Montoyo family. Alexander had open-heart surgery to try to correct or at least control the symptoms of the condition when he was one month old. Although he was healthy enough to go to school during 2012, he faced at least one more heart catheterization and, depending on the results, the possibility of still more surgery.

"Whenever I think about him going through it again, I want to cry," Montoyo said softly. On his desk in Bulls Athletic Park are photographs of his family, including several of Alex right after his first surgery. Underneath one is a caption that says, "Prayer with faith can change things."

Montoyo never prays during a baseball game. He saves it for more important things.

———

As 2012 began, Montoyo had never failed to reach the postseason while managing in Durham. He had reached the playoffs in each of his first five seasons, winning the Triple-A National Championship in 2009. The Rays had played their first season in 1998 and for ten years had been one of baseball's worst teams. But in 2008 the young players they had acquired with high draft picks through the years began to pay dividends, and they won the American League East title and made it to the World Series. They made the playoffs again in 2010 and in 2011, all the while managed by Joe Maddon, who had been hired at the end of the 2005 season, when the Rays finished 67-95.

The team had been sold by then, and new management was in place. After two more horrific seasons (61-101 and 66-96) under Maddon, the Rays took off. The young talent moving through the farm system made the managing job in Durham one of the better ones in Triple-A. Montoyo was grateful to have good players, although he was always aware of the fact that he was expected to deliver those players to the majors with good attitudes, good fundamentals, and an understanding of how Maddon wanted the game played.

Montoyo's success, along with the fact that players universally sing his praises after playing for him, has made his a name that has come up when teams are talking about hiring a manager. Still, he's a realist: the guy in front of him in Tampa isn't going anywhere anytime soon. Maddon is only fifty-eight and considered one of the game's best managers.

That means another organization is going to have to go looking for someone and think, "Hey, that guy in Triple-A with no major-league experience might be the answer." Montoyo knows his best shot to make it to the majors is the Ron Johnson route—as a coach. One reason that most Triple-A managers coach third base is to prepare themselves for possibly being a base coach in the major leagues. Even so, Montoyo doesn't give "the jump," as it is called in Triple-A, much thought—especially once spring training is over and he heads back to Durham.

"When I was a player, there were guys who became obsessed with why they weren't in the big leagues," he said. "They would sit around and wonder why someone else got called up instead of them or what needed to happen to get them up to the majors.

"The same is true when you're managing. It doesn't do any good to sit around and wonder, 'When is my chance going to come? Is my chance *ever* going to come?' Some guys get it when they least expect it. Some guys never get it.

"All I know right now is I have a job and I like my job. I get paid okay, and I like going to work every day. I don't even look at the standings during the season. Believe me, I know when we're winning and when we're losing, and our local media guys always let me know where we are in the standings. In the past, when we've been closing in on clinching the division, our radio guy always lets me know, 'Five more games to clinch, four, three,' so I know what's going on. But I never go out of my way to find out.

"Getting a big-league job often has as much to do with being in the right place at the right time as it does with doing your job well. Just like playing. I always tell my players if they don't get discouraged

WHERE NOBODY KNOWS YOUR NAME

because they're here and keep giving everything they have every day, their chance will come. I tell myself the exact same thing.

"I have one goal in life right now: take care of my family. That hasn't been easy since Alexander was born. As long as I can do that, I'm fine."

———

Of the fourteen men managing in the International League in 2012, two had been managers at the major-league level: Dave Miley, who was in his seventh season managing the Scranton/Wilkes-Barre Yankees, had managed the Cincinnati Reds from late in 2003 until midway through 2005 and had been fired after compiling a 125-164 record. Joel Skinner, in his first season managing the Charlotte Knights—the White Sox' Triple-A team—had been an interim manager in Cleveland in 2002, going 35-41. That record was good enough to get him interviewed for the job at season's end but not good enough to get him hired.

Every manager in the league hoped his time would come—or come again—when he would be in the majors.

Seven of the fourteen had played in the majors, ranging from Montoyo's twenty-two days as a .400 hitter to Lehigh Valley manager Ryne Sandberg, who was in the Hall of Fame. If anyone in the group was considered a lock to manage in the majors someday, it was Sandberg.

"First of all, the guy's really good," said Pawtucket's Arnie Beyeler. "Second of all, the back of the bubble gum card matters."

Among the facts on the back of Sandberg's bubble gum card were sixteen major-league seasons, almost all of them with the Chicago Cubs; ten trips to the All-Star game; nine Gold Gloves as the National League's best defensive second baseman; seven Silver Slugger awards as the best hitter at his position; and the 1984 National League MVP. Most important of course was the last notation: inducted into the Hall of Fame, 2005.

Sandberg had already been mentioned as a future Cubs manager and had been interviewed prior to the 2012 season for the St. Louis Cardinals job after Tony La Russa retired. He was in his second season at Lehigh Valley, and most in the league didn't expect him to be around much longer. Sure enough, at the end of 2012, he was named the Philadelphia Phillies' bench coach. With Charlie Manuel turning sixty-nine before the start of the 2013 season, most looked at Sandberg as the Phillies' manager-in-waiting. The wait was shorter than he expected: Manuel was fired in August 2013 and Sandberg was named to take his place.

"I really admire the fact that he's paid his dues managing in the minors," Beyeler said. "A lot of guys with his background think being in the minors is beneath them. They'll either take a coaching job in the majors or just wait for the phone to ring. Ryne was willing to start at the bottom and work his way up. I think in the long run it'll make him a better manager when he gets up there—which he will, very soon."

Sandberg had managed at Class A, Double-A, and Triple-A for the Cubs and had made no secret of the fact that he dreamed of managing the Cubs. But he was passed over for Mike Quade when Lou Piniella retired in 2010 and again at the end of the 2011 season, when new general manager Theo Epstein hired Dale Sveum. Some thought Epstein passed on Sandberg because he didn't want to ask a Cubs icon to manage such a bad team. The Cubs were certainly bad in 2012—they lost 101 games under Sveum. Others thought Epstein wanted "his own guy," and no one would ever see Sandberg as anybody's guy but his own.

Now that Sandberg is managing in the big leagues, his players would be well advised not to bring what Tony La Russa called the "major-league attitude" with them to the ballpark each day because it won't go over well with the manager.

As his players made their way onto the field for pregame stretching one afternoon in Allentown, someone asked Sandberg how he dealt with a player who was late for stretching. Sandberg looked as if he had been asked if he had ever considered trying to fly to the moon.

"That would never happen," he said quietly, but with steel in his voice. "My players know better."

Clearly, Sandberg could care less what the back of his bubble gum card says. Managing—at any level—is a lot more serious than that. In 2012, there was a sign over the door that leads from the tunnel to the IronPigs' dugout on the third-base side of Coca-Cola Park. It said: "Play like an asshole today."

It is something just about everyone in Triple-A aspires to do.

6

Slice of Life

SENT DOWN . . . CALLED UP . . .

When the 2011 baseball season ended, Washington Nationals pitcher John Lannan was excited. He was also a bit apprehensive.

"I felt like I had lived through a lot of bad times with our team," he said. "I thought we were on the verge of something good happening. I also knew they were planning to do a lot in the off-season. I guess I didn't understand quite how much."

Lannan had turned twenty-seven the day before the Nationals' season finale. He had pitched to a record of 10-13, hardly anything to write home about, but his ERA had been 3.70 in thirty-three starts—the best numbers of his career. He was durable, he was left-handed, and he had battled back after a slump in 2010 that had resulted in being sent briefly down to Double-A—after beginning the season as Washington's opening-day starter for the second year in a row.

"Being sent down was a little bit of a shock to my system," he said. "But I was pitching poorly, and I needed to work on my mechanics and try to get myself straightened out. I knew what they were trying to do, so it didn't bother me very much. I didn't like being there, but I understood the reasoning behind it."

Lannan had made it to the majors quickly after being drafted out of Siena College by the Nationals in 2005. Because the team had so little pitching, a lot of young pitchers were rushed to the majors to see what they had. Lannan was twenty-two when he got the call in the summer of 2007. He had started the season with the Nationals' Class A team in Potomac but had moved quickly up the ladder through Double-A and Triple-A. When his ERA through six starts at Triple-A was 1.66 he found himself in Washington.

"It happened very fast that year," he said. "But to me it was, 'Okay, this is the way it's supposed to be.' I had a lot of confidence in myself. It wasn't as if I started the year thinking I'd be in the majors by July, but I did believe I was going to be in the majors in the near future."

What was hard to believe was where he found himself in his third major-league start. He had gotten a win in his second outing, and his turn came up again on August 6 in San Francisco. As luck would have it, Barry Bonds was sitting on 755 home runs—meaning he was tied with Hank Aaron for the all-time lead in home runs. Lannan didn't really care if Bonds had taken steroids in order to catch Aaron; all he knew was he didn't want to give up No. 756 and become a footnote in baseball history.

Four times Bonds came to the plate that night. Once, Lannan walked him. The other three times he got him out: on a foul to third base; a double-play ground ball; and a strikeout on a 3-2 pitch in the seventh inning.

"The last at-bat is pretty vivid in my mind," he said, smiling. "The place was packed, and here I was a couple of weeks out of the minors. Everyone was standing and it was a 1–1 game. When I got him, I walked off the mound wondering if the whole thing was a dream. I mean, seriously, a year earlier I'd been pitching for the Savannah Sand Gnats, and now I was striking Barry Bonds out when he was trying to break the all-time home run record. Are you kidding?"

Lannan became a regular in the Nats' rotation for the next four years except for the brief stint in Harrisburg in 2010. He had been arbitration eligible for the first time in 2011, meaning his salary had taken a huge jump from the $458,000 he had made in 2010 to $2.75 million in 2011. He was arbitration eligible again for the 2012 season. The previous year, he had accepted the Nats' salary offer without going to arbitration. When the team offered $5 million, Lannan and his agent countered by asking for $5.7 million. When the team refused, that meant Lannan's case would be heard by an arbitrator who would pick one salary or the other. There was no compromise.

Very few baseball negotiations ever actually get to an arbitration hearing because neither side wants to leave themselves in the hands of an arbitrator. More often than not, team and player will meet somewhere in the middle. There's another reason not to go to arbitration: the hearings can get ugly.

"The team's job is to explain to the arbitrator why the player is asking for too much money," Lannan said. "That means they have to say a lot of things about you that you might not want to hear. I don't think I took it personally. I know that some guys do, and that can hurt your relationship with the team."

Lannan had been pleased when the Nationals made a major off-season trade to acquire another left-handed starter, Gio González, from the Oakland Athletics. That appeared to leave them with a rotation of the rising superstar Stephen Strasburg; Jordan Zimmermann, another young talent; González; Lannan; and another young lefty, Ross Detwiler.

"When we got Gio, I was fired up," he said. "I thought it meant we were going to have a deep rotation—young, but deep." In fact, at twenty-seven, Lannan was the oldest of those five.

Then, on February 2, everything changed.

First, Lannan heard that the Nats had signed Edwin Jackson, a talented, though erratic, right-hander, to an $11 million free-agent contract. Later that day, he lost his arbitration hearing.

"When they signed Jackson, I had a feeling my days with the team were numbered," he said. "I knew [manager] Davey [Johnson] loved Detwiler and they hadn't signed Jackson for that kind of money to not start. I did the math and realized I was in trouble. Even so, I went to spring training telling myself to just do my job and the rest would take care of itself. I knew I was still a good pitcher."

It was a completely different sort of camp for Lannan. Twice in the past he had known early that he was the opening-day starter. The spring rotation had been built around making sure he would be ready to take the ball when the season began. Even a year earlier, when the Nationals had brought in veteran Liván Hernández and named him to start the opener, Lannan's only doubt was whether he would start game two or game three.

Now he wasn't sure *where* he would start the season, much less *when* he would start.

Often, he pitched exhibition games out of the bullpen, following one of the four locked-in starters—Strasburg, Zimmermann, Gonzáles, and Jackson—into games. He pitched well, though, and ten days before the team broke camp to head north, Johnson told him that he would be the team's fifth starter. Relieved, he called his wife, and they made plans to go apartment hunting in Washington. They had always rented in-season in the past but this time had waited to look for a place until Lannan was told he was going north.

They found a place they liked in the Foggy Bottom area of downtown Washington, about ten minutes from Nationals Park, and signed a lease just before the Nationals played their annual exhibition game in D.C. Many teams will play one game in their home park to give the stadium a run-through before opening day. On April 3, the Nats played the Boston Red Sox on a cold, sunny afternoon.

"I was sitting in the dugout taking it easy when [shortstop] Ian Desmond came in during the third inning and said he needed a pair of sunglasses," Lannan said. "I went up the tunnel to get him some, and I heard Davey [Johnson] coming up behind me as I got to the clubhouse.

"He said, 'Hey, come into my office for a minute.' I'm not sure why he said it, but he also said, 'Don't worry, you aren't getting traded.' So I had no idea what it was about.

"I got in there and he started talking about making tough decisions and how well Ross had been pitching. After a couple of minutes it suddenly hit me that he was sending me down. I was completely stunned. I'm not even sure I heard anything he said the last couple of minutes. When he stopped, I looked at him and said, 'You're sending me down? Seriously? You're sending me down?' I couldn't believe it. I'm sure I vented for a little while. I was angry. Finally, I went back in the clubhouse and asked to see [general manager Mike] Rizzo.

"I vented some more. I don't think I said or did anything unprofessional, but I was really upset. It just caught me completely off guard. One minute I'm getting Ian a pair of sunglasses; the next minute I'm packing for Syracuse."

———

Lannan's demotion was one of the most stunning anywhere in baseball that spring. Most players know what a call to the manager's office means. "When the manager wants to talk to you in the spring, it's never to tell you how well you've been playing," said Pete Orr, who spent most of his first seven years on the Triple-A/majors escalator. "At best, he's going to tell you that you're going to be playing less than you've been playing. At worst, he's going to tell you that you're being sent down."

The first time Orr made a team out of spring training was in 2005, when he was with the Braves. Just before the team went north, Chipper Jones sat down with him in the clubhouse one day to tell him not to be discouraged if he got sent down.

"It was the 'You're going down but you'll be back' speech," Orr remembered with a laugh. "It was Chipper's way of being a leader, letting a guy who'd had a good spring not feel too bad about going back down."

A few days later, Orr sat in the Braves' spring clubhouse in Orlando and saw players being called into manager Bobby Cox's office. Heart pounding, he waited for someone to come by his locker and say the dreaded words: "Skipper wants to see you."

"Nothing happened," Orr said. "Zach Miner [one of the team's pitchers] came out after they told him he was going down and said I'd made the club. He said his agent had heard we were trading [infielder] Nick Green to Tampa and that's why I was going north. I still didn't believe it.

"Then we broke camp and went to Atlanta. I still hadn't been told I'd made the club, and I wasn't sure. I bought a suit just in case I did make the team so I'd be ready to travel. The day of our exhibition game up there I walked by Bobby [Cox] and he said to me, 'Hey, Petey, how's it going?'

"I think I said something like, 'Great, Skipper, thanks.'

"He got a few feet past me, and then he stopped, turned around, and said, 'Hey, Petey, you know you made the club, right?' I guess it occurred to him that no one had told me. I said, 'I did?'

"He said, 'Yup, way to go,' and kept walking. Just like that I was in the big leagues."

One man walks up a tunnel to get sunglasses and ends up in Syracuse. Another passes his manager in a hallway and finds out he's a big leaguer.

"It's a business," Orr said. "We all know that. Some days it's a great business to be in. Other days aren't as great."

———

One person who wasn't surprised when the call came to go see the manager in the spring of 2012 was Bryce Harper.

Even if he wasn't happy about it.

Harper was baseball's most recent phenom. The Washington Nationals had chosen him with the No. 1 pick in the 2010 draft, although he wasn't yet eighteen. He had split the 2011 season between Class A Hagerstown and Double-A Harrisburg, and it was clear he was close to being ready for the majors—at least as a player.

The question was his maturity. Harper had been ejected from a game while in junior college for drawing a line in the batter's box to show an umpire where a pitch that had been called a strike had—in his opinion—*not* crossed the plate. He wore enough eye-black to be mistaken for someone playing an old-time movie Indian, and he drew a lot of attention when he blew a kiss to a pitcher in Hagerstown as he rounded the bases after hitting a home run.

He was cocky or, more accurately, cocksure, and he tended to draw attention to himself—especially as a No. 1 draft pick—in ways that didn't always make the Nationals happy.

The funny thing about it all was Harper came off as anything *but* cocky in person. He was quiet, self-deprecating, and almost matter-of-fact about the incidents he'd been involved in. He didn't deny them or defend them. They had just happened. He was religious, a Mormon who didn't drink and didn't use profanity, but he wasn't one of those athletes who talked about his faith. It was just part of his life.

When he was invited to the Nationals' big-league camp in the spring of 2012, he knew he wasn't going to make the team even if he hit .500. Part of it was that he was still only nineteen and the Nationals didn't want to rush him. Part of it was business: If the Nationals kept him in the minors until mid-season, he wouldn't become arbitration eligible until after the 2015 season. If he came up sooner, it would be a year earlier. The Nats had done the same thing with pitching phenom Stephen Strasburg in 2010, keeping him at Triple-A Syracuse until mid-June to push his first arbitration-eligible season back a year.

The difference between Strasburg and Harper was that there was no doubt that Strasburg, who had gone to college for three years and was twenty-one in the spring of 2010, was ready to pitch in the big leagues when spring training ended. Harper was a question mark in March, although no one doubted he would be up by mid-season.

Manager Davey Johnson actually believed Harper *was* ready for the majors. Mike Rizzo, the general manager, wanted to go more slowly. That's the way it usually is: managers, who are judged year to year, want the most talented players on the team right away. GMs, who are given a longer rope and take a longer view, tend to be more patient.

"I think I was a lot calmer in the spring than I had been the year before," Harper said. "I wanted to try to make it impossible for them to send me down, but I was okay with it happening when it did. Davey told me they wanted me to play some games down there in center field because they might need me to do that when I came back up. My attitude was, 'Whatever you want me to do, I'll do it.'

"If I needed 250 at-bats down there, so be it. If it was 25, that was fine too."

The Nationals weren't going to just send Harper down to Syracuse and hope everything turned out well there. Triple-A clubhouses are filled with veterans, many in their thirties, many making $12,000 a month and hanging on for dear life. A team didn't just let a nineteen-year-old who had signed for $17.9 million wander in there unprotected. Syracuse manager Tony Beasley assigned two veterans, Jason Michaels and Mark Teahen, both of whom had major-league experience, to "mentor" Harper—which meant keeping an eye on him.

"It wasn't like the kid needed to be watched or anything; he isn't that kind of kid," Beasley said. "But he was still learning. Michaels and Teahen are both guys who know the right way to do things and who would be a positive influence on him."

That didn't mean Harper didn't struggle to find himself in Syracuse. With the *Washington Post* running a daily "Harper watch" that reported on how he was doing game to game, he struggled at the plate and didn't appear comfortable at the Triple-A level. John Lannan, who by this point had been sent down and had arrived in Syracuse not long after Harper and was dealing with his own issues, felt as if he knew exactly what was wrong with Harper.

"He's built for the big stage," Lannan said. "That's just who he is. He wasn't going to do well playing in front of twenty people in forty-degree weather in April in Syracuse or in the snow in Buffalo. I understood what he was feeling because I was feeling some of it myself.

"You get used to the feel of a major-league park—the big crowds, the atmosphere, the noise. Early in the season, especially up north, you feel like you can hear people when they sneeze in the stands. I know Bryce hadn't been in the majors, but that's what he was born to do. He wasn't meant to be in Triple-A. He's got too much star quality for that."

Rizzo came to Syracuse to check on Harper's progress and, even though the numbers weren't great, liked what he was seeing. And so, when two of the Nationals' better offensive players, Ryan Zimmerman and Michael Morse, went on the disabled list, Rizzo decided Harper was the best option available to bring up. On April 27, the agate around the country said very simply, "Washington Nationals recalled outfielder Bryce Harper."

Most players get emotional when they are first called up and can remember almost word for word how they found out they were being sent to the majors. Harper talks about it as if describing how he ordered breakfast.

"Tony called me in and said, 'The team is in California, you've got a flight in an hour,'" Harper remembered. He smiled. "He also said, 'You might be back.' I understood what he was saying, that I was going up because guys were hurt, but to me that was just a challenge. I knew I had to go up and prove that I belonged."

Often when a player is called up to the majors for the first time, his teammates give him a send-off in the clubhouse—nothing formal, just everyone gathering around to offer congratulations. At some point, someone almost inevitably says, "Don't come back." But often as not, players do come back.

No one in Syracuse expected Harper back anytime in the near or distant future. He was one of those for whom promotion to the big leagues was only a question of when, not if.

"If he plays in the minor leagues again, it'll be on a rehab assignment" after an injury, Lannan said. "He wasn't doing anything more than passing through."

Harper's Triple-A career lasted twenty-one games. He hit .243 with one home run and three runs batted in—hardly statistics that jumped off the page. No one really cared. There wasn't any doubt about Harper's talent. Lannan's prediction proved correct: Harper didn't come back. In Washington, he hit .270 in 139 games with twenty-two home runs and fifty-nine runs batted in, setting all sorts of records for a player not yet twenty. He played a sometimes spectacular outfield, showed his speed by stealing eighteen bases, and showed his youth by occasionally making base-running gaffes brought on by overeagerness and a belief that his speed would always allow him to take an extra base. In November, he was voted Rookie of the Year in the National League.

Even though he was overshadowed by another rookie, the Angels' Mike Trout—who is fifteen months older than Harper—he more than lived up to the hype. And, he met the goal he set for himself on that March morning when Davey Johnson told him he was going to "play some games" in Syracuse: "Go down there and try to get out of there as soon as I could. Make them *want* me up here."

"Here" was Washington. It is where Harper will be for many years to come. But Harper's journey was certainly not typical . . . for him, making them want him was much easier than for most.

7

Schwinden and Podsednik

LIFE ON THE ROLLER COASTER

On April 26, the Buffalo Bisons were en route by bus from Allentown back home to Buffalo to begin a series the next night against the Rochester Red Wings.

It was a rare daytime bus trip. The Bisons had wrapped up a series the night before with a 12–1 win over Lehigh Valley, and since the twenty-sixth was one of their eight scheduled days off during the season, they spent the night in Allentown before busing home.

The bus had stopped at a McDonald's so everyone could get something to eat. Twenty-five-year-old pitcher Chris Schwinden, who had been called up to start four games for the Mets at the end of the previous season—and then sent back down to Buffalo to start 2012—was standing in line waiting to order. Schwinden's new season in Buffalo had gone well so far: he had started four times and was pitching to an ERA of 2.05, even though his record was only 2-2. He had been beaten 1–0 the last time he had pitched and was scheduled to open the series against Rochester the following night.

That changed when manager Wally Backman tapped Schwinden on the shoulder. "Just got a call from New York," he said. "You're going up. They need you to pitch in Colorado tomorrow. You need to get to the airport as soon as we get to Buffalo."

Schwinden had gotten a text the night before that Mike Pelfrey had come out of his last start complaining of shoulder soreness and had wondered if he might be a candidate for the call-up if Pelfrey couldn't take his next start.

"It's not as if you root for a guy to get hurt," he said. "But guys *do* get hurt, and when someone does, that can mean you get your chance. That's what had happened when Boof Bonser got hurt in Buffalo the year before. So here was my shot."

Schwinden had been disappointed but not angry when he had been sent down at the end of spring training. "When I looked back on it, there really wasn't much I could have or would have done differently," he said. "I thought I pitched well, but there was nothing I could do to make my twenty days of experience in the majors come close to Miguel Batista's twenty years in the majors." (Schwinden wasn't exaggerating: Batista had first pitched in the majors in Pittsburgh in 1992, and the Mets were his twelfth team.)

"What helped in Buffalo was the weather. It was miserable—cold, windy. That's perfect for a pitcher. The last thing you want is to foul off a fastball when it's forty degrees outside. That's one reason why a lot of pitchers are most effective in April—especially up north."

Of course going to pitch in Colorado wasn't exactly an ideal way to get another crack at the majors. The logistics of getting from Buffalo to Denver weren't all that easy to begin with, and then there was the issue of pitching in Denver's thin air. Even though run scoring had gone down in Coors Field once the Rockies had started putting their baseballs in a humidor so they wouldn't fly quite as far, it was still very much a hitter's park. But Schwinden wasn't concerned with that. He just wanted to pitch—in *any* major-league park.

Which he did the next evening. He wasn't awful—in fact he was the Mets' best pitcher that night in an 18–9 loss. But he wasn't good either, giving up five earned runs in four-plus innings, hurting himself in the fifth inning with a throwing error that led to a three-run home run.

"Easiest throw in baseball," he said, shaking his head. "Pitcher to the first baseman. It's also the hardest throw in baseball because you know it's the easiest. I psyched myself out that night. Everyone kept telling me I had to keep the ball down in that ballpark—which I knew. But I got too focused on it. I do get pitches up; I'm not a ground-ball pitcher. It became kind of a mental barrier for me right from the beginning."

Given the performance of their other pitchers that night, the Mets decided to give Schwinden another start five days later in Houston—another hitter's park, though not to quite the same degree as Colorado.

The results were identical: four innings pitched, five earned runs, meaning his ERA stayed exactly the same: 11.25. The only difference was that he was tagged with the loss.

And with a ticket back to Buffalo.

"Didn't shock me," he said. "It was disappointing, but I could hardly blame them. I tried to take the approach I took when I got sent down at the end of spring training: Be the best pitcher down there. Be the first guy called back up."

It took only fourteen days for him to get called back up. The irony was that it was an injury to Miguel Batista that put him on a plane to Toronto to rejoin the team. He sat in the bullpen on the night of May 20 and flew with the team from there to Pittsburgh. That was when Terry Collins told him he was going back to Buffalo. The team had decided it needed an extra bat—in the person of Vinny Rottino—on the bench rather than an extra arm in the bullpen.

There wasn't much Schwinden could do except pack his bags again and head back to the airport. This time he hadn't done anything to get sent back except for not being a very good hitter.

When a player is sent down to the minors—or comes up to the majors—the team handles all his travel. Mets traveling secretary Brian Smalls told Schwinden he couldn't get him on a nonstop flight to Buffalo, so he was sending him through JFK in New York and then on to Buffalo. Tired and a little bit discouraged, Schwinden said fine and headed to the airport. He got to JFK and was told that his flight to Buffalo was delayed for two hours. He sat and waited until he was told the flight was canceled.

He called Smalls. "Get your bags back," he said. "We'll send a car for you."

He was now eight hours by car from Buffalo. That was twice as far as he had been when he was in Pittsburgh. "Vinny [Rottino] took a car service from Buffalo to Pittsburgh that same day," Schwinden said. "Took him four hours door-to-door."

It took an hour for Schwinden to recover his bags and get to the car, meaning it was nine o'clock by the time he got out of JFK. It was raining, not hard, but enough to make the night even more depressing than it already had been. Schwinden sat back and decided to try to sleep. He was dozing off when the driver woke him.

"One of the [windshield] wipers is broken," he said. "I'm going to have to pull off and get it fixed. Can't drive all the way to Buffalo like this."

Schwinden looked up and realized the driver had gotten off the highway and was in the Bronx. He could see the lights of Yankee Stadium, where the Yankees were in the process of losing to the Kansas City Royals in front of a crowd announced at only 32,093 on a murky, not-made-for-baseball evening.

The driver found a gas station where it took about forty-five minutes to find new wipers and replace them. It was close to eleven o'clock by the time they were clear of New York and heading west on the New York State Thruway. By now it was raining hard. Schwinden settled back to try to sleep again.

Nothing doing.

"Flat tire," he said. "I swear to God you couldn't make it up if you tried."

The car limped to the side of the road. The driver was an older man, and after holding the umbrella and the flashlight for him for a couple of minutes, Schwinden realized it was going to be the Fourth of July before he got to Buffalo if he waited for him to change the tire.

"Hold the flashlight," he said finally and got down on his hands and knees to change the tire.

Finally back in the car, Schwinden sent a text to Joe Gocia, the Bisons' trainer, to find out what time the team was due at the ballpark the next day.

"By then I should have known what was coming," Schwinden said, laughing.

"Game is at one o'clock," Gocia responded. "And you're starting."

It was two o'clock in the morning when both driver and passenger decided they'd had enough and the car pulled in to a roadside motel outside Binghamton—still several hours from Buffalo. Schwinden asked the driver to have someone pick him up at 6:00 a.m. so he could get a few hours of sleep. He finally reached his apartment at 9:30 in the morning—eighteen hours after leaving Pittsburgh.

"I actually didn't pitch too badly," Schwinden said with a laugh. "Went five innings, gave up two earned runs. I was just glad to have my feet on the ground and not be in a car or an airport."

He was back in an airport a week later, this time headed to Philadelphia. The Mets had called again. Schwinden pitched in relief on May 30 at the tail end of a 10–6 loss, giving up two runs in two-thirds of an inning. He knew that another trip back to Buffalo—which would be the fourth time he'd been sent back to Triple-A since the end of spring training—was likely.

Except it didn't happen. On June 2, the Mets designated him for assignment—meaning he was off the forty-man roster and would almost certainly (barring an injury that might make the team change its mind) be put on waivers or released within ten days.

"I was stunned," Schwinden said. "I couldn't believe that just like that I was no longer a Met. They were the only organization I'd ever been in. I went from being in the major leagues one day to wondering if I was going to have a job the next.

"It was discouraging, but more than that it just caught me completely off guard. All I could think was, 'Okay, what happens now?'"

The answer would make the eighteen-hour trip from Pittsburgh to Buffalo feel as if it had been a weeklong vacation in Hawaii.

———

Although May and June would turn out to be roller-coaster months for Chris Schwinden, he could at least say he had a better

April than most players who are sent down to the minor leagues at the end of spring training.

The early weeks of a Triple-A baseball season are not often filled with glad tidings. There are a handful of players who are happy with where they are—players who have been promoted from Double-A; a few pitchers who know they will be called up when their team needs a fifth starter after the frequent off days of the first couple of weeks; the Bryce Harpers and Mike Trouts of the world who know their call-up can come at any minute and may come before April is over—depending on injuries.

For almost everyone else, life is pretty miserable.

Perhaps no one was more miserable that April than the thirty-six-year-old former World Series hero Scott Podsednik, who by his own admission wasn't doing a very good job of dealing with being back in Triple-A. There's an old baseball saying that instructs those playing the game to "try easier." If you grip the bat too tightly, swing it too hard, or try to throw the ball too hard, you are almost guaranteed to fail.

Podsednik knew that. His strength as a player, for as long as he could remember, had been his ability to understand what he could and could not do well. He had never tried to be a power hitter or a pull hitter or anything other than someone who knew how to get on base, play good defense, and be a smart baseball player. He had always understood that his legs—his speed—had gotten him to the major leagues, although it had never been an easy journey.

He was the classic all-around athlete as a kid growing up in West, Texas, a town of about twenty-five hundred people that is fifteen miles outside Waco. His dad, Duane, worked at a glass plant in Waco, and his mom, Amy, was a hospital administrator. Both their children, Scott and Shana—three years younger than Scott—were athletes as kids, and both were track stars in high school.

Scott was also a baseball star, alternating, as most good young players do, between pitching and playing a position, usually shortstop or the outfield. When he was a junior in high school, his dad learned that the Kansas City Royals were holding a tryout camp in Waco and suggested that he and Scott take a drive over, if only to see how Scott stacked up against players who aspired to play at a higher level.

"The big discussion driving over was whether I should sign up as a pitcher or as a position player," Podsednik remembered. "We finally decided I should put down position player because that was the best way to show off my speed." He smiled. "I could run like a deer."

In fact, he clocked the fastest time of anyone in the camp in the sixty-yard dash, and a year later the Texas Rangers made him their third-round pick in the 1994 amateur draft. That left him with another decision: sign with the Rangers or accept the scholarship he had been offered to the University of Texas, the college he had grown up dreaming about attending. In the end, he decided that turning pro was a quicker way to get to the major leagues and, if baseball didn't pan out, his bonus money would pay for him to go to college.

"I wonder now if I missed out on something not going to college for three or four years," he said. "I know it would have been fun. When you're eighteen years old and you sign on to be a pro, you have no idea what you're getting yourself into. You just can't imagine what life in the low minor leagues is like. The next eight and a half years weren't a lot of fun. In fact, they were very hard."

What made those eight and a half years hard, as much as anything, was the fact that Podsednik couldn't stay healthy for any extended period of time. He had three knee injuries, a broken wrist, a sports hernia operation, and various hamstring pulls that kept him off the field.

"I knew nothing about taking care of my body," he said. "And I was someone who had to do that. I wasn't a home run hitter. I counted on my speed. If anything went wrong, it affected me. I didn't even know how to hydrate properly. In the Gulf Coast League they play every day at one o'clock, and it's about a hundred degrees. Didn't even occur to me that I might be cramping because I wasn't drinking enough fluids.

"It took me a while just to figure out what I needed to do to *try* to be a successful baseball player. There's more to it than just getting up to the plate and getting on base."

In the minor leagues—especially the low minors—team trainers have about half a dozen jobs. They are travel agents, clubhouse managers, and, occasionally, Boy Scout pack leaders for players just breaking in. They are less likely to be alert to whether a player is doing the extra little things—like hydrating—that are a given in the majors, where the clubhouses are overrun at times with medical personnel.

Podsednik bounced around the Rangers' farm system for six years before signing with the Seattle Mariners after the 2000 season as a minor-league free agent. By then he was twenty-four and still hadn't been in the majors for one minute. He finally got a chance—briefly—in July 2001, when a slew of injuries got him a call-up to Seattle. In his first at-bat he came up with the bases loaded and tripled. Nothing to it. Except he was back in the minors a few weeks later. He was called up for a short time again the following year but was waived by the Mariners at the end of that season. He would be twenty-seven before the 2003 season started and had a total of twenty-six at-bats in nineteen games of major-league experience.

And then he got the break he needed. The Milwaukee Brewers decided it was worth the $20,000 waiver fee to acquire him. Podsednik made the team as a backup outfielder but played so well early in the season that manager Ned Yost put him into the lineup full-time in early May. Finally healthy, he blossomed. He hit .314, stole forty-three bases, scored a hundred runs, and finished second in the Rookie of the Year balloting behind Dontrelle Willis. A year later he led the National League with seventy stolen bases, but his batting average dropped to .244.

"I hit a few home runs early and forgot what it was that had made me successful the year before," he said. "I was still effective when I got on base, but I wasn't getting on base as much as I did the year before. I ended up with twelve home runs—most in my career. But that wasn't my game."

The Brewers traded him to the White Sox during the off-season, and he found his game again in 2005. He hit .290 and made the All-Star team. The White Sox, managed by the combustible Ozzie Guillén, had one of those dream seasons when everything comes together, and eighty-eight years after the franchise had last won the World Series—a longer drought than the infamous one broken a year earlier by the Red Sox—they found themselves facing the Houston Astros, a team that had never won a Series in forty-four years of existence.

The White Sox won game one at home, and game two went to the bottom of the ninth, tied at 6–6. With one out, Podsednik came to the plate against Astros closer Brad Lidge.

"Needless to say, I wasn't thinking about hitting a home run," he said, a smile lighting up his face as if he were remembering something that had just happened. "I wanted to get on base, try to drive the ball if I could, and get in scoring position. But a single would have been fine too because I would have had a chance to steal second."

Down 2-1 in the count, not wanting to put himself in danger of walking someone with Podsednik's speed, Lidge threw a belt-high fastball. Podsednik drove it—and it just kept going, rising above the right-field fence and into the seats as pandemonium engulfed the ballpark.

"What I remember most is my teammates waiting for me at home plate and thinking, 'Did that just happen, did that just really happen?' How many times as a kid do you dream of hitting a home run to win a World Series game? It doesn't happen very often to guys who hit [a lot of] home runs, so what were the chances of it happening to someone like me?" Not great, especially given that Podsednik was only the fourteenth player in World Series history to hit a game-ending home run.

That hit broke the Astros' spirit. The White Sox went to Houston and completed the sweep.

"There's a video of me running in from the outfield after the last out toward absolute mayhem in the infield," he said. "I have this look of pure joy on my face. I look like I'm a little kid again. The feeling was just amazing."

Then the injuries began to crop up again. As an arbitration-eligible player he made more than $2 million in both 2006 and 2007, but the White Sox released him at the end of 2007 after he played in only sixty-two games. They weren't going to go back to arbitration again with a thirty-one-year-old outfielder who was having trouble staying on the field. The World Series walk-off was a distant memory.

———

And so his odyssey began. He spent a year in Colorado as a part-time player and re-signed with the Rockies for 2009, only to be released in spring training. He had just turned thirty-three, and he didn't have a job. He went home and hoped the phone would ring. It did: the White Sox wanted him back.

"I went from sitting on my couch on opening day wondering if I would play again to my best year since '05," he said. "That year proved to me that if I could stay healthy, I could still be a factor for someone."

He hit .304 in 132 games. He became a free agent at season's end and signed with the Royals, who turned around and traded him to the Dodgers at mid-season. He hurt his foot soon after arriving in Los Angeles, was released at the end of that season, and signed with the Blue Jays for 2011. They sent him to Triple-A Las Vegas—briefly— and then released him in May. Eleven days later he signed with the Phillies and went to Lehigh Valley until another injury—plantar fasciitis in the same left foot that had troubled him in the past—ended his season after just thirty-four games.

All of this left him with a decision to make as 2012 dawned. He was married by then, and he and his wife, Lisa, had two boys, who were three and one. The Phillies had offered him a minor-league contract with an invitation to come to big-league camp and try to make the team.

"I was about to turn thirty-six in March," he said. "I wasn't sure if I wanted to be away from my kids. But I also didn't want my career to end with me being hurt. I still believed I had it in me to be a productive major leaguer again. I decided to work as hard as I possibly could and see what happened in the spring."

What happened was that Podsednik hit .309 in thirty-one spring training games—and thought he was going to make the team. But the business of baseball intervened, which was how he found himself in Charlie Manuel's office on that late March day hearing the "You're still good enough to play in the major leagues but . . ." speech.

"It came down to Juan Pierre or me for the last outfield spot," Podsednik said. "The bottom line was the bottom line. Juan had a contract with a March 30 opt-out, meaning if they sent him down, he could leave right away and sign with another team. I had an opt-out too, but not until June 1. That meant they could send me down and have me available for at least two months in case someone got hurt."

Which meant it was Lehigh Valley or go home. Podsednik's first instinct was to go home—which he did. It was Lisa who talked him into going back ten days later, pointing out that there were twenty-nine other teams that might pick him up and that, worst-case scenario, he could opt out of his Phillies contract on June 1.

"As nice as the home clubhouse at Coca-Cola Field is, it was culture shock for me walking back in there," Podsednik said. "I'd been there the year before, but that felt different, like a stopover. I didn't think I deserved to be there based on the way I'd played in the spring.

"The whole thing hit me hard. We get so spoiled in the big leagues. When you've been there for a while, it's very hard to get up for games in the minors. We're human. I just wasn't in a good place. Fortunately, Ryne [Sandberg] understood. He told me to try not to be one of those guys who was described as being 'bitterly back down in Triple-A.' I didn't want to be one of those guys. But it wasn't easy."

By early May, Podsednik was hitting only .197. He began to wonder if it wasn't getting to be time to go home. In his mind, June 1 remained the deadline. Maybe it was *having* a deadline, self-imposed or not, that kept him from playing well. Then, on May 11, Sandberg called him into his office. "You've been traded to Boston," he said. "They want you to go to Pawtucket, at least for now."

Podsednik knew the Red Sox had lost several outfielders to injury. All of a sudden he saw a light at the end of the minor-league tunnel. "I thought this might be a chance," he said. "I didn't think they'd pick me up if they didn't have something in mind."

Eleven days later, after reporting to Pawtucket, Podsednik found out what they had in mind. PawSox manager Arnie Beyeler called him in and told him he was to meet the Red Sox in Baltimore. A few days after he joined the Red Sox, Daniel Nava—who had been leading off for Boston—went down with an injury. Podsednik got to the ballpark the next afternoon, checked the lineup, and there he was: leading off and playing center field.

He was back. One more time.

8

Slice of Life

WALLY BACKMAN: SECOND CHANCES

The toughest place to be in the International League in the month of April is Buffalo. Syracuse, Rochester, and Pawtucket aren't exactly balmy, but there is nothing quite like Buffalo. That's why in 2012 the Buffalo Bisons—the Mets' Triple-A team—frequently offered two-for-one deals to their fans early in the season: come to one game, get tickets to another.

Snow on opening day in Buffalo isn't uncommon. In 2012, the temperature was a relatively mild forty-three degrees when the Bisons took the field to play the Scranton/Wilkes-Barre Yankees. The Yankees were baseball's version of the Flying Dutchman in 2012—a team, like the hero of the Wagnerian opera, without a home. Only true love could free the sea captain from his curse to sail the seas forever. For the Yankees' Triple-A farm team, it would be a little simpler: once the Yankees finished renovating the ballpark in Scranton, the team would have a home in 2013. That wasn't going to help those on the team in 2012, though: about half of their home schedule would be played in Rochester; the rest of their "home" games would be played in the opponent's ballpark with the Yankees batting last.

Yankees general manager Brian Cashman had hoped to put the team in Newark for the season. The independent league Newark Bears played in a thirteen-year-old sixty-two-hundred-seat stadium that would have fit the Yankees' needs just fine. It would have had the added benefit of being only a few miles from Yankee Stadium when players went up or were sent down.

That, however, was the rub. Because the ballpark was less than seventy-five miles from Citi Field—the Mets' home ballpark—the Mets invoked their territorial rights and refused to allow the Yankees to put the team there. The number of fans who might have passed on buying a ticket to a Mets game to go see Scranton/Wilkes-Barre play in Newark could probably be counted on both hands. But the Mets, who had serious attendance issues and even more serious financial woes, weren't taking any chances.

"I'm not angry," Cashman insisted during spring training. Then he smiled. "But payback can be a bitch."

Cashman's Triple-A players would never have the chance for payback. Like the legendary Flying Dutchman, they were doomed to wander the International League throughout 2012.

Unfettered by the weather—or perhaps encouraged by the fact that there was no snow—10,495 showed up to celebrate opening day for the twenty-fifth anniversary of Coca-Cola Field. The ballpark, opened in 1988, seats 18,025, making it one of the largest minor-league stadiums ever built. It is not to be confused with Coca-Cola Park in Allentown, which was built twenty years later. Seven of the fourteen ballparks in the International League had corporate names. Naming rights have become a major source of revenue for sports franchises at every level of play. Some I-League teams hung on to their stadium names because of tradition; others did so because no one had made them an offer.

The Bisons opened their home season with a 12–3 victory. It was the home debut for Wally Backman as the team's manager. Backman had managed seven minor-league teams in eleven years, after having been a major-league manager for exactly five days in November 2004, when the Arizona Diamondbacks had fired him before he ever put on a uniform.

"I've climbed all the way up the mountain, gone all the way back to the bottom, and now I'm trying to climb back up again," he said, sitting in his office one afternoon, an ever-present pack of cigarettes on his desk. Once it seemed that every manager at every level of base-ball smoked. Now managers like Jim Leyland of the Detroit Tigers (who spent years sneaking into the runway next to the dugout to smoke) and Backman are exceptions, not the rule.

Backman was in the third year of his return to the Mets' orga-nization. He had been brought back into the fold by team COO Jeff Wilpon, in part because he'd had success as a minor-league manager but also because he was a link to long-ago past glory in New York.

Backman had hit .320 in 1986 as the team's spark-plug second baseman, leading off against right-handed pitching as part of a very successful platoon with Tim Teufel—who was also back with the Mets, as a coach at the major-league level. In all, Backman had played fourteen big-league seasons after being the Mets' No. 1 pick in the 1977 amateur draft.

He had gotten into managing in 2002 and had immediate suc-cess with the Birmingham Barons, the White Sox' Double-A team. At the end of the 2004 season, after managing that year in the Dia-mondbacks' system, he was named manager of the Diamondbacks. It seemed to make perfect sense: smart, tough, spark-plug players often make good managers. Backman reminded people a little bit of Earl Weaver—except that he'd had a much better playing career than the Orioles' Hall of Fame manager.

But Backman never got a chance to prove how good he could be at the big-league level. On the day he was introduced by the Diamond-backs, a *New York Times* story revealed that Backman had dealt with legal and financial issues that the Diamondbacks apparently were not aware of when they offered him the job.

He had filed for bankruptcy and had been arrested twice: once for DWI and once for an altercation inside his home that involved his wife and another woman. He had served one day in jail after a judge suspended the rest of a one-year sentence. Initially, the Diamondbacks stood by their hire. But five days later they announced Backman had been fired and said they had failed to do a proper background check on him and he hadn't made them aware of his past.

Backman bounced from the top of the mountain to the bottom in a matter of days.

"I made mistakes and I had to learn from them," he said, eight years removed from the non-stint in Arizona. "It was hell to go through. I paid a major price, but I always believed I was tough enough and good enough to come back from it."

He had to go all the way down to independent league ball for three seasons, managing the South Georgia Peanuts in the South Coast League for a year and then the Joliet JackHammers of the Northern League for a year and a half. He hit rock bottom—or rockiest bottom if there is such a thing—when he was fired midway through his second season by the JackHammers, who, for all intents and purposes, were out of money and about to go bankrupt.

"I really wasn't sure what I was going to do next," he said. "Part of me just wanted to go home [to Oregon] and stay there with my family. They were the ones who were still standing next to me when the Arizona thing happened."

He smiled and lit a cigarette, leaned back in his chair, put his feet on his desk, and shook his head. "I spent a lot of time standing in the middle of Times Square with traffic coming at me in both directions and no one with me except my parents, my wife, and my kids standing by me. It wasn't a good feeling."

In the fall of 2009, Backman was scheduled to make an appearance in New York. Many of the 1986 Mets still make a decent-to-good living off their roles on that team. While Dwight Gooden, Keith Hernandez, Darryl Strawberry, and Gary Carter were the stars, Backman is remembered just about as fondly as any of them.

En route to the airport, Backman, almost on a whim, decided to call Jeff Wilpon, who had succeeded his father, Fred Wilpon, in running the Mets' day-to-day operations. Even before his plane took off, he got a call back. When Backman told Wilpon he was on his way to New York, Wilpon said, "Why don't we try to get together and talk while you're here?"

Jeff Wilpon had been just out of college and already working for his dad when the Mets won the World Series in 1986 and had warm memories of Backman. What's more, with the Mets struggling, bringing people back into the organization who brought back memories of that time seemed like a good idea.

Backman ended up being offered the job as manager of the Brooklyn Cyclones—the Mets' short-season class A team. Technically, the job was near the bottom of the organization's totem pole, but the Cyclones are very important to the Wilpons because of Fred Wilpon's emotional attachment to the Dodgers.

"Managing the Cyclones is a little different than managing your typical [low-A] rookie-league team," Backman said. "For one thing, most of the Mets' best young prospects get sent there, so they're keeping a close eye. What's more, the team is kind of the Wilpons' baby, and since it's right there in New York, they expect a lot—in terms of development *and* wins."

The Cyclones went 51-24 under Backman. The Mets were impressed enough that he was one of the finalists for the managing job at the big-league level after Jerry Manuel was fired at the end of that 2010 season. Terry Collins ended up getting the job, but Backman was promoted to Double-A Binghamton. A year later, when his former platoon mate Teufel was promoted from the managing job in Buffalo to the Mets' coaching staff, Backman was moved up to Triple-A—one step from the big leagues—again.

"My second trip back up the mountain," he said, smiling. "I think I'm as capable as a lot of guys managing in the big leagues. But I like what I'm doing here."

He put out the cigarette and stood up. At fifty-two, Backman is rounder and grayer than he was as a player, his hairline beating a retreat in the wrong direction. But the gleam in his eyes hasn't changed.

There are a lot of jokes made about the weather in Buffalo. Backman didn't mind the cold at all. He was a long way from the low point he had hit back in 2004.

"It's baseball," he said. "It's what I do. It's what I love."

He picked up a bat and walked out the door. It was time for batting practice.

9

Slice of Life

ALL ROADS LEAD TO NORFOLK

Once upon a time, putting together a baseball schedule for an entire season was a long process that involved hundreds—if not thousands—of pieces of crumpled paper and hours and hours of painstaking work.

Nowadays, computers have made life much easier for schedule makers.

Except in the International League. There, the schedule is still done by hand, and it is done by one person—the same person who has put together the schedule since 1969.

Dave Rosenfield has run the baseball team in Norfolk since 1963. He ran it when it was a Chicago White Sox affiliate and a Philadelphia Phillies affiliate in the Carolina League; he ran it when it became the Triple-A affiliate of the New York Mets; and he runs it now as the Baltimore Orioles' Triple-A affiliate—although he did finally turn day-to-day general managing duties over to Joe Gregory in 2011.

Gregory was thirty-two when he got the job, which made him exactly fifty years younger than the eighty-two-year-old Rosenfield, who still holds the title of executive vice president and is in his office every day. Gregory and manager Ron Johnson still run most decisions by Rosenfield, and he is a constant presence in every corner of Harbor Park, which has been the Tides' home since 1993.

Rosenfield also puts together the entire league's schedule every year, as he has done since the Tides came into the league forty-five years ago. Each season he has to figure out how to schedule 144 games for fourteen teams, making sure they can get where they need to go in time for each game, while having only eight off days during the entire season.

"It isn't that hard when you've been doing it as long as I have," Rosenfield said, sitting in his cluttered office one afternoon with several legal pads spread in front of him on which he had been piecing together the 2013 schedule. "I actually kind of fell into doing it after my first year here.

"They handed us the schedules at the [Carolina] league meetings. We were moving into the league for the '64 season. I looked at the schedule and noticed that Winston-Salem, which was where the league offices happened to be, had thirty-two weekend home dates. We had seven. I was sitting in the back of the room, and Bill Jessup, who was the president of the league, was going on about the schedule, and I must have been shaking my head noticeably, because all of a sudden he stopped and said, 'Hey, new boy, you think you can do it better?'

"I looked at him and said, 'A monkey could do it better.'

"He kind of glared at me for a second, pointed his finger at me, and said, 'You've got two weeks.' I went to work, presented him the schedule in two weeks, and the teams voted unanimously in favor of my version. After that, I did it every year. In fact, when we moved to the International League, I kept doing the Carolina League schedule in addition to ours for several years."

Rosenfield isn't a name-dropper; it's not his way. But he's known so many people for so many years there are few names that come up without his having some sort of story to tell about them. He's a natural-born storyteller, not surprising since his mother, Therese Lyon, was an accomplished actress.

She appeared on Broadway in a play written by Groucho Marx called *Time for Elizabeth*. She was also in *The Music Man* and, in 1947, had a role in Charlie Chaplin's *Monsieur Verdoux*.

"Charlie Chaplin and Groucho Marx, now *that's* name-dropping," Rosenfield said with a laugh on a hot summer afternoon. "She didn't even start acting until she was forty-nine. My dad was a co-founder of Piggly Wiggly, and she decided it would be fun to try acting. I was her youngest kid, eighth one."

As Rosenfield talked, Joe Gregory walked in. There was a problem. Like all minor-league teams, the Tides are always looking for promotions that might bring a few more fans to the ballpark. The team draws reasonably well—in 2012 it would average sixty-four hundred fans per home game—but every little bit helps.

That night's promotion was the Cowboy Monkey Rodeo Show. Seriously.

The show involved a guy in a cowboy outfit along with four border collies who were ridden by four capuchin monkeys. The collies and the monkeys, starting from just behind second base, chased four cattle across the outfield grass into a pen on the other side of the center-field fence.

Repeat: seriously.

The problem had nothing to do with the act itself. It was pretty harmless stuff, and the animals all clearly knew what was expected of them. The problem was the heat: it was late June in Norfolk, and the temperature was approaching a hundred degrees with the humidity dripping off everyone.

The show toured the country, apparently doing well enough that it continued to receive invitations to minor-league ballparks. This minor-league ballpark was a little bit different, though: it was located less than a mile from the international headquarters of PETA—People for the Ethical Treatment of Animals.

The folks from PETA were not happy with the notion of the animals being used to entertain fans in the brutal heat. They had organized a protest for outside the ballpark prior to the game, not exactly the way the Tides wanted their fans welcomed on a night when staying indoors had to be very tempting even if you already had tickets for the game.

Gregory reported that he had just consulted with the police about where the protesters would be allowed to picket and that it was pretty clear to him that the police wanted to give the protesters a wide swath. The last thing anyone wanted was to see arrests. There was one piece of good news: it would be very hot for the protesters too. They might not last that long.

There was one other not-so-minor issue: three hours before game time there weren't enough Tides in the building to field a team.

The Tides had played the previous night in Columbus and had been scheduled to fly home at 6:30 that morning—plenty of time, at least in theory—for a 7:15 game against the Syracuse Chiefs.

The trouble began when their flight was canceled due to "mechanical difficulties." Concurrent with this, the East Coast had been hit by a severe storm on Friday night, one that was causing huge travel delays all over the place. With many flights already grounded, finding a way to get thirty-one people—twenty-five players, a manager, three coaches, a broadcaster, and a trainer—back to Norfolk wasn't easy.

After a great deal of scrambling, the Tides had been rebooked on six different flights—three that went to Norfolk and three that went to Richmond. The airport in Richmond was eighty-seven miles from Harbor Park, no more than a ninety-minute trip under normal circumstances . . . but on a summer Saturday with people in the storm-ravaged Washington, D.C., area fleeing to the beach from houses without power, the trip would take considerably longer than that.

Players came stumbling into the clubhouse throughout the afternoon. Manager Ron Johnson stood in the hallway between his office and the players' lockers and shook his head. "I hope we can field a team tonight," he said—joking, but not joking. The last group wasn't due at the stadium—if nothing else went wrong—until 6:30.

"It's Triple-A," Johnson said. "This stuff happens down here. I always say to everyone, myself included, 'If you don't like it, do a better job.'"

Johnson's job had been made a bit more difficult not long after his plane—one of the ones that landed in Norfolk—arrived. En route to the ballpark he received a text from Baltimore: Two Orioles pitchers, Dana Eveland—who had started the game—and Tommy Hunter—

who had relieved him—had been knocked around by the Cleveland Indians that afternoon. Each had given up five runs: Eveland in three and two-thirds innings; Hunter, even worse, in one and two-thirds innings.

"Need González up here ASAP," Johnson's text said.

Miguel González was supposed to be Norfolk's starting pitcher that night. He arrived in the clubhouse a few minutes after Johnson and was about to get dressed to begin preparing for the game. Johnson stopped him. There was no time to congratulate him or wish him luck.

"Go back to the airport," Johnson told him. "They want you up in Baltimore."

González was twenty-eight and had bounced around the minor leagues for most of seven years before signing with the Orioles in the spring. The plan was for him to pitch in Double-A, but he had quickly impressed the team enough to get promoted to Norfolk in late April and Baltimore in June. That call-up had come because the bullpen needed some extra help. When González arrived, Orioles general manager Dan Duquette had been pleasantly surprised by his variety of pitches and his poise.

The Orioles were already desperate for starting pitching. Virtually their entire rotation had struggled since opening day. After consulting with manager Buck Showalter, Duquette decided to send González back to Norfolk to "stretch his arm out"—get him in the starting rotation down there to build his arm strength so he could potentially come back up to start in Baltimore when needed.

Now, less than a month later, González was needed—this time as a starter. He would start in Eveland's spot in five days—but he had to get to Baltimore right away because the team was flying to the West Coast the next afternoon after a day game against the Indians, and management wanted González on the flight so he could begin to get ready for his debut as a starter.

While González raced to the airport, Johnson went and found the relief pitcher Óscar Villarreal to tell him he would be starting the game that night. "I told him if he can get us into the fourth inning, I'll be thrilled," Johnson said. "After that, it's all hands on deck."

Johnson had no issues with the notion that his starting pitcher had been snatched from him a couple of hours before game time. Even though he had spent the previous two seasons as the first-base coach in Boston, the minor leagues had been his home in one form or another for more than thirty years. There wasn't much that was going to happen that would be new to him.

"When Buck [Showalter] calls and says, 'RJ, you got a minute?' I know what's coming," he said, laughing. "He needs something or someone up there, and he wants to know who the best guy is at that moment. My job is to make sure I get the right guy there. If I'm not doing that, what good am I to him and to the club?"

When Rosenfield walked down the hall that afternoon to see how Johnson was doing and to check on the whereabouts of the baseball team, Johnson laughed as Rosenfield sat down across from him.

"This could be a long one, boss," he said. "We might need more than one position player to pitch before we're done."

Rosenfield and Gregory had talked to the Syracuse people about delaying the start of the game and they had agreed. It was now an eight o'clock start—which helped Johnson, although it didn't mean he had a starting pitcher.

"This is why you're better off traveling by bus," Rosenfield said.

"I agree," Johnson said. "I'd much rather ride a bus for eight or nine hours, especially a comfortable one, than get up at four o'clock in the morning for a flight that may or may not take off on time—or may not take off at all."

"I'm making the schedule for next year right now," Rosenfield said. "You want bus trips to and from the Midwest and the North too?"

"Absolutely," Johnson said. "The more bus trips the better. Flying commercial, especially on days like this, is no fun. At least on the bus we know almost exactly when we're going to arrive."

Travel is one of the biggest differences between life in the minors and life in the majors. Major-league teams travel on charter airplanes, and players pass their luggage to a clubhouse attendant after the last game in a city and don't see it again until they walk into their hotel room. Almost everywhere that hotel is a Four Seasons or a Ritz-Carlton. In Triple-A, everyone carries his own luggage, and most of the hotels don't have bellmen. Or room service.

"It isn't as if there's anything wrong with the way you live in Triple-A," Dontrelle Willis said, sitting at the opposite end of the hallway from Johnson's office. He had been one of the lucky Tides who had been on a flight that connected in Atlanta and had landed in Norfolk by mid-afternoon. "It's just the way you live in the major leagues isn't real. Real people don't live like that. But major leaguers do."

Willis had not only been a major leaguer; he had been a star. He had been the National League Rookie of the Year in 2003, when he won fourteen games for a Florida Marlins team that had gone on to win the World Series. Two years later, still only twenty-three years old, Willis won twenty-two games and finished second to Chris Carpenter in the National League Cy Young Award voting.

He was a genuine phenom: a gangly lefty with a delivery that made it tough to follow the baseball as it came out of his hand. He was also a remarkably good hitter for a pitcher, so good that he didn't always hit ninth in the order.

"I think I was good, but I probably wasn't as good as it seemed in '05," he said. "I got a lot of run support that year [his ERA was 2.63, so his success wasn't *just* about run support], and we had a good team. I look back on those years in Florida and realize how lucky I was to be there and to get the chances I got."

If Willis was bitter about the twisted road his career had traveled since the twenty-two-win season, it didn't show as he sat in the middle of the Norfolk clubhouse. He talked easily, almost happily about the struggles he had faced in the five seasons since being taken from the Marlins.

Even though he had pitched reasonably well in 2006 and 2007, his numbers—both in wins and in ERA—hadn't come close to 2005. Prior to the 2008 season he was traded, along with Miguel Cabrera, to the Detroit Tigers in a blockbuster trade that was also a Marlins salary dump. The Marlins got back six low-priced prospects in exchange for Cabrera and Willis (Willis had signed for $6.45 million prior to the season). Even though Willis had pitched to a 10-15 record in 2007, the Tigers believed his best years were still ahead of him. He was still only twenty-five, and he had already won sixty-eight games in the majors. They signed him to a three-year deal worth $29 million.

And got almost nothing out of it. Willis pitched for the Tigers for just under two and a half years. During that time he won two games, meaning he cost the Tigers $14.5 million per win. He struggled with injuries, with wildness, and with an anxiety disorder that landed him on the disabled list twice. Willis went from being a star to a mystery almost overnight.

The Tigers finally gave up on him in June 2010, trading him to the Arizona Diamondbacks. He lasted six weeks in Arizona before being released. He signed with the Giants, and then, at the end of that season, his Tigers contract over, he signed with the Cincinnati Reds. He began the 2011 season in Louisville and pitched well enough to get called back to the majors in July.

"I can honestly tell you I've had some great moments in baseball," he said. "I've been part of a World Series champion; I won twenty [twenty-two] games in a season; I've been paid a lot of money. I'm not sure anything ever meant more to me than being told I was going to Cincinnati.

"I've thought about it, and the reason it meant so much was simple: it was *hard*. For a long, long time baseball was easy for me. I was in the majors at twenty-one. I was Rookie of the Year." He smiled. "Heck, I could even hit.

"Then it got hard—very hard. I couldn't get the ball over the plate. I couldn't get people out anymore. I couldn't stay healthy, and I couldn't stay in the big leagues. I had to *work* to get back to the point where someone thought I could pitch in the majors again. When everyone in that clubhouse came around to congratulate me, I cried. It meant that much to me.

"When I got to Cincinnati, Joey Votto was the first guy to come over to my locker. He said, 'How great does it feel to come all the way back?' I kind of laughed, and he said, 'No, I'm serious. Tell me how you did it. I can't imagine how tough that must have been.'"

Willis didn't pitch especially well with the Reds the second half of 2011. He was 1-6 with an ERA of 5.00, but he was good enough that he kept getting the ball, starting thirteen games. That was why the Phillies, in their constant search for pitching depth, had signed him prior to the 2012 season. When he didn't make the team out of spring training, Willis faced the same dilemma that Scott Podsednik faced: go back to the minors and try to work your way back *again* or go home. His daughters were five, three, and one. Home beckoned. The Phillies released him, and he took off the uniform for—he thought— the last time.

"I enjoyed being home," he said. "But I'm like everybody else. The itch doesn't just go away. I've played sports for as long as I can remember and always been pretty good. As great as it sounds to say, 'I'm going home to spend time with my family,' it isn't that simple."

Which is why, when the Orioles called and asked if he'd like to go to Norfolk, Willis said yes. He knew Baltimore needed starting pitching and thought he might have a chance to get back to the majors fairly quickly.

Only it hadn't worked out. To begin with, the Orioles had thought they were signing a reliever; Willis thought he was going to start. Willis pitched in relief once, got hurt, went home again for a while, then came back to Norfolk after a renegotiation of his role. He finally got a start. It didn't go well—two and two-thirds innings, four earned runs. By late June, no one seemed certain what his status was. Johnson had told him he would be on call that night in the bullpen.

"Which is fine with me," he said. "I need to get innings right now one way or the other."

He pushed back from the table where he was sitting. He was holding a baseball in his hands, just as he had done most of his life.

"I still love coming to the yard every day," he said. "I love the camaraderie of the clubhouse, and I understand it won't be long now before I'm one of those guys sitting around telling war stories. I can say I've been to the pinnacle, and that feels good. But when the day comes that I don't believe I can make it back and pitch in the big leagues, I'll go home. I know it won't be easy, but that's what I'll do."

That night, after long-tossing in the outfield before the game, Willis was designated the first man up in the Tides bullpen. He never got into the game.

"I'd like to say I think he's got a chance to pitch well again," Rosenfield said as he watched him warm up. "But I just don't think it's there anymore. I can't tell you why it isn't there, but it just isn't."

Two days later, Willis decided Rosenfield was right. He retired. Itch or no itch, it was time to go home. Again.

10

Nate McLouth

COMEBACK KID

The Tides won on Cowboy Monkey Rodeo Night.

Even with all their travel troubles and their lack of a starting pitcher, they came back from an early 3–1 deficit to beat Syracuse, 5–3. Five pitchers split up eight and two-thirds innings. The last out of the ninth inning wasn't needed because a huge thunderstorm swept into Norfolk, and even though the umpires tried briefly to keep the teams on the field long enough to get the last out, it wasn't going to happen. They waited thirty minutes to see if the rain would let up before calling it a night.

Nate McLouth was the Tides' hitting star for the evening with three hits and two RBIs. That raised his batting average to .205. As unimpressive as that sounded, it was a long way from where he had been a month earlier.

Literally, McLouth had been in Knoxville, Tennessee. Professionally, he had been out of a job, another example of a fallen star trying to find himself again in Triple-A.

"I believed the phone would ring," he said. "But until it did, I couldn't be certain."

For a long time, McLouth had been on the always-going-up escalator. Growing up in Muskegon, Michigan, he began drawing notice from colleges and professional teams by the time he was a high school sophomore. He could hit, he could run—he stole 179 bases in 180 attempts in high school—and he was an absolute whiz as an outfielder. He was good enough to remind people of the line that Ralph Kiner, the longtime New York Mets TV broadcaster, had used to describe the way Garry Maddox, who won eight Gold Gloves, played center field for the Philadelphia Phillies. "Two-thirds of the earth is covered by water," Kiner said. "The other third is covered by Garry Maddox."

McLouth wanted to go to Michigan to play baseball, and he committed in the spring of 2000 to play for the Wolverines. That's why he wasn't taken until the twenty-fifth round of the amateur draft that spring by the Pittsburgh Pirates. Everyone in baseball knew McLouth was going to college. The Pirates took a late-round flier, figuring they had nothing to lose.

That summer, McLouth played on a travel team and wowed scouts every time out—including those from the Pirates. After seeing him play up close one more time, the Pirates decided it was worth offering serious money to see if there was any chance they could talk McLouth out of going to college.

"I was a few weeks away from enrolling," McLouth said. "There wasn't any doubt in my mind that this was what I wanted to do. Then the Pirates came in with this offer and I had to listen."

The offer was a $400,000 signing bonus, plus money to go to college if he decided at any point that was what he wanted. McLouth talked it over with his parents. "The good news was that they trusted me to make my own decision," he said. "My ultimate goal was to get to the major leagues. I wasn't sure one way or the other was quicker, but there was a lot of money up front regardless of how it turned out. I thought it was the right thing to do."

McLouth progressed steadily through the minor leagues for five years, making it to the majors in 2005 at the age of twenty-three. By 2007 he was the Pirates' starting center fielder, and a year later he was their lone representative on the All-Star team. He also won the Gold Glove that season.

"In some ways, everything was great," he said. "I was playing well, doing what I'd always wanted to do. But the losing in Pittsburgh was tough. You tried to tell yourself that you had to go out every day and do your job even when the team was completely out of contention. But August was always difficult. We were so far out of it, the weather was hot, the ballpark was half full at best. That part was no fun."

That changed in June 2009 when the Pirates, knowing that McLouth was going to begin to cost them big money the following season, traded him to the Atlanta Braves for three prospects. That was one reason the Pirates were so bad for so long: as soon as a good player was in line for a big contract, he would be traded.

But something happened to McLouth after he went to Atlanta— something he hasn't completely figured out to this day. He was still a wonderful outfielder, but his hitting statistics went completely south. During his All-Star season in Pittsburgh, he had hit .276 with twenty-six home runs and ninety-four RBIs—and had stolen twenty-three bases. In 2009, his power numbers were still reasonable—twenty home runs and seventy RBIs—but his batting average dropped twenty points.

A year later, he was involved in a collision in the outfield with Jason Heyward that left him with concussion-like symptoms. Even though he missed a good deal of playing time and struggled after the collision, he insists that wasn't the reason for the falloff.

"The thing is I don't know what the problem was," he said. "I struggled to hit before the collision. It was frustrating because I knew it was in there somewhere, but I couldn't figure out how to find it. That's the thing about baseball, especially hitting. You struggle and you make a small adjustment. That doesn't work, so you make another one. The next thing you know you've made six different adjustments, you have a swing that looks nothing like the swing you had when you were going well, and you still can't drive the ball with regularity.

"It would be easier if you could point at one thing like an injury and say, 'That was it,' because then you think you know the answer. When it isn't one thing, you spend a lot of time wondering if it's ever going to get better."

The Braves sent McLouth to Gwinnett for a few weeks in August to try to take some pressure off him and to give him a chance to work out the issues with his swing. He came back in September, got hot for a while, and then slid back to where he had been during the summer. When Bobby Cox put together his postseason roster that October, McLouth was surprised to find he was one of the twenty-five names on the list.

"After all those years in Pittsburgh, to be in uniform for postseason was a cool thing," he said. "I honestly didn't think I would make it with the way I'd played. I just wish I could have made more of an impact than I did."

Cox kept McLouth on the roster because of his defense, and that was how he got into three games—as a defensive replacement. He did get to bat twice and got a hit, but the Braves lost the division series to the Giants in four games.

In 2011, his play *was* affected by injuries. He was on the disabled list on three occasions and hit only .228 when he did play. The Braves released him at season's end, and the Pirates offered him a chance to return to Pittsburgh. By then, the Pirates had an All-Star, Andrew McCutchen, playing center field for them, but McLouth thought there was playing time there for him—and he would be back where he had enjoyed his best success as a baseball player.

"It made sense," he said. "I knew the organization, and it looked like the team was better than it had been when I was there. I knew I'd have to play well in the spring to earn playing time, but that was fine with me."

He played well enough in the spring to make the team as a part-time outfielder. But his bat was colder than spring in Buffalo. He wasn't accustomed to playing one day and not playing the next, and he couldn't get into any kind of hitting rhythm. "If I ever had a hitting groove in the spring, I lost it when the regular season started. I'm not complaining; I knew the deal when I signed with them. It just seemed like even when I did drive the ball on occasion, I hit it right at someone." He smiled. "Of course that's what everyone says when they aren't going well."

That's true. Chris Giménez, a catcher with the Tampa Bay Rays, spent most of the 2012 season shuttling between Tampa and Durham. After being sent down to Durham in July, he sat in the dugout one night and said, "I'd like to tell you I hit a really *hard* .190 up there, but I can't say it with a straight face."

Just as a bloop single looks the same as a screaming line-drive single in the box score, a screaming line-drive out looks the same as a pop-up. In the end, the numbers don't lie. By late May, McLouth was hitting .140, and it really didn't matter if it was a hard .140. "Actually, there is no such thing as a hard .140," he said, laughing.

It was no laughing matter when Pirates manager Clint Hurdle called him in to his office just before Memorial Day. McLouth knew what was coming. Hurdle told him he had two options: He could go down to Triple-A Indianapolis, play on a more regular basis, and try to work out his hitting problems down there. Being honest, though, Hurdle couldn't promise how much he'd play, because the Pirates had some prospects there who needed at-bats. The second option was to be released and see if he could make a better deal someplace else.

McLouth asked Hurdle if he could think about it overnight. When he thought about it, the answer was easy: he needed to go someplace where he would have a chance to get more at-bats. He wasn't sure where that was, but at the moment it wasn't going to be with the Pirates or, for that matter, with Indianapolis.

The next day he went back to see Hurdle and asked for his release. Hurdle wasn't surprised: players want to play. McLouth is one of those guys everybody likes. Hurdle wished him well, and he went to clean out his locker.

"The next week was torture," McLouth said. "I wondered if maybe I wasn't going to get a chance to go someplace. I was thirty years old, and the thought that I might be done crossed my mind."

One man's bad break is another man's good break. In this case it actually *was* another man's break—Nick Markakis's broken right wrist—that gave McLouth the chance he needed. When the Orioles had to put Markakis on the disabled list in early June, they needed to sign someone for Norfolk after Bill Hall had been called up to the Orioles as an extra bat on the bench.

McLouth's agent, Mike Nicotera, got a call offering McLouth a spot in Norfolk. After ten days at home, McLouth would have walked to Norfolk if need be. The good news when he got there was that manager Ron Johnson had him in the lineup regularly. The bad news was that his bat still hadn't warmed up. He hoped the three-hit, two-RBI performance on Cowboy Monkey Rodeo Night was a start.

"Funny game," he said later. "At 4:55 in the afternoon we're sitting on the runway in Philadelphia, and I'm thinking there's no way we're getting to Norfolk in time for the game. Then we get here, I get three hits, and we win. Maybe it's a sign. Maybe I'm about to get something going."

All Ron Johnson knew as the rain thundered down with the clock about to strike midnight was that his team had won a game he never expected to win. "All I want to do right now is go home and get some sleep," he said. "If those umpires hadn't called the thing, I'd have gone in there and called it for them."

It had been a long, hot, rainy day—and night—in Norfolk.

There were no incidents with the protesters. All the animals survived their romp in the outfield.

11

Elarton

STILL ONE STEP AWAY

The rhythms of a Triple-A baseball season are very different from those of a major-league season. In the majors, stability is a key to success: the fewer roster changes that are made because of injuries or nonperformance, the better off teams are most of the time.

Many players have long-term contracts that include no-trade clauses so they know with absolute certainty where they will be working, which brings a sense of security that can be felt in a clubhouse. For years, when you walked into the New York Yankees' clubhouse you knew that, sooner or later, Derek Jeter, Jorge Posada, Mariano Rivera, and Andy Pettitte were going to be there. They would talk about almost any situation with the calmness that comes from having seen just about everything there is to see.

There's no such calm in Triple-A. No one wants to get comfortable in a Triple-A clubhouse. The air inside a Triple-A clubhouse feels different because there are different people breathing it every day. Players come and go on an almost daily basis: some get called up to the big leagues; some get traded; others get sent down to Double-A; and every once in a while players are released.

"You almost never get too close to anyone when you're in Triple-A, for two reasons," said pitcher Pat Misch, who began the 2012 season pitching in Lehigh Valley. "First, you don't want to get too comfortable at this level. Second, that guy you're having dinner with on Monday could easily be gone on Tuesday."

There's another reason: Triple-A teammates are also competing with one another. When a starting pitcher goes out and pitches well, that's good for the team. But it might not be all that good for the other starters, because he may have leapfrogged ahead of them in the organization's pecking order.

"It doesn't sound very nice to say, but it's true," said Scott Elarton. "You never root against your teammates. But the fact is, in Triple-A, they're also your competition. Everyone has one eye on what's going on with the big-league club—in fact, you have one eye on all thirty big-league clubs because any one of them could be scouting you when one of their guys gets hurt or isn't doing well.

"Am I happy when someone I know and like and share space with in a clubhouse gets called up? Or traded to someone that gets him to the majors? Of course I am. Do I wish it was me? Of course I do."

Elarton had done exactly what Charlie Manuel had told him to do after being sent down to Lehigh Valley. He had maintained a positive attitude, and he had pitched well at the start of the season. Many—if not most—International League hitters had never faced him before, and with his gangly, all-arms-and-legs delivery coming out of a six-foot-seven-inch frame, he was not easy for hitters to figure out the first time around the league.

He started the season 4-0, pitching to an ERA of 2.39 during his first seven outings. He beat the Louisville Bats on May 11, pitching six innings and giving up no runs and one hit in a 4–1 win. The losing pitcher that night was Brett Tomko, who pitched well—three runs in seven innings—but dropped to 0-4 in spite of a solid ERA of 3.55.

The Phillies' pitching staff had been in flux all season because of injuries. Cliff Lee had gone on the DL in April. Elarton had thought he might have a shot to get called up then. Instead, the Phillies had called up Joe Savery, who had been their No. 1 pick in the 2007 draft and also had the benefit of being a lefty. Once Lee was healthy, Savery came back to Lehigh Valley. On May 16, Vance Worley, the Phillies' No. 5 starter, went on the DL. Again, Savery got the call: he was younger (twenty-seven), and the Phillies had a lot more invested in him. When Roy Halladay went on the DL at the end of May, the Phillies decided to stick with the pitchers they had on the roster and called up a catcher to take his spot.

Through it all, Elarton didn't complain.

"They're giving me a chance to pitch here," he said. "I'd like to get the call, we all would, but if I don't, I'm enjoying what I'm doing right now. The best thing about this season is that I've stayed healthy. It's been a long, long time since I could say that about any season."

Elarton was one of those athletes who had ridden his talent for a long time—right into the major leagues in fact. He had grown up in Lamar, a tiny town in southeastern Colorado, and had been a star in both the classroom and as an athlete all through high school. He played football, basketball, and baseball and starred in all three. The son of two schoolteachers, he was the valedictorian of his graduating class in the spring of 1994.

As a senior, he committed to go to Stanford to play baseball, which by then had clearly become his best sport. Then came the baseball draft in June: the Houston Astros used their first pick, the twenty-fifth in the draft, to take Elarton—even though he had told people he was planning to go to college.

After the draft, the Elartons did some research. It turned out that no pitcher taken in the first round who had opted to go to college had improved his draft status by doing so. The Astros offered a $750,000 bonus plus another $100,000 for college down the road. Elarton took it and headed for the buses and the back roads of the minor leagues.

He arrived in the minors when steroids had become a true "thing" in baseball. It wasn't just stars who were using PEDs but minor leaguers, guys who believed if they could get an extra edge, it would make the difference between playing in the majors and playing in the minors.

In those days, even though Commissioner Fay Vincent had banned steroids in 1991, there was no testing. Which was a little bit like posting a speed limit on a highway and not hiring any policemen to patrol.

Elarton saw players around him who were clearly taking steroids. He could see their bodies change, particularly from one season to the next. He was never truly tempted.

"You have to remember that most guys started to use during the off-season," he said. "They'd go home and think, 'If I can recover more quickly when I work out, maybe the extra work will get me to the majors.' It was all very hush-hush. It wasn't something you sat around in the clubhouse and talked about. No one ever said, 'Do you think so-and-so is using?' You just *knew.* I never held it against anyone. It was one of those things where you knew they were just trying to keep their jobs, extend their careers. I guess I didn't begrudge anybody that.

"It's all very different now because of testing," he said. "There's a lot more risk in doing it, and even though there are still going to be guys who think it's worth the risk, you just don't see it now the way you did when I was coming up through the minors, or even my first couple of years in the majors.

"I lived in a very rural area. It's not as if I was going to gyms in the off-season and seeing a lot of bodybuilders who had access to the stuff or knew where to get it—which is what I think happened with a lot of guys. I just never really thought about doing it."

As it turned out, at least early in his career, he never really needed the extra help. His ability was enough.

By 1998 he had reached the major leagues. A year later he had his first shoulder surgery. In 2000, after starting the season on a minor-league rehab assignment, he went 17-7 for an Astros team that finished 72-90.

But his shoulder began to ache again the following season, and he tried to pitch through it. The Astros traded him to Colorado. His shoulder continued to hurt, and he continued to try to pitch through it. By the end of the season his ERA was 7.06, and he needed major reconstructive surgery on the shoulder. He missed the entire 2002 season.

"Looking back on everything now, with the perspective of time, I know that a lot of what happened to me was the result of immaturity," he said. "I don't think I became a grown-up until I was just about done [playing] the first time.

"I lived the major-league lifestyle. I enjoyed it. I was young and I had money and I had fun.

"I made some bad decisions. When my shoulder started to hurt, it never really occurred to me that anything could be seriously wrong—even after my first surgery. I had always been sore after I pitched, even when I was a kid. So now I was a little more sore. I was pitching to big-league hitters, being a little more sore was to be expected.

"My way was to fight through things. Then, when I had surgery, I always tried to come back too fast. Well, it feels better, I'm ready to pitch. Except I wasn't ready to pitch. I'd come back, and people would blow me away. I was terrible because I never let myself get completely healthy."

The Rockies released him midway through 2004 after his ERA had ballooned to 9.80. The Indians picked him up, and he pitched better, most notably in 2005, when he had his best season since 2000—and his healthiest—going 11-9 with a 4.61 ERA. But the shoulder began acting up again after he signed with the Royals in 2006, and he was released again, midway through 2007. The Indians gave him another shot briefly in 2008. It was after his release there in July that he decided it was time to go home.

"I had two young kids," he said. "Everything hurt. I was pitching badly, and I didn't want to go back to the minor leagues again. I had money [his solid 2005 with the Indians had gotten him a two-year $8 million deal from the Royals]. The White Sox tempted me back briefly in 2010, but I was awful, so I decided that was it."

Even before he walked away from Cleveland in 2008, he knew he needed to stop drinking. As his injuries and frustrations had mounted, he had started to drink more.

"At some point in my life I had probably dabbled in a little bit of everything," he said. "You name it, I tried it. But mostly I drank. It wasn't as if I was drinking every single night or drinking all day long; it was never like that. But when I did drink, I drank too much. It could get ugly in a hurry.

"When I came up, a lot of guys were living the hard and fast life. I fell right into it. It got to a point where I knew I had to do something about it before it killed me. I don't think I was ever a bad husband or a bad dad, but I knew it wasn't going to end well if I didn't do something. I didn't feel good physically, and I didn't feel very good about myself either. I just decided it was time to get some help. So I did."

He went away to a thirty-day program but knew he still had work to do when he got back. He didn't think he could handle sobriety and baseball and the frustrations baseball had been bringing to his life all at once. He was sober when the White Sox talked him into his brief comeback. "By then, drinking wasn't the issue," he said, smiling. "My pitching was the issue."

He had pitched in Charlotte for eight weeks in 2010 to an ERA of 8.24. His shoulder hurt even more than it had before he left the Indians two years earlier, and he knew he would need to have surgery again. He was happy to be back in Lamar, until that day in August when he had driven over to Denver with Jake to see his old buddies who were with the Phillies.

Elarton had now rented an apartment in Allentown that was big enough that Laurie and the two children could spend the summer with him. Even with them in Lehigh Valley, the long road trips were tough on him.

"I'm usually okay for about the first six days," he said. "By the seventh day I start to get very cranky. I'm just at a point in my life where I don't like being away from my family at all."

Jake, who was now eight, had vaguely known that his dad was a baseball player and that he knew baseball players. But he had been four the last time Elarton had been a full-time player, and his more vivid memories of his father on a baseball field dated to the August afternoon in Denver when they had stood behind the barrier and watched the "real" players take batting practice.

"For Jake to see me in uniform, and actually pitching and occasionally getting people out, makes this whole thing worth it," Elarton said. "At the very least I know now that he'll remember me as a baseball player. It won't just be some vague, shadowy memory of me playing baseball from when he was very little. He understands the game now; he's really a fan. He thinks being able to come down on the field to be with me is cool.

"I'd love for him to see me in a major-league uniform in a major-league park, but, to be honest, this has been great because down here things are less formal and he gets to be a lot closer to it than in the majors."

He smiled. "Of course I wouldn't mind having to deal with the access issue in the majors if the time came for that."

As May turned to June, Elarton began to lose some of the magic touch he'd seemed to have in Florida and early in the season. A couple of bad outings ballooned his ERA a bit—it was still under 4.00 going into July, which is generally considered good in Triple-A—but he knew he wasn't pitching nearly as well as he had been.

"I'm making mental mistakes out there," he said one night. "I'm not making good pitches when I most need to, and I'm not getting out of innings the way I was early in the season. It's frustrating. I think I'll come out of it, but I hope it's soon.

"Last I checked, I'm not getting any younger."

12

Slice of Life

ON THE ROAD IN PINSTRIPES

When the Scranton/Wilkes-Barre Yankees gathered just prior to their season opener on April 5, their manager, Dave Miley, had spoken to them about the year that was to come, pointing out that they could use the 144-game road trip as an excuse if they wanted to—but not with him.

"None of us signed up for this," he told the team. "But we're here. We can lie down or we can show people that we're competitors and turn some heads that way. It's up to you."

Whether those words got everyone's attention or not, the team played solid baseball right from the start.

"In a funny way I think it's helped bring us together," Miley said after the team had settled into a pennant race with Lehigh Valley and Pawtucket in the North Division. "Adversity can do that. I mean we all have two choices: accept it for what it is and try to succeed or whine about it and not succeed. I don't think anyone in New York is going to say, 'Oh, these guys have it too tough, we'll bring them up even if they're not playing well.' The guys understand that.

"Every spring, before we go north, I always get the players together and say, 'Look, I know there isn't anyone in this room who doesn't want to be up in the big leagues, but we're all here—at least for the moment.' This spring I changed my speech a little, to let them know that I thought the less we talked about it, or thought about it, the better off we'd all be. I brought it up the one time. I haven't brought it up since. Fortunately, I haven't had to."

He smiled. "Of course it isn't exactly one of those things you can prepare for. You just have to take it as it comes."

Two days before opening day Miley had turned fifty and, perhaps more than any other manager in the International League, had learned to take life as it came—the good, the bad, and the tragic.

He had been a hot prospect when he graduated from high school after growing up in Tampa and had been the Reds' No. 2 pick in 1980. He had opted to sign with the Reds—who trained in Tampa when he was a kid and were his favorite team—rather than accept a scholarship to the University of Miami.

Two years out of high school, he blew out his knee and was never really the same player. He bounced around the minors for seven years but never made it to the majors. When the Reds offered him the chance to manage the Greensboro Hornets in 1988, he took the job, figuring he had a better chance to make it to the majors as a manager or a coach than as a player.

He was right. By 1993, he was the Reds' bench coach, before returning to the minors, seemingly to be groomed as a future major-league manager. He managed in Louisville for four years, winning the Governors' Cup in 2001. Two years later, he was the Reds' manager, moved up from Louisville late in the season when the Reds decided to fire both their general manager, Jim Bowden, and their manager, Bob Boone.

Miley was only forty-one when he became the Reds' manager and he was handed a young team that had traded most of its best players away for prospects. The problem with being part of a rebuilding process when you are a manager is that people still judge you on your record. Midway through 2005, having gone 125-164 with a tiny payroll and almost no veterans, Miley was fired.

"It's baseball," he said one afternoon, shrugging as he sat in the small visiting manager's office in Allentown. He had a bat in one hand, and he sat on the one chair in the room. His visitor sat on the floor. Miley is always friendly with the media and never unwilling to talk, but it is clearly not his favorite thing.

One reason for that is that getting fired by the Reds, after twenty-five years with the organization, isn't even close to the worst thing that's happened in his life. He was hired by the Yankees to manage their Triple-A team in Columbus in 2006 and moved with the team to Scranton/Wilkes-Barre a year later.

In May 2008, the Yankees were playing at home when Miley got a call: his seventeen-year-old son, Cody, who had just graduated from the same high school in Tampa that Miley had graduated from twenty-eight years earlier, had been killed in a car crash. To this day, it is difficult for Miley to talk about Cody, to the point where he says he honestly has trouble remembering details.

"It's all a little bit of a blur," he said quietly.

He has a daughter, Courtney, and Miley has been happily remarried for twelve years now. Baseball remains his escape.

"I get asked all the time if I'd like another shot at managing in the majors," he said. "Of course I would. But I like what I'm doing right now. I get paid to put on a uniform every day, and that makes me happy. I like working with young players and trying to help them take that next step. Nothing makes me happier than calling a guy in and telling him he's going up. That's the joy in this job—those moments.

"Especially this year. Because there's no doubt anyone who goes up right now has more than earned it."

———

As much as Doug Bernier enjoyed playing for Dave Miley, he knew it was unlikely he was going to get that call into his office during the 2012 season. Bernier was thirty-one when he reported to spring training in Tampa for his tenth full season as a professional baseball player. He had graduated from Oral Roberts in 2002, thinking he would be taken at some point during the fifty-round amateur draft.

"The decisions I had made up until that point in my life had all been about baseball," he said. "When I was younger, I realized I was probably too small [five feet ten inches] to go very far in football or basketball, but I could play baseball. I was a good pitcher, but when I went to an All-Star camp in high school, I looked around and realized I was the shortest pitcher there. It isn't as if you can't be short and right-handed and succeed [Tim Lincecum comes to mind] but not when you throw it up there at eighty-eight—which is what I was doing. So I focused on playing the infield."

He went to junior college in San Luis Obispo, near where he had grown up (his dad was an aerospace engineer for Lockheed Martin), for two years before deciding to go to Oral Roberts—an interesting choice of college for a California kid who wasn't terribly religious.

"I'd actually never heard of the place," he said. "I got some interest from powerhouse places like Texas and Miami and thought, 'Wow, this is cool.' But realistically, I wasn't going to play at places like that. ORU had really nice facilities, and I liked the idea at that point in my life of getting out of California.

"I'm not sure I realized how different a place it was before I enrolled," he said, laughing. "The first time I went there and saw those giant golden hands [which dominate the central part of the campus], it freaked me out a little. But I liked the baseball aspect of the school, liked the coach and the players. Plus, they were offering a scholarship."

When he first showed up for classes, he realized he hadn't completely understood what the school was about. For one thing, when he walked into his first class dressed casually in the college student's uniform of shorts and a T-shirt, he was quickly informed that no one at Oral Roberts went to class without wearing a tie.

"I went to a Walmart and found a clip-on tie," he said. "I wore it every day for the next two years."

He played well enough, especially in the NCAA regionals his senior year, to think he was going to get drafted. "It wasn't as if I had scouts telling me their team was going to draft me—I didn't," he said. "But a bunch of scouts had seen me when I played well, even though

I knew they were there to watch other guys. I just thought I'd get a shot."

He was wrong. He spent two days trolling the Internet, watching name after name go up on the draft board, none of them his. When the draft was over and no one had taken him, he sat back in his chair and thought, "What do I do now?"

First he flew home. Then he began to consider his options. "I really didn't have any, to be honest," he said, laughing. "I had put all my eggs in the baseball basket. I had my degree [in physical education] but had no idea what I might do with it.

"It really hit me hard. I had played baseball since I was five. It was what I did. And then, very abruptly, it looked like it might be over. Deep down, though, I didn't think it was over. Sometimes when I get discouraged about still being in the minor leagues after all these years, I think about that time I spent at home and realize that I'm fortunate to still be in the game, to still be getting paid to play."

He had been home for three days after college when the phone rang. "It felt more like three months," he said. The Colorado Rockies were interested in signing him as an undrafted free agent. There was no bonus, and the pay was $850 a month. "Where do I sign?" Bernier asked.

The life of an undrafted free agent, especially at the lower levels of the minor leagues, is not an easy one. Players who have been drafted, particularly in the early rounds, are labeled "prospects" by their teams. It is almost as if they walk around wearing a sign that says PROSPECT, because they are placed on a pedestal from the second they report to a team.

"Two things have to happen for someone like me to get a chance to play," Bernier said. "One is to play so much better than a prospect that they have to play you. That one's not easy, because even if a guy is playing poorly, they've got money invested in him, and they're going to want to try to get him to play his way out of it.

"More likely is an injury. Someone gets hurt, you get to play. Or, possibly, someone gets called up, and they give you a shot to play in his place."

Bernier often had to wait his turn throughout his early days in the minor leagues. "I got lucky with my rookie-league team [Pasco, Washington] because they had drafted a guy named Jeff Baker and he didn't sign. That meant they had prospects at three infield spots but an opening at third base. So I got to play some of the time, and I did pretty well.

"You're constantly aware that every baseball organization is a totem pole and you're at the bottom. You can be the first guy to go at any time, and you are almost never going to get the first opportunity."

In fact, during his first nine years, regardless of what level he was playing, Bernier was never an opening-day starter. He was always the guy waiting in the wings. And yet he never let the hard facts of who he was within the baseball pantheon bother him. He kept grinding and slowly made his way up the totem pole. It wasn't until he got to Triple-A in Colorado Springs in 2007 that he even thought about hiring an agent.

"I guess I had a college or high school approach to it all," he said with a smile. "When I first got signed, there wasn't any negotiating to do. What was I going to do, demand $900 a month instead of $850? When I got to Colorado Springs, a couple of guys on the team who had been in the majors—Clint Barmes and Frank Menechino—asked me who my agent was. I said I didn't have one. They said, 'Doug, you aren't in college anymore, you need an agent.' So I ended up hiring Clint's guy."

He was thrilled to make the team in Colorado Springs in 2007. When Tom Runnells, who was the manager, asked if he could fill in at first base if need be, he said, "Of course," even though he had never played first base in his life. Runnells had also managed Bernier at Double-A, and he had become one of the manager's favorites because of his willingness to do anything to help the ball club.

"He kept telling me, 'I have no idea what they see in you, but you're here, so go out and do the best you can.' The first time he put me in the lineup in '05, I got four hits. I think he remembered that."

Bernier was in his second season in Colorado Springs, and his salary had soared to $2,100 a month, the maximum a player not on the forty-man major-league roster could make back then. "Hey, I had almost tripled my salary," he said, laughing. "I thought that was pretty good."

One morning when the team was in Tucson, Runnells came into the clubhouse and asked Bernier to come into his office.

Bernier had been playing well, but given his history and the fact that he was twenty-seven and still expendable, his stomach twisted just a bit. Reading his mind, Runnells said, "No big deal, I just want to talk about some defensive adjustments."

Bernier followed Runnells into his office and was surprised to see the team's coaches in the office too. If they were going to talk about defense, shouldn't the other infielders be in the meeting?

Bernier sat down, and as he did, Runnells's face suddenly broke into a huge smile. Then he said the three magic words: "You're going up."

Bernier was stunned. He knew that Troy Tulowitzki, the Rockies' starting shortstop, was on the disabled list and still a few days from coming back. What he didn't know was that catcher Yorvit Torrealba had just been suspended for getting into a fight with Matt Kemp of the Dodgers. The team needed an extra bat for a few days, and the choice was Bernier.

"I honestly didn't know what to do when Tom told me," Bernier said. "I think I just sat there not really believing him for a minute until he said, 'You better get going.' I remember the guys in the clubhouse all congratulating me. I knew it was probably going to be only a few days, but it didn't matter.

"When I got to Denver, I walked in the clubhouse, and the first person I saw was [likely Hall of Famer] Todd Helton. He ran over, threw his arms around me, and said, 'Dougie, great to see you!' It was really cool that he understood how much it meant to me."

So did (then) manager Clint Hurdle, who put him in as a defensive replacement that first night and then, two days later, knowing that Tulowitzki was about to come off the DL, gave Bernier a start.

"The whole thing really was like a dream," he said. "I tried to drink it all in because I was pretty sure it wasn't going to last long. Tulo was already in the clubhouse taking batting practice and was pretty close to being ready. I wasn't intimidated, at least I don't think I was. It was still just a baseball field. But everything else was different: the size of the clubhouse, the size of the stadium, the *noise*. Sometimes, when you're playing in the minors, you can hear the hum of the lights during a game. Not so in the majors."

Bernier went 0 for 4 in his start. The closest he came to a hit was a line drive toward left field that Cleveland shortstop Jhonny Peralta was able to get to and corral. He played second base flawlessly. When it was over, Hurdle told him that Tulowitzki was being activated the next day and he was going back to Colorado Springs. Which he did— with only one regret.

"I wish I'd gotten a hit," he said. "But just to be there, to put on that uniform, to run out on that field. I reminded myself I'd come a long way and beaten a lot of odds after not getting drafted at all to be able to say I was playing in the major leagues."

Walking out that day, Bernier ran into Torrealba, whose suspension was ending the next day. "I gave him a hug," Bernier said. "I know he didn't get into the fight so I could get to the big leagues, but that's what happened."

If taking the field in a Rockies uniform was Bernier's best moment, his second-best moment came when he received his next paycheck. When a minor leaguer is called up to the majors, he is paid the major-league minimum, prorated on a daily basis over 180 days. In 2008, the major-league minimum was $432,000 (it was $482,000 in 2012). That meant Bernier was paid $2,400 a day—more than he was making in a month at the time. He was in the majors for three days, meaning he earned a total of $7,200.

"It was the first check I'd ever gotten that had a comma in it [after taxes]," he said, grinning. "If I'd been able to afford it, I would have framed it."

As memorable as that June was, Bernier would have liked to have forgotten September. On the last day of the season, playing in Las

Vegas, he was hit in the face by a pitch. He took eleven stitches underneath his eye, and even though it hurt a lot, he figured he was okay. Only it wasn't that simple.

He left the Rockies after 2008 as a six-year minor-league free agent and signed with the Yankees, who were looking for infield depth at Triple-A. The Yankees liked him enough to invite him to their major-league camp—the first time he hadn't reported directly to the minor-league camp.

"It was intimidating to be in that clubhouse and see guys like [Derek] Jeter and [Andy] Pettitte, Mariano [Rivera] and A-Rod," he said. "I was in awe when I first got there. The next thing I know I'm standing there during infield drills talking positioning with Jeter. He acted like he was a baseball player and I was a baseball player, which, technically, we were. Except the reality was a lot different."

Bernier expected to end up in Scranton/Wilkes-Barre, and he did. But the beaning was still on his mind. He found himself worrying about whether he could get out of the way of inside pitches and got gun-shy. Plus, having played in the Pacific Coast League, he had to adjust to International League pitching.

"It is different," Bernier said. "In the PCL, you play at elevation a lot. The pitches break more as a result, and the pitchers throw more breaking stuff. In the International League, you see a lot more fastballs. I didn't adjust well in '09."

Bernier had never been a high-average hitter—except in 2007, when he hit .310 in Colorado Springs—but his average plummeted to .181 in 2009. Not surprisingly, the Yankees didn't re-sign him for 2010. It was January before the Pirates offered him a contract and the chance to play his way back to Triple-A. He did that, playing well enough in Indianapolis that the Yankees brought him back in 2011.

"He's the kind of guy who is good to have in an organization," Yankees general manager Brian Cashman said. "He's a good influence on younger guys, he'll work hard, and you know he can play well enough defensively at any level that you can have confidence he'll get the job done if you need him."

Bernier had a solid season in 2011 and was happy to sign again with the Yankees for 2012. His monthly salary had soared to $12,000, which was helpful since he and his wife, Sarah, had become parents for the first time during the off-season. Bernier arrived in training camp realistic but—as always—hopeful.

"I know that, barring injuries, I can hit .800 in the spring and I'm not making the team," he said. "All I can do is hope I get a chance to show them that I can play a little bit and try to make an impression."

Remarkably, he *did* get the chance to make an impression. Jeter had suffered a calf injury late in 2011, and the Yankees were bringing him along slowly in the spring if only because there was no need to rush him. Eduardo Núñez, who normally would have gotten most of Jeter's time at shortstop, hurt a finger early. All of a sudden Bernier—wearing number 74—was getting a good deal of time as the starting shortstop for the New York Yankees.

Yes, it was spring training, but the uniform had the "NY" on it for home games in Tampa. Robinson Cano was to his left most days, and Alex Rodríguez was to his right. What's more, he was producing. He didn't hit .800, but he did hit .361. Of course once the season began approaching and Jeter and Núñez were ready to play, the inevitable call into manager Joe Girardi's office was just around the corner.

"You showed people you can play," Girardi said. "We all noticed how you performed when you got a chance. Just keep doing what you're doing."

Those words left Bernier feeling about as good as he had ever felt as he headed into a season. The fact that he was in a minor-league starting lineup on opening day for the first time in his career made him feel even better. Living out of a hotel and a suitcase wasn't fun, but it didn't really bother him.

What bothered him was tweaking an oblique muscle—a pulled muscle in the stomach—in early May. He tried to play through it, staying in the lineup for several days before he finally told the trainer he was in pain.

"I thought if I was careful with it, I'd be okay," he said. Then he smiled. "Of course you can't play baseball and be careful at the same time.

"I'm thirty-one," he added. "I can't afford to be hurt at this stage of my career. I need to play."

Needing to play and being able to play are two different things. The season would be almost half over before he would be able to play again.

13

Slice of Life

MANAGING . . . INDIANAPOLIS

In every baseball season, three holidays are important lines of demarcation: Memorial Day, Fourth of July, and Labor Day.

It is often said that there is no point looking at standings until Memorial Day because there are always going to be teams that start fast and fade almost as quickly, and others who look awful in cold weather and then heat up along with the temperature.

By Memorial Day teams have played about one-third of their schedule in the major leagues and a little more than that in the minors since minor-league teams play 144 games—eighteen games fewer than major-league teams. Fourth of July marks the midway point in the majors, closer to the two-thirds pole in the minors, and Labor Day is the start of the final push in the big leagues and the end of the regular season in the minors.

The real difference isn't so much the eighteen games as the fact that no one is paying all that much attention to the standings in Triple-A.

"You go out there every night with the intention of shaking hands in the middle of the diamond at the end of the game," Lehigh Valley manager Ryne Sandberg said. "But it isn't the same as the majors, where you are judged every day based strictly on wins and losses."

Of course the local media and fans don't look at it that way. They want to see their team win. Winning streaks are applauded; slumps are questioned. In every Triple-A ballpark there are photographs of championship teams from the past. Which makes sense. Why keep score if winning doesn't matter?

On Memorial Day 2012, Pawtucket led the International League North with a record of 32-20, followed closely by Buffalo, the wandering Scranton/Wilkes-Barre Yankees (who had been unofficially renamed the Empire State Yankees for marketing purposes for the duration of the season), and Lehigh Valley, which was in fourth place but only three and a half games behind Pawtucket. Gwinnett led the South at 31-20 by two and a half games over Charlotte. Indianapolis, at 29-21, had the largest lead—five games over Columbus—in the West. The Indians were the only team in the West with a winning record.

They also had the only manager in the league who didn't aspire to managing in the major leagues someday. The reason for that was simple. "It's not going to happen at my age," Dean Treanor said. "A team looking for a manager isn't going to hire someone who is sixty-four and has never been at the big-league level."

He smiled. "I'm fine with it. I'm lucky. I love what I do."

Treanor had traveled a very different road from anyone else managing in the IL, arguably from anyone else in baseball. He had pitched in college at Cal Poly–San Luis Obispo and had signed with the Reds after graduating with a degree in math in 1971. "My dad had always wanted one of his kids to be a math major, and I was the last one, so I majored in math," he said. "What I really wanted to do was major in pre-law."

Treanor got as high as Double-A ball, pitching in Quebec in the old Eastern League before rotator cuff surgery ended any dreams he might have had of making it to the majors someday. "I didn't rehab well, and I was a questionable prospect to begin with," he said. "I didn't want to be one of those guys who was lost when the baseball dream was no longer possible. There were other things that interested me, and I decided it was time to move on."

So he did, going back home and joining the San Luis Obispo Police Department. He soon made detective and began working undercover, often in the narcotics division. It was a job he enjoyed, but it was also one that he found extremely stressful.

"You work alone a lot when you're undercover," he said. "You have all sorts of adrenaline pumping all the time because you never know what may happen next. I liked doing what I did. I enjoyed the camaraderie of the police department. Some of the guys I worked with are still some of my closest friends. But I felt like the job was aging me. I was worn out by it."

He had been a cop for thirteen years when he got a phone call in the winter of 1988 from an old friend, Mike Krukow. The two had been teammates at Cal Poly for a year, and their sons had played baseball together. Krukow, who won 124 games in the majors, was pitching for the Giants and knew that the team was looking for someone to manage its Class A team in Fresno. Wondering if Treanor might be tired of life undercover, he called him to let him know the job was open.

"When Krook called, it just hit me that maybe this was the time," he said. "I had never stopped loving baseball, and I was definitely a burnout case doing police work. I decided it was worth taking a shot."

Twenty-four years later, he was still working in the minor leagues. He had managed in Fresno for only one season but had gone on to work for the Padres, Expos, Dodgers, and Marlins at the minor-league level, before being hired by the Pirates as the pitching coach in Indianapolis in 2010. He had done just about everything one can do at the minor-league level. He'd been a pitching coach, a roving instructor, and a manager. When Frank Kremblas was made a minor-league coordinator for the Pirates prior to the 2011 season, Treanor was named to replace him as the manager in Indianapolis.

"I can honestly say I've never looked back," he said. "I love coming to the ballpark every day. To me this is a sacred place—I really feel that way. Every day I walk in here, whether it's home or on the road, I feel good about what I'm doing. How many guys have a job where they feel that way? I don't like to lose, none of us do, but the great thing in baseball is that you get to come back and play the next day. I wouldn't trade being here for anything."

The Indians play their home games at Victory Field in downtown Indianapolis, a short walk from Lucas Oil Stadium, the home of the Indianapolis Colts, and a slightly longer walk from Bankers Life Fieldhouse, where the Indiana Pacers play.

Indianapolis has had a minor-league baseball team since 1887, and the Indians have played at the Triple-A level since they first came into existence in 1902—first in the old American Association, then in the Pacific Coast League, and now in the International League.

Victory Field opened in 1996 and seats a little more than twelve thousand with room for another two thousand people in grassy areas outside the outfield fences. The sparkling new JW Marriott hotel towers over the left-field fence, and the city's downtown skyline backdrops the rest of the ballpark.

The Indians have been the Triple-A affiliate for eight different major-league teams. Their alumni include names like Grover Cleveland Alexander, Mordecai "Three Fingers" Brown, Luke Appling, Harmon Killebrew, Felipe Alou, Larry Walker, Dave Concepción, and many others who went on to distinguished major-league careers. Bob Uecker also played in Indianapolis and, in keeping with his self-perpetuated image, hit .147 there (and in Louisville) during the 1960 season.

Since 2005, the Indians have been the Pirates' Triple-A farm club, which means a lot of players have come through Indianapolis, made brief stops in Pittsburgh, and then, after showing potential, been shipped off to other teams.

In 2011, the Pirates, after eighteen straight losing seasons—a major-league record—finally showed some life. They actually led the National League Central Division briefly in July before tailing off badly to finish with a 72-90 record. For 2012, the Pirates had T-shirts made up for everyone in the organization that had one word on the back: "Finish." Since many of the Indians wear Pirates gear to warm up in every afternoon, the word "Finish" was on the backs of their T-shirts throughout the season.

Like the big-league club, they played very well into the summer
months and found themselves in first place in the IL West by a con-
siderable margin as the weather turned hot. Their best player, without
question, was their young left fielder, Starling Marte. At twenty-three,
Marte had the look of a star. He could hit, he could hit with power,
and he was a superb outfielder.

"If he gets close to it, he catches it," Treanor said. "And most of
the time, he's going to get close to it."

It wasn't a question of *if* Marte was going to get called up; it was
simply when. By late July he was hitting .286 with twelve home runs,
sixty-three RBIs, twenty-one doubles, thirteen triples, and twenty-
one stolen bases. In short, he was doing everything possible to get the
Pirates' attention.

The Indians were cruising along in first place when the Pawtucket
Red Sox came to town on July 25 for a game that started at 11:05 in
the morning. Triple-A teams occasionally play games with morning
starts for one of two reasons: to give teams a head start on a get-away
day when they have a long trip to make and have to play the next day
in another city; or to bring schoolkids to the ballpark as part of a field
trip. The early start means the kids can see the game and get back to
school in time to be dismissed from there.

This was a school-field-trip morning start.

Baseball players—in fact almost all of those associated with baseball in any way—are not morning people. This is especially true when
the game-time temperature at 11:00 in the morning is eighty-seven
degrees and everyone knows it is only going to get hotter as the sun
climbs into the noontime sky.

Whether it was the game time or the heat or the pitching of the
PawSox' Nelson Figueroa, the Indians had one of those days that are
an inevitable part of every baseball season. They were sluggish the
entire game, dropping behind quickly and slogging to a 4–2 loss.

During the game, Treanor got a message from Pittsburgh: Marte
was being called up. He was to leave right after the game to join the
team in Houston the next day. Treanor wasn't surprised at all, even
though he would miss Marte, with whom he had become very close

during the season. Marte had grown up in the Dominican Republic and had been raised by his grandmother, after losing both his parents by the time he was ten. Treanor, who had managed in the Dominican on several occasions during the winter, was comfortable speaking Spanish and had recognized Marte as special from the first day he had managed him. Marte called Treanor his "American *padre*."

Marte doubled in one of the Indians' two runs on that sweltering Wednesday but, like everyone else, wasn't quite with it during the game. When he grounded into a double play in the sixth inning—a rare occurrence for him—Treanor noticed that he wasn't quite giving his all going down the line.

As everyone trudged up the tunnel after the game, Treanor had an idea. As soon as the team was inside the clubhouse, he told everyone to wait a moment before heading for the showers or starting to eat the postgame meal. It was time for a talk—an impromptu team meeting.

Everyone sighed. They knew what was coming. Yes, it had been a morning start, and, yes, it had been a hot day, but the PawSox had played in the same heat at the same starting time. Yes, they were still in first place by a wide margin, but Columbus was heating up, and this was no time to take anything for granted.

Treanor went through all that and mentioned that he understood this was a tense time of year. The July 31 trading deadline was coming up, and everyone in Triple-A was on pins and needles because trades meant movement—sometimes to another organization, sometimes up to the major leagues. It also sometimes meant watching others move up while you stayed put. He understood that everyone in the room was full of hope—and trepidation.

Finally, he turned to Marte.

"Starling, in the sixth inning, did you run as hard as you could to first base on that double-play ball?" he asked.

Marte shook his head. "No, sir, I didn't," he answered.

Treanor nodded. "You know that isn't acceptable," he said. "We don't jog down to first base ever."

He paused for effect, then added, "So, tomorrow, you aren't going to be in our starting lineup."

The clubhouse was completely silent. The players were clearly stunned. They all knew that Marte played hard about 99.9 percent of the time. This seemed harsh.

"I waited about thirty seconds," Treanor said. "Looked around at all of them. Then I said, 'Starling, the reason you aren't going to be in the lineup is because you're going to be in Houston. You're going to be in the lineup there for the Pirates."

This time the silence lasted only about a second before the news sank in with everyone. Then the clubhouse exploded. Everyone forgot how exhausted they were.

When the hugging and celebrating was over, Marte came to find Treanor.

"Thanks, Padre," he said.

"Run everything out in Pittsburgh," Treanor said. "And don't come back."

Marte led off for the Pirates the next night against Houston left-hander Dallas Keuchel. He drove the first major-league pitch he ever saw over the left-center-field fence in Minute Maid Park for a home run. He became the first Pirate to homer on the first pitch of his major-league career since Walter Mueller did it—in 1922.

Treanor was certain that Marte would follow both his instructions: He would run every ball out. And he would not be back.

————

Five days after he got to tell Marte he was going to the majors in front of all his teammates, Treanor had a very different experience. It was trade deadline day, and Treanor wasn't at all surprised when he got to the ballpark to learn that one of his players had been traded. The Pirates were legitimately in the pennant race with a record of 59-44. They trailed the Cincinnati Reds by three games in the National League Central but were tied for the wild card lead with the Atlanta Braves. Not surprisingly, they were looking to make a deal or two to strengthen themselves for the season's final two months.

They had traded with the Miami Marlins to acquire the first baseman Gaby Sánchez in the hope that Sánchez might add some power to their lineup. The price had been a draft pick and, as he was described in every story about the trade, "minor-league outfielder Gorkys Hernández."

Hernández was twenty-four, another player who had been signed out of South America—Venezuela—as a teenager, going to the Detroit Tigers as an eighteen-year-old. He had been traded to the Atlanta Braves and then, in 2009, to Pittsburgh in the trade that had sent Nate McLouth to the Braves. He had reached Indianapolis in 2011 and had a solid year and had briefly been called up to the Pirates in May, where he was used primarily as a defensive replacement: he'd had only twenty-four at-bats in twenty-five games and had gotten two hits before being sent back to Indianapolis.

It was a few minutes before the players were supposed to go out to stretch prior to batting practice when Treanor got the call telling him that Hernández had been traded to the Marlins. The problem was the Marlins hadn't told the Pirates where they were sending Hernández. It could be Miami, or it could be Triple-A New Orleans, or it could even be Double-A Jacksonville. Things were so chaotic in south Florida that no one seemed certain what was going to happen to anyone next, much less the fate of a "minor-league outfielder."

Treanor hung up the phone and went to find Hernández, who was in uniform, ready to go out and stretch. Hernández was no longer a member of the Pittsburgh organization, so he couldn't go out and take BP with his now-former teammates. Treanor waved him into his office. Hernández, knowing what day it was, knew something was coming—he just didn't know what it was.

"I figured it was a trade of some kind," he said later. "I was nervous. I mean, they can send you anywhere."

Hernández's nerves weren't just focused on his baseball future. He and his wife had a two-year-old daughter and were expecting their second child in early to mid-September. Traveling anywhere at this point—much less trying to pack and/or find a place to live—was going to be just about impossible.

"Gorkys, you've been traded to the Miami Marlins," Treanor said, figuring there was no point beating around the bush. "Right now, I don't know where they're sending you. The general manager has your cell phone number, and they promised they would call as soon as they know."

Hernández was a little bit stunned, not so much by the trade—he'd been traded twice before—as by being told he was supposed to sit and wait to be told where he was going to go next.

"I'm a little bit confused at that moment," he said. "I could tell Dean was confused too."

Treanor was more angry than confused. Telling a player he was traded or even that he was being sent down was one thing. Telling him he'd been traded to nowhere was another. "Never happened to me before," he said.

Hernández walked back into the clubhouse and told his ex-teammates what had happened. When Treanor had called him in, most had figured he was being traded. When they asked where he was going, he gave them the same confusing answer Treanor had just given him.

There was nothing anyone could do. Good-byes were said quickly. Everyone else headed out the door and up the tunnel to the field. Hernández was left in an empty clubhouse. He called home and told his wife what was going on. He was going to be getting on a plane soon; he just didn't know where the plane would be going.

"She was very calm," he said. "Calmer than me."

He took off his uniform, showered, and was walking back to his locker when he saw his phone ringing. It was Michael Hill, the general manager of the Marlins.

"Gorkys," he said. "I'm sorry for the delay getting in touch with you, it's been kind of hectic here. I want to welcome you to the Marlins."

Hernández told him it was no problem and waited. "The team is in Atlanta," Hill said. "We need to get you on a flight so you can meet them there as soon as possible."

Hernández felt his heart rate go up. He was going to the big leagues, not to New Orleans or Jacksonville or anyplace else.

"If I have to leave my family now, I want to do it to go back to the majors," he said after hanging up with Hill. "An hour ago I had no idea where I was going to be. Now I know I'm in the major leagues."

He sent Treanor a text, and Treanor passed the good news on to the players. After batting practice, when Hernández had left for the airport, Treanor sat in his office and smiled.

"Well, I've lost my two best outfielders in five days," he said. He paused for a moment and smiled. "I couldn't be happier."

14

Schwinden and Lindsey

HOME SWEET HOME

While players like Marte and Hernández were making the giant leap from Triple-A to the majors, Chris Schwinden was just happy to be back in Buffalo.

Schwinden had just endured thirty-seven days that were tumultuous even by tumultuous minor-league standards. Following his one-day sojourn in Toronto that was followed by the eighteen-hour odyssey that took him from Pittsburgh to JFK Airport . . . to a gas station in the Bronx . . . to the side of the road on the New York State Thruway . . . to a motel in Binghamton . . . and finally to the mound at Coca-Cola Field, Schwinden had spent a week back in Triple-A before getting called back to the Mets for a third time in under five weeks. Three days later he had gone from the major leagues to unemployed—when the Mets stunned him by designating him for assignment, meaning Schwinden would be on waivers for ten days, and if someone didn't pick him up, he would be released.

He had just cleared security at LaGuardia Airport and was going to get on a plane to go back to Buffalo, to start packing up his apartment and wait for his phone to ring. As he was standing in the airport, his phone did ring. It was his agent, Brian Charles.

"Where are you right now?" he asked.

"Just cleared security at LaGuardia," Schwinden said. "Heading to Buffalo."

"No you're not," Charles said. "You need to go get yourself on a flight to Las Vegas. The Blue Jays just claimed you. They want you out there as soon as possible."

Schwinden wasn't looking forward to another odyssey to get to a Triple-A town, but he was relieved that someone had picked him up so quickly. He found a flight to Las Vegas and, a day later, was on the mound in a Las Vegas uniform. But not for very long.

He didn't pitch very well that day; in fact he was awful: three innings, seven earned runs. Oh well, a bad outing after a long trip. There would be time to settle in. The team was heading for Fresno—forty-five minutes from Visalia, his hometown—and at least there he would get a chance to pitch in front of a lot of family and friends.

"I was still in a little bit of shock going from the Mets, after being a Met my entire career, to finding myself in Las Vegas," he said. "But I was happy at least about going home and having everyone get a chance to see me pitch. I had about 150 people coming to the game. I was fairly convinced I would pitch a lot better the second time out."

He never got the chance to find out if he was right. Four days after acquiring him, the Blue Jays put him on waivers. The bad news was Schwinden never got to pitch in Fresno. The good news was he was unemployed for only a few hours.

"Congratulations," Charles told him on the phone. "You're now a Cleveland Indian."

Or, more accurately, a Columbus Clipper. Schwinden got on another airplane, flew back across the country, and presented himself to manager Mike Sarbaugh in Columbus. The Clippers, it turned out, had some guys on the roster he had played with in the past.

"I'd pitched on the East Coast and in the International League my whole career," he said. "It was just a more comfortable feeling to be back in the East—even if I wasn't out west for very long."

His stay in Columbus lasted considerably longer than his stay in Las Vegas: twenty-three days.

He started three times for the Clippers and wasn't as god-awful as he had been in Las Vegas, but not nearly as good as he'd been in Buffalo, where he had been pitching to an ERA of 2.70 before the

Mets let him go. On June 29, after his third start, the Clippers put him on waivers.

By now, it had all become ritual for Schwinden. He didn't even try to go anywhere. He just sat and waited for the phone to ring. It rang: this time he was heading for Rochester to join Scranton/Wilkes-Barre. He was a Yankee—not the kind who plays in the Bronx—the kind who was wandering the International League in 2012.

He packed again, not even certain what town he would be staying in since the Yankees didn't have a home. Three days later he pitched for SWB and lasted four innings. In five weeks he had pitched seven times for five different teams—Buffalo, the Mets, Las Vegas, Columbus, and Scranton/Wilkes-Barre—in four different baseball organizations.

His outings had ranged from brutal to mediocre—at best. Twenty-four hours after his start for the Yankees, he was on waivers again. That made four organizations that had given up on him in thirty days.

He was a little bit dizzy and a lot discouraged. Understandably.

"The whole thing was draining," he said. "To begin with, just the process each time: you find out you've been waived, and you sit there and wonder what you should do next. Get on a plane and go home? Sit in a hotel room and wait to hear if someone's picked you up?

"I did a lot of that because my agent kept saying, 'Sit tight, someone's going to call.' He was right—thank goodness—each time, but when you've been waived, everyone else kind of moves on without you. I ate a lot of meals alone in a lot of empty food courts and restaurants. It wasn't for that long a period of time, but it *felt* like a long period of time.

"Then you get word you've been picked up, and you have to pack and get to an airport and figure out how to get to wherever your new team is at that moment. I'd go out to pitch, and I wanted to make a good impression on my new bosses, so I was probably trying too hard, overthrowing, getting myself into trouble right away. Then, when I did, I started to think, 'Here we go again,' and it would snowball. I almost found myself thinking, 'Am I going to get waived *again*?'

"Every time you get waived, it feels lousy. It's even worse when they take one look at you and say, 'We don't want you.' On the one hand, you tell yourself that it's good that there are people out there who want you, who think you're worth a shot. But the negatives during a time like that completely overwhelm any positives you might try to come up with. It was not any fun."

The day after he was waived by the Yankees, Schwinden was sitting in another hotel room contemplating yet another meal by himself when he got a text from Bobby Parnell, an old friend from his long-ago (at least it felt that way) Mets days. Sitting in the Mets' bullpen, Parnell had heard about Schwinden's latest release and that he might be on his way back—remarkably enough—to the Mets, which would mean a return to Buffalo.

"Hearing you might be a Met again soon," the text said.

Schwinden almost held his breath hoping. It took two more days for the phone to ring again.

This time it wasn't Brian Charles. It was John Ricco, the Mets' farm director. "We'd like to bring you back," he said. "Do you think you can report to Buffalo right away?"

By then, Schwinden was actually *in* Buffalo. He'd driven there from Rochester after the Yankees had released him, since he still had his apartment there and had never had a chance to get back to pick up his things. He had sublet it to Matt den Dekker, a Bisons outfielder, but there was enough room for two.

"I was ecstatic when I got the call that I was a Bison again," he said, smiling. "I was going back to a place that was familiar, with guys I knew. I felt like I had been on the longest, strangest road trip in history."

He didn't even mind it when he walked into the Buffalo clubhouse on July 5 and his new/old teammates kept asking him how many Sky-Miles he had rolled up in the previous five weeks.

It had been thirty-seven days since he had pitched for the Mets in Philadelphia and thirty-four days since his first release. He had appeared in "transactions" fourteen times since being sent down by the Mets at the end of spring training.

Perhaps no one in baseball history has ever been happier than

Chris Schwinden to learn he was being sent back to Buffalo. He was home again.

———

John Lindsey's spring hadn't been nearly as hectic as Schwinden's, if only because his phone hadn't been ringing at all since he had signed to play in Mexico.

Although the Mexican League is generally considered to be on about the same level as Triple-A, Lindsey didn't find the pitching to be quite as challenging. Very few of the pitchers in the league had been in the majors—unlike Triple-A, where almost every night you faced at least one pitcher with major-league experience.

"I felt comfortable playing there," he said. "I could tell right away that the work I had done in the off-season, losing the weight, getting into better shape, had helped me. My dad had been right—my body still had something left to give."

Lindsey had been a consistent Triple-A hitter for several years, and he was even better playing for Laguna. By mid-June he was hitting .341 and had hit twenty-one home runs and driven in sixty-four runs. He knew that scouts from major-league teams were in the ballpark most nights, so he remained hopeful he would get a call.

Finally, on June 21, he did.

The Tigers wanted to sign him and send him to Toledo. The Mud Hens were struggling and needed an extra bat with some power. In truth, the Tigers were having a tough time getting going at that stage, after being picked in the spring by many experts to reach the World Series. If he played well and Detroit continued to struggle at the plate, who knew?—maybe he would get a chance to build on that one hit he had gotten back in 2010.

"All I knew was I would be going to a ballpark that was an hour away from the big-league team," Lindsey said. "I didn't see any way that could be a bad thing."

Within twenty-four hours of being signed by the Tigers, he was in Toledo. He wondered if he would have trouble adapting to the International League. He'd been in the Pacific Coast League in recent years, where the pitchers tended to throw more breaking pitches than fastballs because of the altitude. It didn't turn out to be an issue.

"I'm a fastball hitter anyway," Lindsey said. "I was very happy to be in a place where they were going to throw me a lot of fastballs."

Manager Phil Nevin put him in the lineup right away, often having him hit cleanup. Lindsey was comfortable in the Toledo clubhouse right from the start. "One of the advantages of playing in so many places is that you're used to going to new places," he said. "Plus, in the minors there's so much turnover on teams all the time that there are new guys coming in every day. You learn how to get along with people pretty quickly because if you don't, you aren't going to have a very happy life."

Just as Schwinden was delighted to find himself in Buffalo, Lindsey was thrilled to be a Mud Hen. He was thirty-five years old, and he was still playing high-level professional baseball.

"It's funny, because if you had told me when I first signed that I would play this long, I would have told you no way," he said. "And if you had told me I would play this long and almost all of it would be in the minor leagues, I'd have laughed at you and said you had no idea what you were talking about.

"That's the thing about baseball. No one knows. None of us know what it's going to be like when we start out, and none of us know how tough it's going to be when the day comes we have to walk away. We all know it's coming, but we want to push it back—and push it back for as long as possible."

Lindsey knew his day was coming. But he wanted to keep pushing it back for as long as he could and *hope* he might push it back far enough to get one more shot at making the one-hour trip up I-75 to Detroit.

15

Slice of Life

JAMIE FARR WOULD BE PROUD

If the Durham Bulls are minor-league baseball's most famous team, the Toledo Mud Hens must be second.

Part of it is simply the team's name. In recent years, minor-league teams have become much more creative with their names than in the past. Nowadays there are teams like the Savannah Sand Gnats, the Richmond Flying Squirrels, the Charleston RiverDogs, and the Augusta GreenJackets.

Toledo had the Mud Hens long before any of those teams—or names—existed. In fact, the name dates to 1896, when the team played in a place called Bay View Park, which was next to some marshland that was inhabited by American coots—also known as marsh hens or mud hens. People in Toledo took to calling the team the Swamp Angels or the Mud Hens. It was Mud Hens that stuck, and it became the team's official name when it rejoined the American Association in 1902.

Prior to that, the Toledo Blue Stockings had been "promoted" to the American Association in 1884. In those days, before there was what is today's American League, the American Association was a major league, and minor-league teams were occasionally invited to join. The Blue Stockings had two African Americans on the team, Moses Fleetwood Walker and his brother, Welday Walker.

According to historical accounts, the Hall of Famer Cap Anson, then with the Chicago White Stockings, told management he wouldn't take the field to compete against the Walker brothers. Soon after, the brothers were gone from Toledo, and the next African American who played major-league baseball was Jackie Robinson—sixty-three years later.

The Mud Hens have been in Toledo for most of the last 110 years. They won a Double-A championship in 1927, when Casey Stengel was their manager. There were two brief periods when they played under other names, and there was no team in Toledo at all from 1956 to 1964—after the Milwaukee Braves moved their Triple-A farm team from Toledo to Wichita. In 1965, the Yankees moved the Richmond Virginians to Toledo and rechristened them the Mud Hens, and there has once again been Triple-A baseball in Toledo ever since. For the last twenty-six seasons, the Mud Hens have been the Tigers' Triple-A team, which makes geographic sense since Fifth Third Field, their home since 2002, is fifty-eight miles south of Comerica Park, a straight shot up I-75.

Nowadays, the Mud Hens embrace their unique name. Their mascots are named Muddy and Muddonna, and their newsletter is the *Muddy Times*, except online, where it is the *Mud-E-Times*. The kids' club is, you guessed it, the Muddy's Buddies Kids Club.

The second reason for the popularity of the Mud Hens is one man: Jamie Farr. The actor grew up in Toledo, and when he became one of the stars of *M*A*S*H*, his character, Max Klinger of Toledo, Ohio (also of Lebanese descent like Farr), often wore a Toledo Mud Hens baseball cap. Farr frequently referenced Toledo and the Mud Hens during the nine years he was a star on the show (he appeared in six episodes the first year and in twelve episodes the second).

To this day, Farr remains Toledo's most famous celebrity. Starting in 1984, his name was on the LPGA golf tournament that is played in Toledo, and the most popular bobblehead night of the year at Fifth Third Field is—not surprisingly—Jamie Farr bobblehead night.

"The 2012 version was the second one they've done," Farr said one afternoon from the apartment he was renting in Hamilton, Ontario, where he was starring in a play called *The Last Romance*. "They're doing a third one for 2013. I told [general manager] Joe Napoli I wanted to be in a tuxedo. Very un-Klinger-like, I guess."

Farr still gets back to Toledo and to a Mud Hens game at least once a year. He grew up as a fan of the Mud Hens and the Detroit Tigers, going to games at Swayne Field, which was the Mud Hens' home until 1955.

"I was part of what they called the Knot Hole Gang," he said, laughing. "You paid fifty cents and they let you watch the game through a hole in the fence. I loved going to games back then. I worked as a paperboy for the *Toledo Blade* and the *Toledo Times*. The guy who was in charge of the neighborhood I worked would take us to a Tigers game in Briggs Stadium whenever we sold a certain number of subscriptions. I loved that too. I was a huge baseball fan then; I'm a huge baseball fan now."

Farr's real name is Jameel Farah. His dad was a meat cutter who opened his own grocery store—Farah's Meats—when Jamie was a teenager. The grocery store still exists but, according to Farr, isn't in very good shape. "It's like a lot of places in Toledo," he said. "Hit hard by the economy."

Farr is seventy-nine now—thirty years removed from the last episode of *M*A*S*H*. He considers himself lucky to have played Klinger, although like many actors who have had an iconic role, he finds that it can be a burden at times.

"It's not an issue in the theater," he said. "I've been lucky that way. But TV and film are different. If I want to be cast as, say, a murderer, the fact is a lot of directors, even now, will say, 'How can I cast a guy who is famous for dressing in women's clothing as a murderer?'"

"Alan [Alda] tells me to this day, for all he's done since *M*A*S*H* when he's onstage someone will invariably yell out, 'Nice going, Hawkeye.' It's a blessing to have had a role like that, but there are times when it's a bit of a curse. I *love* that I was Klinger. I'd just love for someone to call and say, 'Okay, here's that next great role.'"

When Klinger was created—initially for one show before the character took off—it was *M*A*S*H*'s co-creator Gene Reynolds, who was from Cleveland, who suggested having him come from Toledo.

Larry Gelbart, who co-created the show with Reynolds, decided to name him after an old friend of his and make him Lebanese, in honor of the great comedian Danny Thomas, who had also grown up in Toledo, under the name of Amos Jacobs. Farr, who had first come to Hollywood in 1955 and had been a second banana on (among others) *The Red Skelton Show*, read for the part and got it almost instantly.

"It probably helped that I *am* Lebanese American and that I'd been in the army and was in Korea on a couple of occasions," he said. "Or maybe it was just meant to be."

Ken Levine, one of the show's writers, also dabbled back then in baseball announcing. He had worked for the Tidewater Tides (and has since worked for several major-league teams, most recently the Dodgers) and was familiar with the Mud Hens. He began writing references to the Mud Hens into the script for Klinger. When Gene Cook, then the Mud Hens' general manager, sent Farr a Mud Hens cap, he began wearing it on a regular basis.

"Gene told me that they began getting calls from all over the world from people looking for Mud Hens gear," Farr said with a laugh. "A lot of people weren't even sure it was a real team. Once they found out it was real, they wanted caps and T-shirts and coffee mugs—everything. Joe Napoli tells me they still get calls all the time for stuff."

In the meantime, Farr is always welcome at Fifth Third Field. "I love Muddy and Muddonna," he said, laughing. "Where else but in Toledo could someone famous for cross-dressing throw out the first pitch at a baseball game?"

Where indeed?

16

Slice of Life

WEEKEND IN TOLEDO

Fifth Third Field is like many of the newer Triple-A parks. It sits smack in the middle of downtown Toledo, and as with Victory Field in Indianapolis the local skyline can be seen behind the outfield fences.

Because the Mud Hens have been part of Toledo's fabric for so long, special events are frequently held inside the ballpark—including weddings, church services, and graduation parties. On a Saturday in July 2012, several Mud Hens arrived at the ballpark early one afternoon to take extra batting practice prior to a game against the Louisville Bats and found a wedding party standing on the pitcher's mound having their photographs taken.

"Happens all the time," manager Phil Nevin said, feet up on his office desk. "You get used to it after a while."

Nevin might have been tempted at that moment to see if any of the groomsmen might be available to pitch for his team that night. By any definition, the Mud Hens were having a tough summer, and they had bottomed during a five-game series in Columbus earlier in the week.

"We caught them while they're playing well at a time when we're playing badly—and pitching badly," Nevin said. "All you can do is hope you pull out of it soon. If not, it can be a pretty miserable August."

Minor-league managers dread the month of August—especially when their team isn't in contention. August 1 is a tough day in Triple-

A for everyone, because the trade deadline has passed. No one has traded for you. Your team hasn't made a trade that has opened up a spot for you. You are in the minor leagues, and if you aren't a prospect, chances are good your season will end in early September without a September 1 call-up to the big leagues.

"August 1 is the day it really sinks in with guys," Nevin said. "All season they've told themselves they're either going to play their way onto the big-league club wherever they are, or someone else is going to notice them and trade for them. That's why you hear guys around here say, 'I'm playing for thirty teams, not just one,' all the time. August 1 comes around, they know they're pretty much stuck where they are. They can do the math. They know which two or three guys on the team are considered prospects by the organization. That means the other twenty-two or twenty-three guys are playing for maybe one or two or, at most, three September call-ups. Those numbers are real—and they aren't encouraging."

The Mud Hens were not going to be contending when August rolled around. They had managed to win the second game of a five-game series in Columbus, but then had given up forty runs in the next three games. Nevin had used twelve different pitchers in those games, and each had failed more miserably than the previous one. The Hens had limped home on Saturday morning with a 42-66 record. The only good news was that they were starting a four-game series with the Louisville Bats, the one team in the league that had a worse record than they did.

"Baseball, especially when things are going like this, is a motherf——," Nevin said. "It will just tear your heart out." He smiled. "Of course everything I've ever gotten in life—going to college, meeting my wife, making the living I've been able to make—is because of baseball. So it's tough for me to complain."

Nevin had played an indirect role in shaping baseball history. In 1992, he had been the College Player of the Year at Cal State–Fullerton, capping a three-year career in which he had hit .364. Since he was twenty-one and considered not far from being ready for the major leagues, he was very high on most draft boards that spring.

The Houston Astros had the first pick in the draft. Their lead scout, Hal Newhouser, had told them they *had* to draft a high school infielder from Michigan named Derek Jeter. The Astros weren't sure that was the right move: For one thing, Jeter and his family were telling people he was going to college, specifically the University of Michigan. For another, the Astros had lost their No. 1 pick, John Burke (whom they had taken at No. 6 in the first round), a year earlier when he had opted to turn down their offer of a $500,000 bonus in order to go to college. Jeter, the Astros figured, would cost at least double that and even that might not be enough.

So they passed on Jeter and took Nevin. Four other teams passed on Jeter before the Yankees took him at No. 6. According to legend, when concern was expressed in the Yankees' predraft meetings that Jeter might go to Michigan, Dick Groch, who had scouted him for the team, answered by saying, "The only place Derek Jeter is going for sure is to Cooperstown."

Jeter ended up signing with the Yankees for a $700,000 bonus, and the rest, as they say, is history. The other players taken before Jeter became—along with Nevin—the answer to a trivia question. The answer is Nevin, Paul Shuey, B. J. Wallace, Jeffrey Hammonds, and Chad Mottola. It is not all that different from the Portland Trail Blazers' decision in 1984 to take Sam Bowie ahead of Michael Jordan, because they didn't think they needed another guard. When his team passed on Jeter, Newhouser, the Astros' scout, was so angry he quit his job.

Nevin had the best career of the five players taken before Jeter. But it wasn't easy. After playing on the U.S. Olympic team in 1992, he was sent to Triple-A to begin his pro career. "I thought I'd only be there a little while," he said. "I figured I was passing through. I never thought it would be such a struggle to get to the big leagues and stay. I got sour pretty quickly and was probably pretty bitter about the whole experience before it was over."

Nevin ended up playing a total of eighteen games in the majors for the Astros. He was traded in 1995 after he and the team had a preseason dustup over his refusal to work out with so-called replacement players, the nonunion players brought in by owners during the 1994–95 players' strike. Like a lot of younger minor leaguers, Nevin didn't want to be involved with the replacement players, and that led to hard feelings between him and the Astros.

They traded him to Detroit midway through the 1995 season, and the Tigers converted him into a catcher to try to find more playing time for him. Two years later, after bouncing between Triple-A and the majors, he was off to Anaheim—which produced more of the same. It was only after he was traded to San Diego prior to the 1999 season, and manager Bruce Bochy moved him back to third base, that Nevin finally blossomed.

"One thing I learned through my own career is that guys find their potential at different times," he said. "Not everyone does it at twenty-two or twenty-three. The best thing that ever happened to me as a hitter was becoming a catcher, because I had to learn so much more about hitting in order to try to catch.

"I tell my guys every chance I get that there are lots of ways to improve and it may not happen for them right away. It didn't for me. I was almost thirty before I got to that point. Problem is, a lot of times, you get to be twenty-four or twenty-five and teams give up on you. I was lucky because I had been the No. 1 pick once upon a time; people were willing to give me more than one chance."

He hit 24 home runs and drove in 85 runs in 1999 in San Diego. A year later those numbers were 31 and 107, and the following season, when he was an All-Star, they soared to 41 and 126. That led to serious big-money contracts. Over the last five years of his career, Nevin was paid almost $35 million. It took him a while, but in the end he beat the motherf—— that is the game he loves.

"That's why, without sounding corny, I like the idea of giving something back to the game," he said. "I'd like to manage in the big leagues someday, but there's a lot of gratification in this job. The best part is always sending a guy up for the first time. Thad Weber [one of his pitchers] sat in my office and wept when I told him he was going up.

"The worst part is releasing a guy, because you're killing their dream. I try to be very honest with them. If I think they're still good enough to play, I'll tell them that. If not, I'll tell them that too. Sometimes the biggest favor you can do a guy is to tell him, 'It's time.' They may not *want* to hear it, but sometimes they *need* to hear it.

"The first year I managed in independent league ball [2009] I had a guy playing for me named Frank Lonigro. He had talked about going to firefighter's school. I called him in one day and said, 'You need to go to firefighter's school.' For some reason I knew there was a school starting the next week—maybe he had mentioned it. I told him it was time, that I was releasing him.

"He was angry; he vented. A couple years later I heard from him. He said, 'I hated you at the time, but you did the right thing for me.'"

Nevin retired in 2007, tried broadcasting for a while, but missed being in uniform. That was how he came to manage the independent league team in Orange County in 2009. A year later the Tigers hired him to manage their Double-A club in Erie, before promoting him to Toledo in 2011. Although the Mud Hens had been 67-77 in Nevin's first season and were struggling in his second, Nevin was still considered a prime candidate to succeed Jim Leyland whenever he decided to retire as the manager in Detroit. For the moment, that wasn't Nevin's main concern. Finding a pitcher who could keep the Louisville Bats in single digits on a July night in Toledo was far more important to him.

"We'll be okay tonight," he insisted. "The guy we've got pitching gets people out."

———

That guy was Adam Wilk, and Nevin was right. For seven innings, Wilk shut the Bats out. The Mud Hens, in front of a packed house of 11,500 on a gorgeous night, built a 4–0 lead. Even with the team struggling, Toledo still loved its baseball team.

The highlight of the evening came when John Lindsey, still very much enjoying being in Toledo after his stint in Mexico, hit a long home run over the left-field fence in the bottom of the first to put Toledo up 2–0. The ball flew out of the ballpark and landed on Monroe Street, which runs directly behind the fence. A man passing in his car at that moment apparently saw the ball clear the wall and bounce, because he stopped his car, jumped out, chased the ball down, picked it up, got in his car, and drove away.

It had to be one of the most unexpected souvenirs in baseball history.

Sadly for the Mud Hens, their worn-out bullpen couldn't hold the lead for Wilk. The Bats scored eight runs in the final two innings, even though the Hens came within one out of holding on for the win. The final score was 8–4.

The next day, the teams were scheduled to play a six o'clock game. Most minor-league teams move their Sunday games to evening starts in July and August to dodge the heat. On this afternoon, a daytime start would have worked just fine since the temperature was in the eighties in the afternoon.

The first two men to reach the Toledo clubhouse that day were Lindsey, who had hit the Monroe Street homer the night before, and hitting coach Leon Durham. The two were markedly different men whose careers had also been markedly different.

Durham had been a No. 1 draft pick for the St. Louis Cardinals in 1976 and had been in the big leagues before his twenty-fifth birthday. He had played in the majors for ten years, mostly with the Chicago Cubs. He had been in 1,067 games and had been to bat 3,587 times—hitting 147 home runs and driving in 530 runs. His nickname was Bull, because he was big and strong and had the kind of personality that came right at you.

He was about as no-nonsense in dealing with his hitters as anyone you might meet in any walk of life. Outside the office he shared with pitching coach A. J. Sager, there was a whiteboard. On it, Durham had written his theory of hitting for everyone to see: "You can't make a living looking to hit a breaking ball. You *can* make a living looking to hit a fastball . . . Look for a fastball."

Lindsey had hit a lot of fastballs in the eighteen years he had played professional baseball. He had been drafted in the thirteenth round in 1995 and hadn't gotten above Class A ball until 2003. In all, he had played in 1,787 minor-league games in fourteen different cities—several for more than one stint—and had 6,347 at-bats. He had hit 268 home runs and had driven in 1,195 runs. All impressive numbers—none of them in the major leagues.

His major-league career consisted of the one month he had spent with the Dodgers in September 2010.

Through all the stops and all the letdowns, Lindsey had managed to keep an upbeat outlook on both baseball and life, even though his father's warning to him when he first signed (that getting to the majors would prove to be harder than it looked) had turned out to be more accurate than either man could have known at the time.

It took Lindsey seven full seasons even to reach Double-A ball. He had issues with injuries but also struggled at times at the plate when he was healthy. After he had hit .208 in 1999 (and had been forced to have shoulder surgery after hurting himself diving back into a bag on a pickoff play), he wondered if it wasn't time to look into going to college.

"I was talking to my uncle about it all one day, and he said, 'When was the last time you had your eyes checked?'" Lindsey said. "I'd had them checked, and I was twenty-twenty. He said it might not be that simple and sent me to a specialist he knew at Mississippi State [Lindsey is from Hattiesburg]. Sure enough, I *was* twenty-twenty, but I had an astigmatism that was causing me to react just a split second too slowly at the plate. He gave me some lenses to correct it, and I began to see things more quickly."

Even then, his progress was slow. He finally made it to Double-A in 2003 after hitting .297 with twenty-two home runs and ninety-three RBIs at high-A San Bernardino a year earlier. He had two solid years at Double-A San Antonio, a Seattle farm team, and signed a free-agent contract with the Cardinals prior to the 2005 season. But the Cardinals released him in spring training, and at the age of twenty-eight Lindsey didn't have a job.

By then, Lindsey was convinced his dad had been wrong when he said baseball was a big pond. "Baseball," he said, "is an ocean."

He turned to independent league ball, signing with the New Jersey Jackals of the Canadian-American Association. He played well enough there to be signed by the Marlins, who returned him to high-A ball for the rest of that season. The next spring, again without a contract, he was back in New Jersey.

His time with the Jackals extended his career and also produced a nickname that stuck with him: "the Mayor." The Jackals' radio play-by-play man was Joe Ameruoso, who was old enough to remember that John Lindsay had been mayor of New York City from 1966 through 1973. Lindsay had been reelected in 1969 in large part because of the good feeling in the city generated by the Mets' miracle run to a World Series title. Lindsay had clung to the Mets for dear life after losing the Republican primary. Running on a third-party ticket, he was reelected three weeks after the Mets won their championship.

In spite of the different spelling, Ameruoso started calling Lindsey "the Mayor." The nickname not only stuck, but teammates—who have never heard of New York City's John Lindsay—use it today.

With or without holding political office, Lindsey played solidly in 2006, hitting .311, but by the end of the season he had decided to retire and go to college. Major League Baseball has a program that helps players pay for their college education after they retire, but they must be enrolled within two years of having last been on the payroll of a major-league baseball team—whether they are in the majors or the minors. But independent league ball doesn't count, so Lindsey had until the fall of 2007—two years after he had last been under contract to the Marlins—to enroll.

"I didn't want to commit myself to another season of independent league ball, because it would have ended too late for me to enroll before the deadline," he said. "I was thirty and I was playing independent league. It just seemed like time."

He had actually enrolled at Pearl River Community College when he got a surprise call from the Los Angeles Dodgers. Lorenzo Bundy, who had been a minor-league instructor when Lindsey was with the Rockies, and Mike Easler, one of the Dodgers' minor-league hitting instructors, had recommended trying to sign Lindsey to a minor-league contract. Both men saw him as a solid minor-league hitter who was a good clubhouse influence on younger players.

Lindsey still didn't have any children at that point in his life. He decided if Bundy and Easler thought he was worthy of another chance, there must still be something in him that perhaps even he wasn't seeing. What's more, he knew if he was under contract to a major-league team in 2007, he could still get his education paid for at the end of the season (or begin a new two-year window of eligibility) if things didn't pan out.

So he accepted the invitation to Dodgers camp in the spring of 2007. He was assigned to Double-A out of camp but played well enough to quickly be called up to Las Vegas—where Bundy was managing. Twelve years after signing his first pro contract, he had finally made it to Triple-A. He was bigger by then and stronger and a smarter hitter. In a little more than half a season in Vegas, he hit .333 with nineteen home runs and eighty-eight RBIs. A year later, in a full season, he hit .316 with twenty-six home runs and a hundred RBIs—the best numbers he had ever had at any level in his career.

He spent the next year in New Orleans, having signed with the Marlins again, but returned to the Dodgers a year later. With the Triple-A team now in Albuquerque, he had his strongest season ever: hitting .353 with twenty-five home runs and ninety-seven RBIs. Even so, there was no sign at all that he was ever going to get the call to the majors. That is, until he was summoned to Tim Wallach's office in Round Rock, on the penultimate day of the season.

That moment was different from J. C. Boscan's in Gwinnett, because no one in the clubhouse had been clued in beforehand. And yet all the elements of *The Rookie* were there again. No one in history had spent more time in the minor leagues before getting a major-league call-up than Lindsey. The celebration was spontaneous but unrestrained.

"If you know John Lindsey at all, you know why guys would react that way," said Phil Nevin. "He's one of those people who is impossible not to like."

Lindsey's major-league stint was cut short soon after he got his "Carlos Lee" hit, when he was hit on the right hand by a pitch and broke it. He was back in Albuquerque the next year but found himself out of work at the end of the 2011 season. Again, retirement crossed his mind. Again, he began thinking about college. Again, he decided to heed his father's words. He spent the off-season working out harder than he had in years. He lost thirty pounds and, after his half season in Mexico, had been signed by Toledo in June. "I'll tell you what," Nevin said. "The guy can still hit."

At thirty-five, Lindsey still didn't believe he had used it all up. "I'm an accident away," he said, repeating the minor-league mantra. "It happened once. I still believe it can happen again."

Still believing is what keeps everyone in Triple-A coming back— day after day, year after year.

———

The day after Lindsey's home run and the bullpen's late meltdown, it was a surprisingly comfortable summer Sunday in the Midwest— largely because the humidity was low enough that being in a ballpark wasn't at all unpleasant.

Two hours before the Toledo Mud Hens were scheduled to host the Louisville Bats, a middle-aged man stood on top of the Mud Hens' dugout wearing a white straw hat with a Greg Norman shark logo on it, a yellow shirt, blue shorts, and flip-flops. He was giving his testimony—at length—and about three hundred people sat in the sun and drank in every word.

"I was born again on November 6, 1983," Frank Tanana was saying. "That was the day I gave my life and my soul to Jesus Christ."

Tanana was thirty years old when he was born again both as a Christian and as a pitcher. He had made it to the major leagues as a twenty-year-old flamethrower with the California Angels and had eighty-four wins by the time he was twenty-five years old. In those days there weren't pitch counts or inning counts or young pitchers being shut down at 160 innings to protect their arms. You just went out and threw until your arm fell off—which, in many cases, it did, at least as far as throwing ninety-five-plus miles an hour was concerned.

In his first full season in the majors, 1974, Tanana pitched more than 268 innings. He turned twenty-one in July of that year. A year later it was 257 innings, and the year after that, when he was 19-10, it was 288 innings. These days, for a young pitcher to pitch 288 innings in *two* seasons is considered a tad risky.

In 1979, Tanana hurt his throwing shoulder and missed almost half the season. He never threw as hard again and had to learn how to pitch all over again. Instead of getting hitters out with power, he learned to get them out with finesse. Pitching with a fastball that rarely got into the high eighties, he had a second career in Texas and Detroit—his hometown—that kept him in baseball until 1993, when he retired with 240 career victories.

The line used most often to describe Tanana's career was "he threw in the nineties in the '70s and in the seventies in the '90s." It was very close to being true. Because he pitched for so long, he had the unusual distinction of being one of two pitchers (Rick Reuschel was the other) to have given up home runs to both Henry Aaron and Barry Bonds.

Now, at fifty-nine, Tanana lived back home in Michigan and was part of something called the Pro Athletes Outreach group. That meant he spent quite a few Sundays in ballparks like Fifth Third giving his testimony. Sitting among the fans as Tanana talked were a handful of the Mud Hens, in uniform. They all knew who Tanana was, even if he hardly looked like someone who had once overpowered major-league hitters.

As Tanana spoke, the dichotomies of minor-league baseball were evident all around him. Down the left-field line, the Bats players stretched, going through their Sunday pregame routine. Sunday is never a day of rest in baseball, but it is often a day with no batting practice, which means players can report to the ballpark later than normal. On the scoreboard behind Tanana, various future promotions were repeatedly flashed, including—most notably—Jamie Farr bobblehead night, which was twelve days away.

All in a day's work in the minor leagues.

As Tanana was winding up his forty-five-minute talk, another ex-pitcher was drawing a small crowd himself: out on the concourse, Denny McLain was signing copies of his autobiography, *I Told You I Wasn't Perfect.*

That might have been one of the most understated book titles in history. McLain was baseball's last thirty-game winner, having gone 31-6 for the Detroit Tigers in 1968 with an ERA of 1.96. A year later he won twenty-four games. After that, his life pretty much crashed.

In 1970, he was suspended twice by baseball commissioner Bowie Kuhn—the first time after revelations that he had been involved in a bookmaking operation, the second time for carrying a gun onto a Tigers team plane. Later that year, he filed for bankruptcy, apparently having lost most of his money gambling. He was traded to the Washington Senators—a deal that, for all intents and purposes, destroyed baseball in Washington. He spent the entire season fighting with Washington manager Ted Williams while going 10-22. He also hurt his arm during the season, which ended with the Senators leaving Washington to become the Texas Rangers.

He bounced from Washington to Oakland to Atlanta and last pitched in the majors in September 1972 at the age of twenty-eight. He had been so good at a young age that he had 131 career victories—114 of them by the age of twenty-five. His post-baseball life had been filled with arrests, drug issues, and several stints in jail, most notably when he spent six years there after being convicted on charges of embezzlement, mail fraud, and conspiracy. His weight had ballooned to a reported 330 pounds, and while he didn't look quite that heavy anymore, he still had to weigh close to 300. His 1968 baseball card listed him as six feet one and 185 pounds.

Now he was sixty-eight and still able to make some money through various media outlets in Detroit and by trying to sell his book. Fifth Third Field was a fairly typical McLain stop. He signed books for a while and then appeared on the Mud Hens' TV pregame show, which was on local cable television.

While Tanana was testifying and McLain was signing and fans

were making plans for Farr bobblehead night, the team was currently preparing for Toledo Fire Department Night.

All in a day's work in the minor leagues.

This was a fairly complicated operation since it involved fire trucks and firefighters; one firefighter rappelling down a rope behind the right-field fence and then jogging the game ball into the pitcher's mound; several mascots and the two teams—who were expected to be on the field when the festivities climaxed with the singing of the national anthem.

Shortly before six o'clock, the fire trucks came rolling down the third-base line. One carried the mascot for the Toledo Fire Department. Another carried Muddy and Muddonna. Trailing them was yet another mascot called BirdZerk!, who appeared at various minor-league parks as part of the entertainment. Firefighters were everywhere. The players appeared, poking their heads gingerly from the dugouts. The firefighter rappelled; the ball was delivered to starting pitcher Casey Crosby; and, with just about every inch of the field covered by people and trucks and mascots, the anthem was played.

Finally, it was time to play baseball.

As the Mud Hens' PR staff settled back to announce the game-time temperature and slip into the routine of a baseball game, their walkie-talkies crackled. It was the marketing assistant who had been in charge of the on-field activities.

"What in the world," she asked, "am I supposed to do with all these fire trucks and mascots?"

17

Brett Tomko

MORE THAN NINE LIVES

Brett Tomko was on the field with the rest of the Bats during the pre-game tribute to firefighters, mascots, and rappellers. To him, this was just another day at the ballpark. At thirty-nine, he had pretty much seen it all.

He was in his eighteenth season as a professional baseball player and had pitched in twenty-five different cities—ten in the major leagues; fifteen in the minors. That didn't count two stints in the Arizona Fall League. He was scheduled to pitch the following day for Louisville, and he knew there was a possibility it could be his last start. Even though he had a respectable ERA of 3.43, his record was 0-6, and he knew that the Cincinnati Reds, the Bats' parent club, might be thinking about giving him his release. He didn't believe the way he had pitched merited that kind of treatment, but he also knew that stranger things had happened in baseball.

"I've been done [finished] in this game so many times I don't worry about it anymore," he said, sitting in the dugout, wearing the kind of bright smile that isn't seen that often in Triple-A—especially from someone who has won a hundred games in the major leagues. "I'm way past sitting around being bitter—maybe because I've been able to play for a lot longer than I ever thought I would play."

He smiled. "Last year, when I was pitching in Round Rock, we went to Omaha on a road trip. I was scheduled to pitch against Jeff

Suppan. Now, think about it, we've both been around forever and had a lot of time in the major leagues. But here we are in *Omaha* getting ready to pitch against each other. The night before we pitched, we were talking and he said to me, 'BT, I may never get back up and you may never get back up. For now, right here in Omaha tomorrow, we're pitching the seventh game of the World Series. That's the only way to look at it. Otherwise, why be here?'

"That was a good punch in the gut for me. He was right. We were both in Omaha because we *wanted* to be."

Suppan has won 140 major-league games and in 2006 was voted the MVP of the National League Championship Series while pitching for the Cardinals—who went on to win the World Series. And both men *did* make it back to the majors after their talk in Omaha—Tomko later in the 2011 season, Suppan in 2012.

As much as he loves baseball, Tomko didn't set out necessarily to become a baseball player. Growing up in Euclid, Ohio, he actually thought his best sport in high school might be basketball . . . until he encountered someone named Tess Whitlock one night. "I had scored fifty-five the game before," Tomko said. "They put him on me and said, 'Stop him.' He did—completely. Late in the game he had the ball on the break, and I got back to try to stop him. He just jumped right over me and dunked. At that moment I thought, 'Maybe I should start taking baseball more seriously.'"

His dad, Jerry, was the sports fan in the family. In fact, Jerry Tomko was responsible for naming Cleveland's NBA team, the Cavaliers. In 1970, when Cleveland was granted an expansion team, the *Cleveland Plain Dealer* staged a contest to name the team. There were eleven thousand entries, and readers voted to select one of the five finalists. Cavaliers won.

"My dad got an autographed basketball and a one-year season ticket," Tomko said. "That was it. And that season they won fifteen games and lost sixty-seven."

His mom was more artistic. In fact, she insisted that Brett take an art class as a teenager, and he got hooked. To this day, he brings drawing materials with him on the road and almost always spends some time working in his hotel room before bed. "Great stress reliever," he said.

He also has talent and has sold a couple dozen pieces through the years. It's something he wants to spend more time on when he's at home more often—after baseball is over.

"If you've spent any time in the majors, there's no point lying to yourself about where you are," he said. "The postgame spread in a Triple-A clubhouse might be the same food as in a major-league clubhouse, but it doesn't *taste* the same. In the majors you stay at the Ritz or the Four Seasons. Here . . ." He paused and pointed at the Park Inn, looming over the left-field wall at Fifth Third Field. "You stay at the Park Inn, and it's just fine. You have a roommate, and that's just fine too.

"But there are moments when it hits you. Earlier this season we were up against some pitcher I'd never heard of, and we couldn't touch him. Willie Harris [another veteran major leaguer] says to me in the dugout, 'That dude is nasty, really nasty.' I said, 'Dude, he's pitching in Triple-A. If he was *that* nasty, he wouldn't be here.'"

For most of his career, Tomko was one of those pitchers described as an "innings eater." He rarely dominated or overpowered anyone. In 266 major-league starts he had thirteen complete games and two shutouts, the second one coming in the game in which he badly hurt his shoulder in 2009. But he consistently got his team into the sixth or seventh inning with a chance to win, which kept him around for a long time with a lot of different teams.

"The not-so-funny thing, looking back, is I was pitching about as well as I've ever pitched when I got hurt," he said. "Not just that day, but the whole time I was in Oakland that summer—which was only six starts. It was such a strange feeling that day. There I was throwing as well as I ever had, and I threw a 3-2 fastball to Chris Davis and felt something pop near my shoulder bicep. I remember thinking, 'Please don't be something serious.'

"I tried to throw another fastball, and I think it got halfway to the plate. I called Kurt Suzuki, who was catching, out and said, 'Just call curveballs.' Somehow, I got three outs. I think I threw ten straight curveballs. When everyone came out to the mound to celebrate, all I could think was, 'Is this it? Am I done?'"

The A's were celebrating the hundredth win of Tomko's career. A major milestone. But Tomko was in no mood to sit back and enjoy what he had accomplished.

He went back to the hotel and had a drink with Nomar Garcia-parra, who was in town broadcasting the game for ESPN. "I was holding the drink in my hand, and suddenly it felt very heavy," he said. "I had to put it down.

"I went to bed hoping it would feel better after ice and with some rest. I woke up about five in the morning screaming in pain. I sat up in bed with my arm up against my chest and waited as long as I could before I called the trainer. I was crying by then I was in so much pain."

He had fractured the biceps muscle in his shoulder. The doctor in Texas gave him painkillers so he could fly home to witness the birth of his twin sons, who were due to be born on September 18—four days after he was injured. "By the time they were born, I couldn't move my arm," he said.

He had surgery soon after that and then had to decide if he wanted to put himself through the rehab process to try to pitch again. "Part of me was thinking this was the time to stop," he said. "I'd just become a father. I had made pretty good money. But every time I was ready to make up my mind and retire, I'd think about that day in Texas and the memory wasn't happy, it was bleak. There was this black cloud because of the injury and the pain.

"My wife and I talked about it, and she said, 'You have to see this through until you *know* it's time to stop.'"

He had not yet reached that moment. Every time he thought it might be time to go home, he thought about something he had read years earlier. "You're an ex-ballplayer for a lot more years than you're a ballplayer," he said, smiling. "So I stuck with it and here I am."

In spite of his god-awful (7.52) ERA during his stint the following year at Stockton, early in 2010, the A's moved him up to Triple-A

Sacramento, where he pitched marginally better, but not well enough to merit a new contract at the end of the 2010 season. "My ERA in Sacramento wasn't a lot better than in Stockton, but I can honestly say it was deceiving," he said. "The first time I pitched there I didn't get anybody out. I got blasted. But after that I actually did get a little better."

But not well enough to get another contract in Oakland. The Rangers were willing to give him a chance, though, and he decided to take one last shot—hoping that some rest and a little more arm strength might make a difference.

He pitched better at Round Rock at the start of 2011 and was called to the majors as a relief pitcher—something he hadn't done much in his career. He wasn't complaining.

"Just to get back to the majors after all that had gone on was thrilling," he said. "That's why I lost it that first game back when I got through that inning. I remember thinking, 'At least now I can tell the boys they saw me pitch in the majors.' We took pictures that day of them on the field with me before the game. I'm not sure I ever enjoyed a day in my baseball career more."

He lasted forty-three days in Texas, a number he remembers because his contract said if he was in the majors for forty-five days, he was guaranteed major-league pay regardless of where he was pitching for the rest of the season. He went back to Round Rock, finished the season, and then signed one more contract, this one with the Reds—the team he had started with eighteen years earlier—for 2012. Which was what landed him in Toledo in a Bats uniform in late July.

Being in uniform—ready to make a start—was no small thing at that point in the season. Tomko had pitched well for the Bats for two months. His ERA on May 30 was 3.15 when he went out to pitch against Syracuse—even though he hadn't yet won a game. Early in the game his spikes caught on the rubber just a tad, and he felt a tug inside his shoulder.

"It wasn't anything like that day in Texas when I knew I'd done something serious," he said. "But I knew it wasn't good. At thirty-nine, *no* pain is a good idea. Anything else is trouble."

It turned out Tomko had strained his shoulder and the biceps muscle. He ended up missing almost two months before coming back to pitch again for the Bats on July 25. The shoulder, he insisted, felt fine. "Let's put it this way," he said. "It feels good enough. That's all I can ask for at this point."

Every time he took the ball to start, Tomko felt as if he had beaten the odds—for at least one more day.

"To say I don't think about the end at this point would be lying," he said. "I've probably thought about it almost every day since I hurt my shoulder back in '09 because it was staring me right in the face. I'll be forty in April. Knowing I'm going to stop playing baseball soon and that I'm going to be forty does make you think about things like your mortality. You can't help it. I mean, my manager [David Bell] and I were teammates once upon a time [in Seattle] and he's six months older than I am."

He sat back and folded his arms. "When I was in rehab, there was a sixteen-year-old kid from the Dominican who had just signed, I can't remember his name, but he was rehabbing too. I looked at him and thought, 'Oh my God, this kid wasn't *born* when I signed my first contract.' That was a dose of reality."

Tomko was quiet for a moment, staring at several teammates playing catch in front of the dugout. "As difficult as the shoulder injury was, I think it *did* make me appreciate how lucky I've been to do this for so long. When I was rehabbing, if I was riding a bike or something and a baseball game came on, I couldn't watch, I'd go turn it off. It occurred to me in very real terms that the game goes on just fine without all of us. Not just guys like me, everyone who has ever played—Ruth, Cobb, Mays, Aaron—the game went on.

"We all get a little window to play and be part of it. Not many people get that chance. I'm almost forty, and I still get paid to play the game I loved to play as a kid. Whenever I walk away now, I'll have no regrets."

He stood up to go back to the clubhouse to get ready for the game. There were perhaps half a dozen fans standing at the corner of the dugout looking for autographs. Tomko stopped and signed. When one of them asked if he could get a picture taken with him, Tomko said absolutely.

He walked out of the dugout and leaned into the seats so he could get close to the fan. The smile on his face as the photograph was snapped was completely genuine.

18

Mark Lollo

TRAVELING THE UMPIRING ROAD

Brett Tomko wasn't the only one feeling a bit insecure about his future in July. Mark Lollo was also wondering about his future. And he was starting to get nervous.

He had worked two major-league games in June but hadn't gotten a call since then. As one of eighteen Triple-A umpires on the major-league call-up list, he was keenly aware of which guys were getting major-league games and which ones were not.

Lollo was one of the "were-nots." Which he knew wasn't a good sign.

"One thing that was making me nervous was that I was working with a third different supervisor in four years," he said. "You never know how you're going to get along with a new boss. More important, you don't have a feel for how they feel about your work."

The new boss was Cris Jones, a longtime Triple-A umpire who was thought of as a hard-ass by the umpires working for him. "I'd say no-nonsense," Lollo said. "Which I didn't really mind."

Umpires are like players in that they travel a long way to get to the cusp of the big-league life. Lollo had been a football player and a baseball player as a kid growing up in Coshocton, a small town in east-central Ohio. He was better at football than baseball, but he loved baseball.

"Problem was I couldn't hit," he said. "Most games I spent a lot of time hitting ground balls. One day I changed my stance and got three hits, but that was the highlight."

He was recruited by his dad's alma mater, Otterbein, to play quarterback and linebacker. By then, he was also working as an umpire, working three or four Little League or youth-league games a day and making $70 to $80 a day at it. He enjoyed it and took it seriously. "I even went out and bought my own equipment," he said. "I wanted to be good."

There was an umpire working in Triple-A at the time named Scott Nelson, who was from Coshocton. Knowing of Lollo's interest in umpiring, he invited him to drive with him to a game in Columbus one night. Lollo liked the whole atmosphere surrounding the umpires, from the room where they got ready to the game itself to their little postgame meal.

By the time he was ready to graduate from high school, he had three choices on what to do next: go to Otterbein; go to umpiring school; or join the marines. The marines were eliminated because he didn't especially like the recruiter. He decided to give umpiring a shot and signed up for the umpiring school in Florida run by the former major-league umpire Jim Evans.

At the end of the school, 25 umpires out of about 150 students were selected for membership in the Professional Baseball Umpire Corporation. The other major umpiring school, run by another former major leaguer, Harry Wendelstedt, also had 25 umpires selected. That meant 50 new umpires who started to receive minor-league assignments. Lollo didn't make the cut.

"They told me I was on the reserve list," he said. "They encouraged me to get some more experience and come back in a year. It was hard. I'd never failed at anything before." He smiled. "Except hitting a baseball. I went home to decide what to do."

He was working a local college game when his mother showed up one afternoon with a letter inviting him to umpire in the Northwoods League, a high-level collegiate summer league which had a total of eight teams that were located in Wisconsin, Iowa, and

Minnesota. Apparently, the Evans people had recommended him to Dick Radatz Jr., the league president.

Lollo took the job and spent the first few weeks of the season being miserable. "To begin with, I wasn't very good," he said. "I can remember calling breaking pitches a strike just before they bounced on home plate. Plus, I didn't like my partner very much and we were traveling together. I was so discouraged I was ready to quit and go home. Dick Radatz asked me to hang on until the All-Star break, and I said okay.

"I called my parents to tell them what I was doing, and my dad said, 'I'll get you a car to drive the rest of the season so you don't have to travel with the other ump. But you don't quit.' He didn't believe in quitting."

Thanks to the car and his father, Lollo stuck with it. By the end of the season he had come a long way. "No more breaking pitches called strikes that hit the plate," he said, smiling. "Dick Radatz told me at the end of the year that one of the reasons the league existed was to train guys like me."

He smiled. "The only problem was my diet. We had meal cards [from the league] for KFC and Country Kitchen. It was a lot of that and a lot of ballpark food all year. That wasn't especially good for my weight, although the price was right."

A year later, Lollo went back to umpiring school. This time he made the cut. He was assigned in June 2002 to the Gulf Coast League.

From there, just like a player, he began working his way through the minors. Of course, in umpiring, there are no phenoms. You move up one step at a time, and sometimes you take baby steps. In 2006, while he was working in the Carolina League, the minor-league umpires went on strike for more money. Some of the umpires were willing to cross the picket line to work. Lollo wasn't one of them.

"My grandfather was a plant manager at General Motors," he said. "I remember when I was a kid he told me to never cross a picket line."

The strike ended in June, and Lollo's pay increased by $100 a month and $1 a day in per diem.

Soon after that he was promoted to the Texas League (Double-A), and after filling in on Pacific Coast League games in 2008, he made the jump full-time to Triple-A when he was assigned to the International League in 2009. At that point his chances of working in the major leagues had gone from 1 percent (when he graduated from the Evans school) to 33 percent. It had taken him seven years to get that far.

Two years later, in 2011, he was assigned to work major-league spring training—a very encouraging sign and a financial boon. Triple-A umpires make $3,200 a month and are guaranteed five months of work. If they make the playoffs, they make extra, but typically they are paid between $16,000 and $18,000 a year.

Working spring training basically doubles a Triple-A umpire's pay because umpires are paid $420 a day in per diem (the major-league rate) for thirty days plus $175 for every game they work. Most work between twenty-two and twenty-eight games. "I made almost as much in March the last two years as I made during the season," Lollo said. "That was a big help in justifying what I was doing to my wife. With two young kids [three years old and less than one during 2012] the travel is very tough on her."

The minimum pay for a big-league umpire is $90,000 per year. Like the players, umpires are paid on a prorated daily basis when they sub in the majors. They also fly first-class between cities. Lollo, like most minor-league umpires, was used to *driving* first-class between cities.

Lollo got his first call-up to the majors in 2011, working six games, including a game behind home plate. All the feedback was encouraging, and he was asked again to work both the Arizona Fall League and major-league spring training.

"Which is why, I guess, I thought I'd get more games in 2012, not less," he said. "No one ever indicated to me, based on my work in the majors in '11 or on anything else, that I wasn't still on the fast track—or at least a good track. Then again, maybe it was just opportunity. I knew I wasn't in the top five [on the call-up list], but I figured I was doing okay. I tried to tell myself that I was jumping at shadows."

Eleven years after his summer of KFC and Country Kitchen, weight—and avoiding fast food on the road—were still issues for him.

"It's a very competitive situation, especially when you get that close to the majors," he said. "I've always been a big guy." He smiled. "When you're my size, you can either be big boned or fat. I needed to make sure I wasn't seen as the latter. When they look at a guy's potential as a major leaguer, they aren't just looking at how you call balls and strikes. They look at your demeanor, how you handle tough situations, or how you handle missing a call—because we all miss them. They also project out and say, 'What is this guy going to look like ten years from now? Fifteen?' I knew that was a potential issue."

Lollo was a stocky five feet ten inches and had weighed as much as 250 pounds. After he first made the call-up list in 2011, he had worked very hard and gotten his weight down to 215. During most of 2012, he weighed about 230. "I still think I move well and get to where I need to get," he said. "But I know I always have to be aware of it."

During his six-game major-league stint in 2011, Lollo made $3,000 plus the major-league per diem. He even got a plane flight out of it. But then it was back to his car and to the back roads, hoping his phone would ring. Major-league umpires get four weeks off for vacation during the season. Minor-league umpires get zero weeks during the season for vacation. An umpire in Lollo's position, on the call-up list, waits for the phone to ring to be told he's going to the majors to replace someone for a few days or, he hopes, perhaps a week or so.

A year later, by late June 2012, Lollo hadn't gotten a call. He was getting antsy. Finally, on June 23, while he was in Indianapolis preparing for game two of a series between the Indians and the Rochester Red Wings, Lollo got the call: the Reds were hosting the Minnesota Twins, and veteran umpire Jerry Layne had gotten hit in the nose by a broken bat and had a broken nose. Lollo was only 112 miles away— could he get to the ballpark for the game that night?

"If they needed me to walk to get there, I'd have been there," Lollo said, grinning.

Walking into a major-league ballpark to work again was a thrill for Lollo, just as it had been a year earlier, when he had made his major-league debut in Washington. Beyond that, it was a relief. Lollo was keenly aware of which umpires also on the call-up list were actually getting called up, and he was beginning to wonder when his turn would come. Once it came, he relaxed a little bit.

"It's my second year on the list, and generally speaking, it isn't until the third year that you begin to wonder if you aren't moving forward enough," he said. "None of us actually knows where we are on the list, but we can make some kind of educated guess based on how often we're going up. I knew I wasn't at the top of the list, but at least when the call came to go to Cincinnati, I figured I was still in the mix and, I hoped, moving up based on my work."

Lollo worked two games in Cincinnati. He was at third base the first night and second base the next afternoon. He actually flew to Minnesota to begin a series there the next night but got a call saying he wasn't needed and should head back to Triple-A.

"You know that call is coming sooner or later," he said. "You just hope it will be later. It felt good, though, to be back in the majors. I didn't have a lot of calls, but felt like I handled the ones I had well." Lollo had a lot of confidence in his work behind the plate and in his demeanor. "I feel like I handle myself pretty well now when a manager gets hot," he said. "I get along well with most of the guys in the league, and I feel as if they respect me. Occasionally, you know someone is coming out to make some kind of point—to you or to his players. You can tell that they want to get run. When I sense that, I just say, 'Do you want to go? Because if you do, just tell me and we'll get it over with.'

"But if someone just thinks I missed one or he's trying to let his players know he's got their back, I'm not going to let that get to me. With the players, I try to give them some space too. They're trying just as hard to get to the big leagues as I am. Most of them are good guys. They know we're all trying really hard and not getting paid a lot of money to work in a place we would love to be leaving soon.

"Every once in a while you see a guy who is completely bitter about being in the minors. Usually, it's a guy who has been in the majors—and thinks he has a *right* to be there."

He smiled. "Last season [2011] I had Brendan Harris in a game when he was in Norfolk. He was being paid $1.7 million for the year and was back in Triple-A. I called him out looking, and he got back to the dugout and was screaming at everyone in sight. He went through about twelve batting helmets while I was standing there, just flinging them everywhere.

"Finally, I just looked at him and said, 'Hey, Brendan, why don't you just keep your head up.' What I wanted to say is, 'You're making $1.7 million and I'm working for about 100 bucks a day—grow up.'"

He paused.

"There are two ways to look at where I am in my career," he said. "One way is to say that I'm not where I want to be. I want to walk into those major-league parks every day. It isn't so much the money or the lifestyle—although both would be very nice—but the feeling that you've beaten the odds and become one of the best at what you do.

"This has been my life's work. It's all I've ever done since I got out of high school, and it's all I've ever wanted to. My goal has always been to be a big-league umpire, and although I've tasted it, I haven't achieved that. On the other hand, when I started out eleven years ago, there were a lot of guys who had the same dream who haven't come nearly as far as I have.

"Late at night, when I'm in the car, that's what keeps me going. As long as I'm still moving forward, I still have a chance. That puts me in a lot better place than most guys I started out with.

"There's one last hurdle. It's right there in front of me. All I need is the chance to jump over it."

Clearly, Randy Mobley, the president of the International League, was in his corner. Lollo was selected to work the plate for the Triple-A All-Star game between the International League All-Stars and the

Pacific Coast League All-Stars. He was pretty certain he would be a crew chief once the playoffs began. Mobley had even made a point of telling his father one night at a game, "Mark is exactly the kind of person and umpire we like to see succeed."

All well and good. But even though the major-league supervisors might accept input from Mobley, they would be the ones who would ultimately decide Lollo's professional fate.

He knew that. Which was why as the days in the season dwindled and he continued to work in Triple-A one night after another without another major-league call-up, he wondered exactly where he stood.

Finally, while he was talking to Mobley on the phone one afternoon late in August about how to deal with potential hurricane conditions in Gwinnett that evening, Mobley asked him straight out, "Do you want me to see what I can find out?"

Lollo wasn't sure if he did. Then again, he needed to know. "Why don't you," he said.

"I'll get back to you," Mobley said.

It wasn't Mobley who called back. It was Lollo's supervisor, Cris Jones.

Mobley steeled himself when he heard Jones on the phone. He had wanted to know where he stood. He suspected he was about to find out.

19

Slice of Life

MANAGING THE HIGHS AND LOWS

Almost without fail, the first person in any clubhouse on a given day—other than trainers and equipment people—is the manager. Occasionally, a coach might arrive first, but 90 percent of the time it is the manager.

"I like the quiet," David Bell was saying on a Sunday morning about six hours before game time. "I like to kind of review what happened the day before, see what's going on with the major-league club, work on a lineup, and decide if there's anyone specific I want to talk to when the players get to the ballpark."

If there is anyone in the world who should be comfortable inside a baseball clubhouse, it is Bell. In a very real sense he was born to the game. His grandfather Gus played in the major leagues for fifteen years and was a four-time All-Star. His dad, Buddy, played eighteen seasons in the majors, and his career numbers merit at least some Hall of Fame consideration: 2,514 hits; six Gold Gloves as a third baseman; one Silver Slugger as best hitter at his position; five All-Star game appearances. If his batting average—.279—had been a little bit higher, he would have received serious consideration.

David and his brother Mike both played in the majors too—making the Bells the fifth family to have three generations reach the majors. Mike's major-league career was brief—half a season in Cincinnati. David's didn't quite measure up to his father's or grandfather's but was very solid: twelve years with six teams, a .257 career average with 123 home runs and 589 RBIs.

"My grandfather was a very good player, and my dad was a great player," he said. "I just wasn't in their class."

At five feet ten inches and 170 pounds, he was never blessed with his father's (six one, 180) or his brother's (six two, 195) size, but he was one of those players who kept making themselves better.

After graduating from Moeller High School in Cincinnati (a school much better known for football than for baseball), he was drafted in the seventh round by the Cleveland Indians. His first instinct was to follow through on his plan to attend the University of Kentucky, but when the Indians offered a $50,000 signing bonus, he decided to make the leap.

"The funny thing is a lot of kids who make that decision because they think it's a quicker route to the big leagues regret it, because they find life in the minors to be so tough," he said. "Because I'd been around baseball clubhouses my whole life, including the smaller ones in spring training, it never bothered me at all. I got sent to the Gulf Coast League and felt right at home from day one.

"Of course my problem was simple: I didn't have great talent or size."

Perhaps not, but a twelve-year big-league career is nothing to thumb one's nose at by any means. Most of Bell's players in Louisville would have killed to have their manager's career. What's more, he had scored the winning run in the deciding game of the 2002 National League Championship Series for the San Francisco Giants and was also involved the following week in one of the more bizarre plays in World Series history.

The Giants were playing the Anaheim Angels, and Bell was on first base, J. T. Snow on second base, in the sixth inning of game five. Kenny Lofton tripled in the gap. As Snow and Bell flew around the bases, Dusty Baker's three-year-old son, Darren, who was in uniform and serving as a batboy/mascot for the Giants, wandered out toward home plate to pick up Lofton's bat.

At the last possible second, Snow saw the little boy and, as he crossed home plate, scooped him up in his arms to avoid running into him. Bell, not far behind Snow, was more than relieved when he saw that Snow had gotten Darren out of the way because he was concerned there might be a play on him at the plate with Darren somehow in the middle of it.

"All was well that ended well," Bell said, years later. "But it was a good idea for baseball to pass the rule that you had to be fourteen to be in uniform after that happened. I'm not so sure I would have been as quick thinking as JT was in that situation. Plus, I tended to run with my head down, so I shudder when I think about what could have happened if JT hadn't gotten him out of there."

Bell played until 2006. The desire to play was still there, but his body wouldn't let him. He'd had back problems and had surgery on one knee and one hip. "Mentally I wasn't burned out, but physically I was," he said. "Some guys can lose a step, and because they're so talented, they can still play effectively. I didn't have that margin for error. When my body started breaking down, it became harder and harder for me to compete."

Bell had just turned thirty-four when he retired. He didn't want to try to hang on, perhaps find himself back in Triple-A because he wasn't quite the player he had been. He had become a father for the first time earlier that year. Being home felt like a good idea. After two years, not surprisingly, he decided to get back into baseball.

"I'm an expert at one thing," he said. "Baseball. I honestly believed I had something to contribute, that I could help players get better. I knew a lot of people in the game—obviously including my dad [who was managing in Kansas City at the time and is now a Chicago White Sox vice president]—but I didn't want to do it that way. I made six phone calls—the sixth one was to Billy Doran, who I'd known for years. He was working for the Reds, and he said they had a job open managing at Double-A in Carolina. That was the good news. The bad news was I had to make a decision by the next day because they were about to start interviewing guys."

Because of his father, Bell grew up around ballparks. He can remember sitting in the dugout (à la Darren Baker) when he was a kid and how much he and Mike looked forward to going to games with their dad.

"The best thing my dad did for us was to never make us feel any pressure to succeed in baseball," he said. "That's a tough thing when your dad has been playing in the majors your whole life. He got to the majors the year I was born. He retired one year before I was drafted. So when I say he was in the majors my entire childhood, I'm not exaggerating.

"But he never coached us in baseball. He coached us in basketball and we loved it. He didn't want us to feel like he was looking over our shoulder when we played baseball. I think that's why Mike and I both grew up loving the game."

And wanting to stay in it. Today, Mike is the Arizona Diamondbacks' farm director. It made sense for David to return to the one thing in which he was, in fact, an expert. He spent three years in Carolina before being promoted to Louisville prior to the 2012 season. Even though the team's record was awful, Bell was enjoying most of what he was doing.

Like most minor-league managers, the thing he enjoyed most was telling players they'd been promoted to the majors. The first time he'd had a chance to do that had been in his second season at Carolina when his closer, Jordan Smith, was jumped straight from Double-A to the majors because he had been performing so well and the Reds needed relief help.

"I got the call in the morning, and they wanted him to get on a plane and get to Cincy right away," Bell said. "They wanted him available that night. The thing to do, of course, was to pick up the phone and call him so he could pack and get going. But I knew he had a little time to make his plane, so I called him and asked him to meet me in a shopping center near where he lived. I told him I was going to buy him lunch—or something like that. I just wanted to *see* his face when I told him.

"He got out of his car and I said, 'Jordan, I have to tell you something.' For a split second I think he was nervous, but he was pitching too well for that. I'm sure he thought I was going to tell him he was going [up] to Louisville. When I told him he was going to Cincinnati and he had a plane to catch, I could see him processing it in his mind for a minute and then he broke into this huge smile. The first thing he said was, 'I gotta go call my dad.'

"It's funny, because the first time I got called up [in 1995] I think those were my exact words." He smiled. "It's interesting to me, being the son of a player who was also the son of a player, the number of guys whose relationships with their father were about baseball in a lot of ways. I guess it's the oldest cliché in the book, but there is something to the idea of fathers and sons playing catch in the backyard. I know I remember the first time I did it with my dad. Obviously, I'm not alone in that."

On Bell's list of things to do on this particular Sunday morning was to talk to Denis Phipps. It had been Phipps who had started the five-run ninth-inning rally the night before by lining a single to center field with the Bats trailing Toledo 4–3 and two outs from another loss. When he stepped to the plate in that ninth inning, Phipps was hitting .200 and was already 0 for 4 on the night.

"What I want to do is remind him that winning players find a way to make something good happen, even when they're struggling," Bell said. "He's had a tough year and I know there have been moments when he's been discouraged, but he's never hung his head. Last night, he came up to the plate in the ninth not thinking about being 0-fer, but about finding a way to get something started for his team. And that's what he did."

Phipps was twenty-seven and had grown up, like so many good players, in San Pedro de Macoris in the Dominican Republic. The town of just under 200,000 people had produced more than seventy major leaguers—among them Sammy Sosa, Alfonso Soriano, and Robinson Cano—and so many shortstops had come from there that it had been dubbed "the cradle of shortstops."

Phipps was an outfielder in his seventh minor-league season and had never spent a moment in the major leagues. Bell believed he had the talent to play in the majors.

"One thing I know, because I never had overwhelming skills, is that the difference between most major leaguers and guys at this level isn't physical; it's mental or emotional. Every guy in our clubhouse has the physical ability to play at the major-league level.

"But some don't have the confidence; some don't have the attitude or the work ethic. I tell the guys all the time that most major leaguers have two hot streaks a year at the plate, maybe three in a good year. That's the time when they feel like they're going to get a hit every time they come up.

"Most of the year isn't like that. Most of the year is about grinding. It's about being 0 for 4 and finding a way to get a hit in that fifth at-bat. It's about taking an extra base when you can to help the team or moving a runner or making a play on defense. The guys who make it are the guys who do that, because managers notice that, coaches notice that, personnel guys notice that. You can be in the worst slump of your life, and there's still a way to help the team. The guys who grind through those periods and find a way to contribute are the guys who ultimately make it. If you compete when it's hard to compete, when lying down would be easy, that's when you become a real baseball player.

"Denis could have lain down last night. We did nothing for seven innings, and we're two outs from losing. But he had a good at-bat against a good pitcher [Chris Bootcheck] and started what turned out to be the game-winning rally. That's what a winning player does."

Bell spent some time that day with Phipps reminding him of all those things. Coincidence or not, Phipps raised his batting average by 20 points starting with that ninth-inning single in Toledo in late July and, on September 3, when Louisville's season ended, got his first call-up to the majors.

"That's the kind of thing that makes managing at this level worth it," Bell said. "It makes up for those moments when you have to send a guy down or, worse, release a guy. Those are the moments you dread."

Four days after his encouraging talk with Denis Phipps, Bell had one of those dreaded moments. Brett Tomko had pitched the third game of the series in Toledo and had been neither awful nor good—

somewhere squarely in between. He had pitched six innings and given up five earned runs. The Bats had actually broken a 5–5 tie in the top of the seventh to take a 6–5 lead, putting Tomko in position to win his first game of the season. But, as had been the case all summer whenever Tomko left a game with a chance to win, the bullpen couldn't hold a lead. The Mud Hens rallied to win 10–9 in eleven innings.

Three days later, after the team had gotten back to Louisville, Bell got one of those phone calls a Triple-A manager doesn't want to take. The Reds had decided to release Tomko. The major-league team was flush with pitching, and with several prospects at both Double-A and Triple-A who needed innings, there was no reason to keep a thirty-nine-year-old pitcher around who was muddling through with a respectable ERA of 3.78. Plus, Pedro Villarreal, a twenty-four-year-old right-handed starter who was considered a prospect by the Reds, was coming off the DL. A roster spot was needed.

When Tomko reported for work that afternoon, Bell was waiting for him.

"Hey, you got a minute?" he said as Tomko walked in the direction of his locker.

At first, Tomko didn't think anything of it. He and Bell often talked baseball early in the day when the clubhouse was quiet. They went into the manager's office, and Bell shut the door.

"That was my first clue," Tomko said later. "David was an open-door manager. He wouldn't close the door to talk about what a nice day it was outside."

Even so, Tomko was stunned when Bell told him what was happening.

"I hadn't been pitching that badly," he said. "I mean, if I was getting killed, I would have said, 'Yup, you're right, I get it.' But the fact is, I didn't get it."

Bell was completely honest with Tomko. This had nothing to do with the way he was pitching. He had told the Reds that if someone was needed for an emergency start or if someone got hurt, there was no doubt in his mind Tomko could get the job done. But it was late in the season, and the Reds believed they had enough backup that they could afford to use Tomko's roster spot on a younger player. It was baseball math: all things being equal, the old guy goes overboard.

"He was really, really disappointed," Bell said. "Hurt. Surprised. Pick a word. But he didn't vent or take it out on me at all. He handled it as well as you could handle it—which didn't surprise me at all.

"Funny thing is we were teammates for two years, and I always felt I knew Brett well. I always liked him. But I also had the sense that he was a guy who people often didn't understand. In baseball, if you have any outside interests, people look at you as if you're weird. Brett was into art, and some guys just couldn't understand that. I thought it made you better rounded and more interesting.

"There was this notion that he wasn't tough. Believe me, he's tough. I felt as if I got to know him more in Louisville than I did in Seattle. His attitude was so good.

"We talked that day for an hour. I told him that I knew this was hard to understand but this was the best thing for him—fair or unfair. He's so competitive it's going to be hard for him to stop playing, but at some point he's going to stop playing.

"The Reds weren't going to call him up before the end of the season. They'd made that decision. This was a chance to maybe catch on with a team that would call him up. Or, if this was the end, well, it was meant to be the end. It might be time to move on.

"Easy for me to say, no doubt. Probably hard for him to hear."

Ten days later, Tomko was signed by the Arizona Diamondbacks, whose farm director is Mike Bell.

"Sheer coincidence," David Bell said, laughing. "But I suspect he was highly recommended."

20

Slice of Life

I-75

While Brett Tomko was trying to keep his job in Triple-A during that late July weekend in Toledo, Danny Worth was trying to figure out how he could put Toledo in his rearview mirror once and for all.

It wasn't that he disliked the town. He liked the people, he liked his manager, and he liked his teammates.

He just wished he wasn't their teammate.

"When I got back the other day, several guys came up to me and said, 'It's great to see you, but it sucks to see you,'" he said. "I felt exactly the same way."

Worth had been sent back to Toledo from the Tigers on July 24—the ninth time he had been sent down since his first call-up to Detroit in May 2010. In all, including spring training, he'd gotten—as he called it—"the tap on the shoulder" to be sent down eleven times in his career.

"Usually, there's a routine to it," he said. "Jeff Jones [the pitching coach] will give me the tap and tell me that [manager] Jim [Leyland] wants to talk to me. It isn't always that way. Once [in 2011] we had flown from Anaheim to Chicago, and we got to the hotel at about four o'clock in the morning. I got off the bus, walked into the lobby, and [general manager] Dave [Dombrowski] and Jim were standing there waiting for me. I was pretty sure it wasn't to ask me what I thought about the in-flight movie."

Worth's most recent return to Toledo had not come as a shock, although he readily admitted that every time it happened it was tough to take. Shortly after getting back to town, he did a pregame TV interview. He said all the right things: he knew he just had to hang in there; this was part of the game; he had to keep his head up and play hard and hope the call to go back up would come again soon.

"I fake it," he said, smiling. "The fact is, every time you get sent down, it's crushing because no matter how you rationalize it, the reason it happens is because you aren't a good enough player to stay up. I simply haven't been able to hit enough to stay in the majors. Every time you get sent down, they tell you, 'Hey, you'll be back up soon,' and you know it's entirely possible. But you also know it's possible you might never get back. Maybe they make a trade at your position. Maybe you get hurt. Maybe they've decided you're out of chances. That's the fear: that maybe this time down is the last time."

It had been a trade that had sent Worth back to Toledo this time. The Tigers, looking to strengthen themselves for the second half of the season, had acquired pitcher Anibal Sánchez and second baseman Omar Infante from Miami. The acquisition of Infante meant a position player had to go down. There were three candidates: Worth, Don Kelly, and Ryan Raburn. As a player with five years in the majors, Raburn couldn't be sent down unless he agreed to the demotion; the Tigers would have therefore had to release him, and they didn't want to do that. Kelly was out of minor-league "options"—which are so complicated most players don't understand them—and would have had to pass through waivers to get to Toledo.

Rather than take that risk, the Tigers decided to send down Worth. They had just finished a series at home and were flying to Cleveland when Worth heard that the trade had been made. He got on the plane with the team, wondering if perhaps he might avoid the dreaded "tap." Kelly and Raburn were on the flight too, so he knew it might still be coming.

"We got to the hotel, and Jim grabbed me getting off the bus," he said. "They had to wait until we got to Cleveland because the trade hadn't been final before we left."

The only good news was that the Mud Hens were playing two hours away in Columbus. Worth called his wife, Bree, and told her it had happened again and that she would need to pack their things in the apartment they had been renting in Detroit for another move back to Toledo. They had both been through this before.

"I remember the first time I got called up in '10," he said. "Needless to say, I wanted to call everyone I knew. We packed the car, and I told Bree to drive so I could make all the calls. The problem is she's a terrible driver, and she was so excited I finally had to take the wheel from her about halfway to Detroit. I couldn't take it anymore."

So what became of all the phone calls and texts?

"I made them anyway," he said, grinning.

His first major-league at-bat was against John Lackey, who had first come up to the Anaheim Angels in 2002—when Worth was in high school in Valencia, about sixty miles north of Anaheim. "I remembered watching him pitch back then," Worth said. "Now here I am in the majors and he's pitching to me. It was a little bit scary but also quite cool."

Sent up to pinch-hit with the bases loaded, Worth hit a roller down the first-base line and beat it out for a single and an RBI. A nice moment. It is one he thinks back to when he starts to feel depressed about the literal ups and downs his career has gone through since that night.

"I try to remind myself that ten years ago, when I was a high school senior, if you had told me I would get to the majors, I'd have said, 'I'll sign for that right now,'" he said. "I played on a really good high school team. I probably wasn't the best player—in fact, I *wasn't* the best player. We had six guys who people thought had major-league potential. I'm the only one who has ever gone past A-ball, much less played in the majors.

"When I sit back and think about things like that, it makes me feel good and it makes me feel lucky. On the other hand, when you're a kid and you dream about being in the major leagues, you don't dream about being a backup shortstop or second baseman. You don't dream about being the guy who is up for a month, then down for a month.

You dream about being a contributor, being a star—not the guy who gets sent down eleven times."

He sighed. "This is a really good place to play Triple-A ball. Really nice ballpark, good crowds, good people. But when you've been in the majors . . ." He shook his head. "Every time I hear the crowd at Comerica [Detroit] my body goes numb. I get goose bumps on my arms. It's *so* loud up there. You can't make ten thousand people sound like forty thousand people. I guess the only good news is I can make the drive up and down I-75 blindfolded by now.

"I still remember going to see the Dodgers play when I was thirteen. Alex Cora was the shortstop. He made a couple plays, and he made an error too. I remember thinking, 'I can do that; I'm good enough to do that someday.' I was right. I have been good enough to do that. I just need to be good enough to do it more consistently—with my bat."

As difficult as it was to be back in Triple-A, Worth was a long way from giving up. He had played for Steve Rodriguez in college at Pepperdine. Rodriguez had produced many top players, nine of whom had been drafted by major-league teams.

"I still go back during the off-season and take BP at Pepperdine and I talk to Steve," Worth said. "We talk about all the guys who have played for him and how tough it is sometimes to keep your head up as a baseball player. The game can be so negative. I asked him what he says to guys when they get down and talk about quitting.

"He said, 'I tell them, guys, the grass outside the ballpark may look greener sometimes, but believe me it's not. It's a lot better to be inside the park than outside the park.'"

Whether the park seats ten thousand or forty thousand.

21

Elarton

PIGS (NOT) IN THE BIGS . . . AND
THE EVER-PRESENT REVOLVING DOOR

The newest franchise in the International League is the one in Allentown—the Lehigh Valley IronPigs.

The Pigs, as they are called throughout the valley, came into existence in 2008 when the Ottawa Lynx were moved by the Philadelphia Phillies to the brand-new ballpark that was only sixty miles from Citizens Bank Park in South Philadelphia. The Phillies had taken over the Lynx from the Baltimore Orioles in 2007 while that new ballpark—Coca-Cola Field—was being built, fully intending to move the team in a year.

The IronPigs have been a huge success almost since day one. The team's affiliation with the Phillies helps greatly because there are lots and lots of Phillies fans in the area. Not only do the Pigs wear Phillies colors, but one of the first things people see when they walk into the ballpark is a mural that is called "Pigs in the Bigs." On it are the names and uniform numbers of all the Lehigh Valley players who have gone on to play in Philadelphia.

Next to the elevator that leads to the suite level in the ballpark is an actual iron pig—complete with a definition for those who have never seen one before.

1. Derived from Pig Iron, raw iron that is melted down, refined and then used to make steel, which is one of the strongest metal alloys

known on earth . . . (A) The iron was called pig iron because it was melted into molds said to resemble a row of piglets.

2. Name of AAA baseball team in Lehigh Valley, Pennsylvania. Name was derived from steel making heritage that existed in Lehigh Valley . . . (A) team name was chosen by a name-the-team contest. Eight finalists were: Woodchucks, Crushers, Gobblers, Phantastics, Phillies, Keystones, Vulcans and IronPigs.

Certainly IronPigs was by far the best choice on that list.

The ballpark is full of reminders regarding the team nickname. During 2012 if you went to look for Ryne Sandberg, you didn't look for the manager's office—you looked for the office marked "Head Pig."

The best one-liners in the ballpark, however, can be found in the men's rooms. In a minor-league ballpark, every inch of real estate is for sale—including space in the bathrooms. The urinals in the men's rooms are sponsored (seriously) by the Urology Specialists of the Lehigh Valley. That means when someone walks into the bathroom and steps to a urinal, he will be greeted by signs posted in the urinal.

Among the messages are:

"Standing here longer than the National Anthem? . . . Urology Specialists of the Lehigh Valley . . ."

"Back again? It might not be the beer's fault."

"Has your bat gone silent?"

"Can't reach home plate like you used to?"

And, last but not least: "The only place for dribblers in the ballpark is down the first and third base lines."

You simply *cannot* get entertainment like that in Yankee Stadium.

Which might explain why the IronPigs play consistently to sellouts or near sellouts. In 2012 they drew a total of 688,821 for seventy-six home dates—four more than normal because Scranton/Wilkes-Barre played four games as the home team in Allentown. For their seventy-two official home games, they averaged 9,034 fans per game—which is pretty good given that the ballpark seats 8,089. Frequently, the Pigs draw crowds of more than 10,000—many fans paying for the right to stand or sit on the grassy knolls beyond the outfield fences.

"I honestly didn't think you could have an atmosphere like the one we have night in and night out in a minor-league park," said Sandberg, who managed in Lehigh Valley in 2011 and 2012. "One of the hard parts about being in Triple-A is that a lot of nights there's no buzz in the ballpark. That's not a problem here."

The IronPigs' clubhouse is comparable to many visiting club-houses in the major leagues and much roomier than those in older parks like Fenway and Wrigley Field. The visiting clubhouse—as in the majors—is considerably smaller than the home clubhouse.

"If you have to be in the minor leagues, this is about as good as you can possibly hope for," Scott Elarton said. He smiled. "Of course it's still the minor leagues."

On an early summer night, Elarton was the starting pitcher for the Pigs against Pawtucket. His mound opponent was Brandon Duckworth, who also had extensive major-league experience. In fact, the two men were almost the same age: Duckworth had been born January 23, 1976, and Elarton had been born exactly a month later. The matchup could just as easily have taken place in the big leagues except that both pitchers had gone through enough ups and downs that they found themselves trying to pitch their way back to that level.

They had been teammates briefly, in Kansas City in 2007, and had pitched against each other in 2008 after Elarton landed in Cleveland. That was the last year either had pitched in the majors. "We were joking that we've come a long way since we last pitched against each other," Elarton said. "Problem is we've gone in the wrong direction."

Both men pitched reasonably well in their rematch. Duckworth came out in the fifth inning in large part because his pitch count had reached ninety. He had given up three earned runs to that point, which pushed his ERA to 4.34 for the season. Not awful, but probably not good enough to merit a serious look from the Red Sox.

Elarton was a little better. Even though he gave up ten hits, he kept pitching out of trouble and left a tie game having given up four runs—three of them earned. His ERA crept up a little bit to 3.55—again, not bad, but not as good as he had been hoping for when he had walked out of Charlie Manuel's office in Clearwater back in March after being sent down.

"I was lucky," he said afterward. "I really didn't throw the ball very well, but I got some outs when I had to."

Which is what good pitchers do. Like hitters, they know they aren't going to have their best stuff every night. How they perform on those nights when they are being knocked around the ballpark a little usually determines how their season—and ofttimes their career—will turn out. Elarton was old enough and wise enough to understand that, but it still bothered him that he wasn't pitching better.

"The funny thing is it's no different now than when I was young and pitching well in the major leagues," he said. "There are very few nights when I walk off the mound feeling good about the way I've pitched. Sometimes I'm being hard on myself. Other times I'm not."

And other times—most times—the truth lies somewhere in the middle. Elarton knew that the middle wouldn't be good enough to get him to the major leagues. At thirty-six, he had to be better than that to get the Phillies' attention, even with the team having its worst season in years. In fact, the team's struggles made it more likely that a young pitcher would be called up, if needed, because the focus would be more on the future than the present.

"I don't have a single regret about doing this," he said the morning after getting the win against the PawSox. "Just being healthy and being able to take the ball every time it's my turn has made it fun."

Elarton sighed. "But there are days and nights when it's tough. The road trips are tough, especially those last few days when you feel like you've been looking at the same walls in the same hotel room for a month. I miss my family at that point. I occasionally catch myself saying, 'Do I want to be *here*?' I want to play baseball, I know that, but do I want to be back at this level?

"I think every guy who has ever been in the majors, especially for an extended period, is going to have issues with coming back down. You do it because you believe you can get back up. But if you're looking in the mirror at night and you know the person looking back is pretty much stuck in Triple-A if he's being realistic . . . sometimes it's tough."

Elarton had his hand on his forehead as he spoke, as if he were thinking the whole thing through one more time. He paused, then nodded. "The easiest thing in the world is to say, 'I'm done, I'm going home.' I did that once when it wasn't time yet. I'm going to make sure I don't do that this time around."

———

Lehigh Valley's starting third baseman in the game Elarton had pitched on that Saturday night had been Timothy Craig Hulett Jr., known to one and all since he was little as Tug—because his mother's second-favorite major-league baseball player was Tug McGraw, the great and colorful relief pitcher for the Mets and the Phillies.

Her favorite major-league player was Tim Hulett, Tug's father, who had played in the majors for twelve years with three different teams. Tim Hulett was never a great player—his career batting average was .249—but he was a solid infielder and was always considered a positive clubhouse presence wherever he played.

Tug was the oldest of the four boys born to Tim and Linda Hulett. The three other boys—Joe, Sam, and Jeff—all came along within the next five years. They were a close family, although, ironically, it wasn't Tim who taught his sons to play baseball, it was their two grandfathers.

"Dad was on the road a lot playing," Tug said. "He helped us whenever he could, but I can remember my dad's dad taking me to the park all the time for batting and fielding practice. I was a field rat right from the beginning. Always loved to play, to practice, just to be around baseball."

When Tug was nine, his dad was playing for Baltimore, and the four brothers walked to a nearby apartment complex that had a baseball field to play one July afternoon while the Orioles were in Chicago. It was only a short walk to and from the little park, and after they had played, the boys started home. They were about a block from their house when, for some reason, Sam, who was six, darted into the street. Tug remembers yelling at him and grabbing Joe—two years older than Sam—before he could follow Sam.

He probably saved Joe's life by grabbing him. He couldn't save Sam. A car coming down the street couldn't stop in time, and Sam was hit. He died several hours later. Phil Itzoe, the Orioles' longtime traveling secretary, got the phone call in the press box that afternoon while the Orioles were playing the White Sox. Itzoe had to go down to the clubhouse to tell manager Johnny Oates that Tim needed to come out of the game and get home as soon as possible.

"It's a little bit hard to focus on whether you need to make a pitching change when you've just heard news like that," Oates said later. "It just doesn't seem to matter much."

Needless to say, Tug Hulett was crushed by his little brother's death. "For a long time I blamed myself," he said. "I kept saying, 'I'm sorry, I'm sorry.' I became very introverted. In the end, what brought me out of it was my faith."

The Huletts were a deeply religious family before Sam's death, and they turned to their religion afterward. Tug finally found a passage in the Bible that resonated with him: Philippians 4:7—"Peace through understanding." It made him realize that if he understood what had happened—and that it was *not* his fault, that in fact he had probably saved Joe from the same fate—he could begin to move on with his life.

"I felt an overwhelming peace afterward," he said. "My dad had always talked about baseball giving him a platform to talk about his faith, and I came to believe that too. I don't think I force it on anyone, but I like people to understand what it's meant to me."

Tug's mother, Linda, was as big an influence on his athletic career as his father. It was Linda who insisted that her son learn to hit left-handed. "Every time I'd pick up a bat and try to swing righty, she'd say, 'No, son, wrong side,' and I switched," he said, laughing.

When Tim retired after the 1995 season, the family moved back to his hometown, Springfield, Illinois, where Tug started high school before finishing at Evangelical Christian High School in Shreveport Louisiana. He played all sports but loved baseball most and ended up going to Auburn on a baseball scholarship. He was drafted in the fourteenth round of the 2004 draft by the Texas Rangers (his dad had been a No. 1 pick), which was a disappointment because he had been told he would go somewhere between the third and the fifth rounds.

"After the fifth round I stopped paying attention," he said. "I figured someone would call when I got picked. I remember hearing guys who were taken in the second and third rounds talking about how disappointed they were not to go in the first round. I didn't feel a lot of sympathy for them."

Tim Hulett wasn't very big—six feet and 185 pounds—and Tug wasn't quite as big: closer to five ten with a fireplug body type. He could always hit, though, and was willing to play anywhere on the field to get in the lineup. He made it to Triple-A three years later—in 2007. He was traded to Seattle during the following off-season, and was hitting .301 midway through the 2008 season in Tacoma. Then he got a post-midnight phone call one evening when he was in bed in a Salt Lake City hotel room. It was Daren Brown, the manager of the Rainiers.

"You're going to the majors," he said, not wasting any time. "There's a flight out of here at four a.m. You're booked on it. You're meeting the team in Oakland."

It was not the way Hulett had envisioned his first call to the big leagues, but he wasn't complaining. He got to the ballpark that evening with no equipment. He had to borrow a glove, cleats, batting gloves, and a bat. Manager Jim Riggleman sent him up to pinch-hit in the eighth inning and he struck out. Two nights later, in Kansas City, he was the DH and singled off Gil Meche for his first big-league hit. A week later he was back in Tacoma. But he was called back up soon after that and spent the rest of the season in the majors.

A year later, he got some more time in the majors in Kansas City, but the Royals released him at the end of the season. He signed with the Red Sox and then became the classic journeyman, moving from the Red Sox back to the Mariners, then to the Rockies and the

Nationals—all in two years. He signed before the 2012 season with the Phillies and started the season with Double-A Reading before being called up to Lehigh Valley in May.

"There is a lot of failure in this sport," he said, holding a bat in his hands as he sat in the third-base dugout at Coca-Cola Field waiting to start batting practice. "I've played in ten different places in the last six seasons. The irony is teams sign me because they say they need guys in the system with big-league experience. Then, when I don't get the chance to go back up, they either say it's because I don't have enough experience up there or they want to go with a younger guy. I'm caught in the middle: I'm twenty-nine. I have *some* big-league experience but not enough. I often want to say, 'How am I supposed to have enough big-league experience for you if you won't call me up to the big leagues?'"

Hulett knew his call-up to Lehigh Valley in mid-May might be temporary. The Phillies had infield prospects they were looking to move up in the system, and Hulett understood that twenty-nine-year-olds with sixty-seven major-league at-bats (and thirteen hits) were not looked upon as prospects.

"Ryne [Sandberg] is good about getting everyone in the lineup," he said. "That means I'll get chances—and as long as I have a chance, I'm not going to complain." He smiled. "Heck, I'm not going to complain regardless.

"I remember when I was fourteen I told my dad I really wanted to focus on baseball. School was always a big deal in my family. My mom didn't let us play sports if we weren't making A's. But I told Dad I wanted to be a baseball player. He looked me in the eye and said, 'That's fine, Tug, now tell me how you plan to separate yourself from the twenty million other kids who want to be baseball players.'

"Well, I think I separated myself from most of them. I made it to the big leagues, and I still believe I can make it back there again. I know I can still hit."

That night Hulett was 2 for 3, including an RBI double. It raised his batting average to .321 since he had escaped Reading. He started again the next day and got another hit. Six weeks later, he was in the lineup on a Saturday night in Norfolk, playing third base. By then, he was getting into the lineup sporadically. The Phillies had sent the veteran Pete Orr down in early June, and he was playing third base most nights. Kevin Frandsen, the team's best player, was at second base, and the primary backup to the two of them was Michael Martínez, who had also seen major-league time during the season.

Hulett was the odd man out.

But he kept taking advantage of the chances he was given. On the night of July 14 he went 2 for 4 and upped his batting average to .325 in 37 games and 120 at-bats. For the next four days, Hulett didn't see the field. Which is why he wasn't shocked when Sandberg called him into his office with the team in Durham to tell him he was being sent to Reading. The Phillies had activated pitcher Justin De Fratus off the disabled list, and he needed innings to get his arm back into shape. Hulett was hitting well and his numbers were strong, but at this moment in time he was also the most expendable player on the Lehigh Valley roster.

Hulett didn't complain. All he could do was keep playing and, he hoped, keep hitting while waiting for another chance.

———

Hulett's demotion, brought on by De Fratus's coming off the DL, is a microcosm of the life led by what are called organization players—guys who have reached a point in their careers where getting to the majors or returning to the majors isn't impossible but isn't likely. As Phil Nevin, Toledo's manager, had pointed out, once the trade deadline passes at the end of July, a Triple-A manager is faced with a clubhouse of twenty-five guys who know that—at most—they are playing for two or three guaranteed major-league spots in the month of September. And, as any manager will tell you, almost everyone knows who those two or three guys are going to be long before the September call-ups occur.

The harshest description of the life led by most minor leaguers might have come in 1970, when Tommy Lasorda was managing the Dodgers' farm club in Spokane and the team had a twenty-year-old hotshot named Bobby Valentine on the roster. Valentine had been the fifth pick in the draft two years earlier and had briefly made the Dodgers in 1969 as a September call-up. He was about as cocky as any player who had ever set foot in a clubhouse, and a lot of the older players in Spokane resented him and went out of their way to make his life difficult.

Which led to Lasorda's calling the players together and, as legend has it, telling them what he wanted them to do before the game that night.

"First I want you all to go and get Valentine's autograph," he said. "Because someday it'll be valuable to you when he's a star in the majors. Then I want you to thank him. You know why? Because we need the rest of you guys around here so we can field a team for him to play on. If not for him, we wouldn't need the rest of you."

Hyperbolic, certainly. Also brutal. But there was a large chunk of truth in it too. That's why minor leaguers are always aware of who the "prospects" are in an organization. That's why being on the forty-man roster, even if it doesn't mean you're playing in the majors, is so important. It has financial advantages, but it also means the organization sees value in you at that moment—and believes you have a future with the major-league team.

Players like Tug Hulett and Pete Orr were always aware of where they stood in a team's pecking order. They were never going to be considered prospects—Hulett had been a fourteenth-round draft pick, and Orr, after choosing to go to junior college instead of signing out of high school as a thirty-ninth-round draft pick, ended up signing with the Atlanta Braves two years later as an undrafted free agent.

"The funny thing is, when I was in high school, I never even thought about getting drafted," he said. "In Canada [Orr grew up in Richmond Hill in Ontario] the draft wasn't that big a deal. I was sitting in a math class, and I was told to go to the principal's office. I figured I was in trouble for something. They said I needed to call my mom. Then I figured I was really in trouble. So I called and she said, 'Congratulations, the Texas Rangers just called and said they drafted you in the thirty-ninth round.' That was how I found out."

Orr decided not to sign because he didn't think he was ready for the minor-league life, having not yet turned eighteen. He had split time between hockey and baseball until he was sixteen and felt that he could improve as a baseball player if he went to college before trying to turn pro. Dick Smith, the coach at Galveston College in Texas, had made a habit of recruiting in Ontario after stumbling over a couple of good players there while recruiting a player who had moved north from Puerto Rico. He offered scholarships to Orr and another local kid, Jeremy Walker. Orr decided to accept. Once he got over the culture shock, he liked the school and played well enough to be offered a scholarship to Nebraska two years later.

"I was ready to go to Nebraska but figured I'd see what happened in the draft," he said. "I thought with two years' more experience I'd go higher than I had in high school. Then I didn't get drafted at all. It was very disappointing. I found out later that the scouts who'd been watching me thought I was locked into going to Nebraska and they didn't want to waste a pick on me."

Orr was playing for a semipro team back home (for no money so he could retain his college eligibility) when he got a call saying that the Braves were interested in him. They were offering $10,000 to sign. That seemed like a lot of money, so he took it.

Moving up in the Braves' system wasn't easy. The Braves were in the midst of their fourteen-year run, during which they made postseason play at the major-league level every year. They had a deep, well-stocked farm system, and there wasn't a lot of turnover in Atlanta, because the team was good. Orr chipped away, finally making it to the majors in 2005—even though Bobby Cox didn't get around to actually telling him he had made it until their chance encounter in the hallway in Atlanta, on the eve of opening day.

Orr stuck with the Braves for the next two years. He even hit .300 in a part-time role in 2005 and became one of the team's most popular players because of his productivity, his versatility, and his attitude. But he was sent to Richmond, which was then the Braves' Triple-A team, midway through the 2007 season and released that winter.

"It's a business," he said with a shrug. "They had some younger players coming up through the system, and they needed a spot. You can't take it personally, because it isn't personal. If it had been personal, I would probably still be there because I know Bobby liked me and I think the organization did too. But that's not the way it works."

He signed with the Washington Nationals and spent parts of the next two seasons in Washington—which was a shock to his system. "I went from one of the best teams in baseball to the worst," he said. "They were building, and you could see the potential in some of their young players. But at that moment, when I was there, we were a bad team. I was spoiled. I was used to contending."

A job was a job, though, and he shuttled between Washington and Syracuse until the end of 2010. By then the Nationals were ready to bring up young infielders like Ian Desmond and Danny Espinosa and had signed veterans like Alex Cora and Jerry Hairston Jr. to back them up. Orr was the odd man out, and signed with the Phillies for the 2011 season. He spent that year in Lehigh Valley but came to spring training in 2012, thinking he might have a shot to make the team as a backup infielder. He had a good spring and thought he might be making the trip north, especially when second baseman Chase Utley went on the disabled list. Then, a little more than a week before the team was supposed to break camp, the Phillies signed veteran Luis Castillo, a three-time All-Star who was trying to make a comeback at the age of thirty-six.

"That was demoralizing," Orr said. "I thought I had outplayed the other guys who were competing for utility jobs in the infield, and then they signed Luis. There was certainly no comparison in our résumés, so I thought maybe I was going to be sent down again."

Nine days later, the Phillies released Castillo after realizing he wasn't even a shadow of his former self. Orr felt better—but still not safe. "Cliff Lee kept asking me, 'Have they told you, have they told you?'" he said. "The answer was no."

There are very few boundaries when it comes to locker-room humor, especially in baseball—where players spend far more time with one another during the course of an eight-month season than they do with their families. Orr spent most of the spring being ribbed about his uncertain status with the team. After the Castillo signing, Shane Victorino put a printout in Orr's locker that listed potential housing opportunities in the Lehigh valley.

"All the guys were messing with me," he said. "But I knew they wouldn't be doing it if they didn't want to see me make the team."

Just as he had done in 2005 with the Braves, Orr made the trip north with the Phillies, still uncertain if he was going to be on the opening-day roster. Hector Luna, another backup infielder, also made the trip. Orr was sitting in the dugout during the Phillies' last exhibition game—played in Citizens Bank Park—when Lee asked him again if anyone had told him he was on the team. Again, Orr told him no.

"Well, I'm going to find out," Lee said—and stalked away.

In the ninth inning, Lee came back and sat down next to Orr. "You're in," he said.

"You're sure?"

"Yup. You're in."

Sure enough, after the game Charlie Manuel called Luna into his office. Orr could tell by the look on Luna's face when he walked out that he had been sent down. A few minutes later, it was Orr's turn. He was on the team. Whether Lee had said something to Manuel about telling Orr the news or whether Manuel had been waiting to see if the Phillies made some kind of a deal that would have sent Orr to Lehigh Valley along with Luna, he didn't know. Regardless, he was ecstatic. "I hadn't been in the majors at all in 2010, and just briefly in 2011," he said. "It meant a lot to work my way back there."

Orr played well when he got to play in Philadelphia. He knew his time there might be brief once again because he was the most likely guy to get sent down when Utley came off the disabled list. "I knew it was probably coming," he said. "I just didn't expect it to happen when it did."

It happened on June 7—the day before he turned thirty-three. The Phillies decided to call up Michael Martínez, who had been playing well at Lehigh Valley, and send Orr down in his place. It was one of those player swaps that go virtually unnoticed even by those who read the agate, but that profoundly affect the people involved.

Orr was in the lineup almost every day back in Triple-A. The person most affected by his presence was Tug Hulett, who had been playing more often when Martínez was on the team. On July 22, Hulett was told he would need to pack up his locker and head back to Reading.

The revolving door of baseball never stops.

22

Slice of Life

COLUMBUS

There is one player currently employed by a Major League Baseball team—in this case the Cleveland Indians—who has a degree in economics from Harvard. That would be Frank Joseph Herrmann, Harvard class of 2006, Columbus Clippers bullpen 2012.

"If I had a dollar for every time I hear, 'Hey, you should know the answer to that question, you went to Harvard,' I could probably retire," Herrmann said one night with a smile. "When you're the only one of anything, especially in a clubhouse, people are bound to notice."

Herrmann doesn't mind being the only Harvard grad around. He made it to the big leagues for the first time, in Cleveland, in 2010. That made him the fifteenth Harvard man to pitch in the majors, but the first since Jeff Musselman had pitched for the Mets in 1990.

"When I was coming out of high school, I thought I had a chance to play in the majors someday," he said. "But when the chance came to go to Harvard, there was no way I could say no. I mean, how do you pass up a chance like that?"

Actually, athletes who have pro ambitions often pass up that chance. In 1995, Frank Sullivan, the basketball coach at Harvard, thought he was about to pull off a recruiting coup when Wally Szczerbiak told him he was going to come to Harvard that fall. Szczerbiak was from Long Island and had somehow slipped under the radar of the

big-time college programs. Late that spring, Miami of Ohio, hardly
a powerhouse but still a more highly regarded basketball school than
Harvard, offered Szczerbiak a scholarship. He accepted and went on
to be the No. 6 pick in the NBA draft and play ten years in the NBA.

"I still think about what might have been if Wally had come,"
Sullivan has often said. "Then again, the decision worked out pretty
well for him."

Herrmann was also recruited by some of the big-name jock
schools. He was a three-sport athlete in high school, perhaps as good
a prospect in football as he was in baseball, and a thousand-point
scorer in basketball. But he had made up his mind to apply early decision to Harvard after baseball coach Joe Walsh invited him to campus
for a visit. Once he got in, there wasn't any doubt about where he was
going to go to college.

"I don't think my parents would have ever forgiven me if I didn't
go," he said. "Maybe in the next life, but not in this one."

Herrmann pitched and played the outfield as a freshman. That
summer he played for a team owned by former Montreal Expos and
Boston Red Sox general manager Dan Duquette in the New England
Collegiate Baseball League.

"I think Dan saw something he liked in me," Herrmann said.
"I remember he told me that I had some qualities that could help a
major-league team. That was a nice boost for my confidence because
I knew that he knew what a big-league ballplayer looked like."

As a sophomore Herrmann became a full-time pitcher. By the
time he was a junior, he was attracting some attention from major-
league clubs but had no intention of entering the draft or even thinking about turning pro until after he had graduated. In fact, he had
an internship on Wall Street that summer, which made sense for
someone majoring in economics. He didn't especially like the job, and
when he got a call from a friend who said he could spend the last six
weeks of the summer in Hawaii playing in a new collegiate summer
league, he quit and decided to go pitch.

While he was there, Don Lyle, the Cleveland Indians' Northern
California scout, saw him pitch and recommended to the Indians that

they try to sign him. "He said I had life in my arm and they liked my potential," Herrmann said. "They offered me $30,000 and one semester's tuition."

At that point, Herrmann was two semesters from graduation. Hearing what was going on, Duquette called Indians general manager Mark Shapiro and asked him to excuse Herrmann from pitching in the fall for two years so he could get his Harvard degree. When Shapiro agreed, Herrmann decided to sign. Even with that proviso, his parents weren't thrilled.

"It was a leap of faith—in myself, I guess—on my part," he said. "I figured I'd be getting a year's head start and I could still get my degree. My parents were adamantly against the idea, but they said it was my decision to make."

In fact, when he and his parents went to a minor-league game that summer in Vermont, Frank Herrmann turned to his son as they left the ballpark and said, "You're giving up Harvard for *this*?"

He was. He kept his word to go back to school and even wrote a column for the *Harvard Crimson* while he was back on campus about his experiences pitching in the minor leagues. His rise through the minors was steady, and after he had pitched to an ERA of 0.31 at Columbus during the first two months of the 2010 season, he got the call to join the Indians in Cleveland. He made his debut in early June, facing four batters and getting them all out.

Nothing to it.

Except that facing big-league hitters wasn't the same as facing Triple-A hitters, and Herrmann figured out why pretty quickly. "What you find out is that there are no easy outs in the major leagues. The worst hitter in a lineup is usually a guy who has hit Triple-A pitching very well or he wouldn't be there. And the best hitters in a lineup are guys who crush Triple-A pitching. In Triple-A there are times— not all the time, but some of the time—when you can get through an inning without throwing very many good pitches. That's never true in the majors. Never."

Herrmann knew when he arrived at spring training in Arizona in 2012 that he would be fighting for one of the last bullpen spots on the Indians' roster. He didn't get off to a good start when he gave up four runs to the Reds in an inning of work the first week in March. He pitched better after that, but the die seemed cast. On April 2, three days before the Indians opened the season, he was sent back to Columbus.

"Disappointing to say the least," he said. "It's definitely tougher coming back down because you know what you've lost—tangibly and intangibly. The first time I made it up to Triple-A, I was making $2,000 a month, and that was completely okay by me. I've had two years in the majors now. Even at the minimum [$482,000 in 2012] that's a far cry from what you make down here. You get spoiled, used to the idea of being able to do things and buy things without worrying about money because you have money.

"It isn't as if I'm broke. My wife [Johanna] has a very good job [in corporate communications for Coca-Cola] and we've done well while I was in the majors. But it *is* different.

"We just got back from a twelve-day road trip to Syracuse, Rochester, and Buffalo. The last couple of days of that trip I was dragging. Those days this was a *job*. I think 80 percent of the time this is fun. I like doing my work, I like getting a chance to pitch, and I still believe I'm good enough to be back in the majors."

He smiled. "Of course as the days dwindle and the trade deadline gets close, you see that window closing. The thing you have to understand is that for every guy at every level of the minors, the stakes every day are very high. But I think they might be highest at Triple-A because you know how close you are. If you've been up, you know you have it in you to get back. And yet you look around and know there are twenty-four guys on your team thinking the same thing and twenty-five guys in the other dugout also thinking the same thing.

"The day I look around and say, 'What am I doing here?' is the day I walk away. I've never had that thought. I know I want a second career out of baseball, and having a Harvard degree helps me think there's a soft landing for me out there when I'm done. A lot of guys don't have that. For them, it's baseball or bust."

He looked out at the rain pelting down on Huntington Park in downtown Columbus. Two nights earlier, the Clippers and the Mud Hens had been rained out, and they had played a doubleheader the night before.

"Last thing we need is to have to play two again tomorrow," he said, shaking his head. "The only thing worse would be to sit around for three hours and *then* have to play two anyway. Down here, they don't like to call off games. They want the gate."

The way rainouts are handled in Triple-A is very different from in the majors. When a game is rained out in the majors, it is rescheduled either for an off day or as part of a day-night (separate admissions) doubleheader. A rainout still costs a team money because the walk-up crowd for a rescheduled game is almost always very small, but season-ticket holders have to pay for the game whether they show up or not.

In the minors, because there are so few days off during the season, it is almost impossible to schedule a makeup game on an off day. What's more, since teams travel by bus or on commercial airplanes, it is much more difficult to get to and from a city for one day to play a makeup game the way major-league teams—which fly charter—often do.

There is also a rule that allows for only one separate-admission doubleheader in each city each season. That is also due to the lack of off days: the thinking is you get games in as soon as you possibly can. The only break the minor leaguers catch is that the games in a one-admission doubleheader are reduced to seven innings.

Herrmann wasn't really thinking about any of that as he watched it rain. Manager Mike Sarbaugh had moved him into the role of closer recently, and he had pitched well three straight times since taking over the ninth inning for the Clippers.

"I like it," he said. "I like the challenge. I like the idea that no one's behind me, that the game is mine to try to finish. And, if it gets someone's attention, whether it's the Indians or someone else, all the better."

Herrmann did get the Indians' attention. On August 7 he was

called back up to Cleveland to try to help a struggling bullpen. Seventeen days later, he was back in Columbus. Nine days after that, he made it back to Cleveland for the rest of the season.

Escalator up, escalator down. Even with a Harvard degree, nothing in baseball is guaranteed.

———

Herrmann's manager, Mike Sarbaugh, had never had to worry much about the escalator when he was a player. "Once I got to Double-A, I began to notice there were a lot of guys who had more talent than I did," he said. "The problem was I had gotten hooked on the game by then."

If Ryne Sandberg in Lehigh Valley ran the International League's tightest clubhouse, Sarbaugh probably ran the loosest. A few feet from the door of his office, in the open area where players often sat to eat before and after games, there was a Ping-Pong table. At almost any hour of the day, there was a game going on because the team ran a never-ending Ping-Pong tournament during the season. Players came and went, and the Ping-Pong tournament continued, much like Nathan Detroit's longest-running floating craps game in the musical *Guys and Dolls*.

This was proof, if nothing else, that there was more than one way to run a successful minor-league team. Sandberg, the Hall of Famer, had been a winner wherever he managed and was generally considered the most likely of the fourteen International League managers to run a big-league club someday soon.

Just behind him on that list was Columbus's Sarbaugh, whose career had peaked in 1994, his final season as a player, when he made it to Triple-A Charlotte for four games and five at-bats. He had gotten one hit and retired the following spring when he was offered a coaching job at Class A Kinston in the Carolina League by the Indians.

"Baseball got me into college [Lamar University] because I was a decent high school shortstop," he said. "I was figuring I'd go to a DIII school and play baseball and soccer, but a college friend of my dad's, Ron Rizzi, who was a Pirates scout, knew Jim Gilligan, the coach at Lamar, and recommended me. I signed there without ever having seen the school.

"Even so, I never figured I would stay in the game after I graduated. Both my parents were teachers, and I figured I'd be a teacher and a high school coach. That's why I majored in kinesiology. It was something I figured I'd use as a teacher and as a coach. The only sport I really dreamed about playing professionally was basketball. I thought I'd play in the NBA. By high school I knew that wasn't going to happen."

Sarbaugh was crushed when no one drafted him coming out of college. By then he was hoping at least to get a shot to play professionally. "I went home and was trying to decide what to do next," he said. "Get a job? Go to grad school? Sulk?"

While he was weighing his options, he got a phone call from Walter Yauss, a Brewers scout who had seen him play in college. The Brewers were short an infielder on their Helena, Montana, rookie-league team. Yauss asked Sarbaugh if he would be interested in signing with the Brewers and going to Helena.

"I jumped at it," Sarbaugh said, laughing at the memory. "My bonus was a plane ticket to Helena. My salary was $850 a month."

Sarbaugh worked his way up to Double-A over the next few years but understood he had hit his ceiling when he got there. That's why when he was offered the coaching job he took it.

"I knew I was on shaky ground as a player," he said. "I was twenty-eight and, at best, a Double-A talent. It's funny because when I signed with the Brewers out of college, I figured I'd do it a year and then go teach. When I took the coaching job, I figured I'd do it a year and then go teach. Now I'm twenty-three years out of college and I'm still here."

But he does teach. He met Nicole Paul on a blind date not long after he had become a coach, and they were married in 1998. They settled in Shillington, Pennsylvania—not far from where Mike grew up in Lancaster. Every off-season since, Mike has gone home to teach. He has a full-time job at a middle school and also subs at the high school level.

"It just seemed like a natural thing for me to do," he said. "A teacher's lounge isn't unlike a baseball clubhouse. There's a lot going on in there, and you have to hope that personalities will mesh well."

Sarbaugh got his first chance to manage in 2004, in the rookie-level New York–Penn League running the Mahoning Valley Scrappers. They won the league title. Two years later, promoted to single-A Kinston—where he had previously been on championship teams as a player and as a coach—he won the Carolina League title as a manager. In 2009, the Indians moved him up to Columbus, and the Clippers had won both the Governors' Cup and the Triple-A national championship game in 2010 and 2011.

It wasn't so much the winning that had put Sarbaugh into conversations as a future major-league manager as the way he handled his players. Even though he had turned forty-five before the start of the 2012 season, he looked as if he could still be playing. His players liked the fact that he was always straight up with them but didn't feel the need to micromanage them.

"The hardest part, day in and day out, is knowing you've got twenty-five guys in the room who all think they should be in the majors," he said. "They should feel that way—whether it's true or not. When a guy gets sent down or doesn't make the team out of spring training, I always sit down and say to him, 'What do you think you need to work on to get up there?' I let him tell me. Usually, they know exactly what it is. And then I say, 'Okay, let's see if we can work on that and get you up there.' Are they all going up? Of course not. But my job is to help them make the best of things, regardless of what direction they're heading in."

At that moment the Clippers were headed in the right direction. After struggling for much of the season, they had won eight straight games and, at 57-50, had become a factor in the wild card race. Indianapolis still led the West Division by nine games at 66-41, but the Clips were only two games back of Pawtucket for the wild card spot.

"Winning is a lot more fun than losing—that's obvious," Sarbaugh said. "But it still isn't the primary job. Managing games comes second. Managing people comes first."

Sarbaugh sat back in his chair just as the phone rang. The rain, he was told, should slacken enough to allow the game to start on time.

"That will make everyone very happy," Sarbaugh said. "The less these guys sit around and think about things right now, the better."

The trading deadline was five days away. Which meant that August 1—the day Triple-A managers dread most—wasn't far behind.

23

From Montoyo to Longoria

HOT SUMMER NIGHTS IN DURHAM

Charlie Montoyo sat in a chair next to the desk in his office, having given up his usual pregame spot behind his desk to his nine-year-old son, Tyson, who was engrossed in a computer game his father had no chance of understanding.

For Montoyo, the best part of June and July is that his family flies east to join him in Durham. On a typical day, when the team is in town, Tyson goes to the ballpark a few hours before game time with his dad. Samantha and four-year-old Alexander usually come later.

Most Triple-A managers join the major-league club in September once their season is over, helping out around the ballpark since there are extra players to work with when the rosters expand. It is considered a perk—a chance to enjoy big-league life for a few weeks after a season of long bus rides and motels.

Montoyo is an exception. As soon as his season ends, he flies back to Arizona to rejoin his family—which has to head home in mid-August so the boys can start school. In spite of his heart issues, Alexander is now going to school. Montoyo doesn't want to be away from his boys for one minute longer than he needs to be, and the Rays understand.

The 2012 season had been—from a baseball perspective—Montoyo's most difficult. The Bulls had opened the season at home and gone 5-2 before going on one of those Bataan Death March road trips that International League teams face a couple of times every season. They had gone from Gwinnett to Charlotte to Pawtucket and then to Norfolk. That meant a six-hour bus trip to Gwinnett, a relatively easy three and a half hours to Charlotte, a 4:00 a.m. wake-up to fly to Pawtucket, and then eleven more hours on a bus to get to Norfolk to play the next night. They had lost thirteen of fourteen on that trip and then tacked on three more losses when they finally got home, meaning they had lost thirteen in a row and sixteen of seventeen. That left the Bulls at 6-18, and in a hole from which they would never completely climb out.

A couple of times in early July they had gotten to within four games of .500 before sliding back—often on nights when Montoyo had to hold pitchers out of games or use backup catcher Craig Albernaz to mop up games on the mound. The Rays had placed nine important players on the disabled list at one time or another during the season, which meant they were constantly pillaging Montoyo's roster for replacement players. That, plus their never-ending search for bullpen help, meant that Montoyo found himself looking at a different group of players on an almost nightly basis. By the end of July the team had been involved in 112 transactions—players going up to the majors or coming back to Triple-A; others going down to Double-A or coming up to Triple-A; a few being released; a few more going on or off the DL. There had also been a fifty-game suspension for drug use involving Tim Beckham, who had been the No. 1 pick in the entire draft in 2008 but was now struggling to get his life together while playing in Durham.

Through it all, Montoyo's demeanor never changed.

"That's the great thing about Charlie," catcher Chris Giménez said. "He's trying to get the team to win every night, but he's still managing us as individuals. We all know that his door is always open for us whenever we want to talk about anything. And he's not going to bury anyone. If you're on his team, you're going to play. That makes life down here a lot more bearable for everyone."

Montoyo completely understood how tough it was for someone like Giménez to be on the Tampa-Durham shuttle. Giménez had started the season in Durham and had been called up in mid-April. In late May he was back in Durham being kidded by his teammates because when he rejoined the team in Indianapolis he didn't have any of his Durham equipment with him. So he warmed up in Rays gear before games.

"They started calling me 'big-league Jimmy,'" he said, laughing on a hot summer night. "It's kind of stuck. Of course that's not the kind of big leaguer I want to be." He shook his head. "I know how this sounds when I say it, but I swear to God when I was up there I couldn't get anything to fall. But that's the way it works. No one is looking at the type of outs you make up there. I get it."

Giménez, who was twenty-nine, and fellow catcher Stephen Vogt had both been on the shuttle all season because the Rays' catching situation was in flux. Vogt, who was twenty-seven, had been sent to the minor-league camp midway through spring training but then had been called up to the team before opening day; the Rays had decided they needed more offense in their lineup after outfielders Sam Fuld and B. J. Upton went on the DL.

Vogt had been drafted out of Azusa Pacific University in the twelfth round in 2007 as an outfielder but had been converted into a catcher. He'd come back from major shoulder surgery in 2009 to be the Rays' Minor League Player of the Year in 2011. He was sitting in the training room in Durham getting ready for the Bulls' last preseason workout when coach Dave Myers came in and told him he needed to get dressed and get to the airport because he needed to catch a plane to Tampa.

Vogt was stunned and thrilled. It would turn out to be the first of three times he would get the call to Tampa during the season— meaning he was sent back down twice. He spent the majority of the season in Durham, getting only twenty-five at-bats in the major leagues—without a hit.

"I honestly believe I'll get another chance," he said one night. "Just being in the major leagues was great. I want to go back and prove that I can stay there. I've come a long way in a fairly short time—

especially after my surgery." In 2013 Vogt *did* get another chance—in Oakland.

There were two disappointed people on April 4, the day Vogt was called up: Jeff Salazar, who thought he had made the team but found himself on the way back to Durham; and Montoyo. Montoyo was out for his daily five-mile run when the call came from Tampa for Vogt. Normally, Myers would have waited to let Montoyo get back to give a player the news he was going to the majors for the first time, but there was no time because Vogt had to leave for the airport right away.

"I hate missing those moments," Montoyo said. "They're the best part of the job. I don't even like to tell a guy on the phone unless I have to. I like to call him in, sit him down in my office, and see the look on his face when I tell him. With Steve, I missed it completely."

Of course, seventeen days later, when Vogt came back, the first person to greet him was Montoyo.

"You have to deal with each guy coming back differently," he said. "Most of our guys handle it well. I haven't had too many pouters on my teams through the years. A guy like Steve, he's come so far, he's not likely to get down. And I could say to him, 'Look, with your ability to catch and play outfield, they're going to be keeping a close eye on you.' I never lie to a guy. I try to tell him what he needs to do to get back up, because if I lie, one of two things will happen and both are bad: He'll believe it's not his fault, and he *will* get bitter, and he won't work on his weaknesses. Or he'll know I'm lying and I'll lose his respect."

Sometimes the toughest conversations were not with the guy who had gone up and come back but with the guy who didn't get called up. On August 2, the Rays decided they needed some more punch on their bench, so they sent veteran Brooks Conrad to Durham and called up Will Rhymes—swapping backup infielders. Rhymes had been hot, hitting .368 over a ten-game stretch—so the Rays thought he might be able to help their anemic lineup.

Montoyo had the pleasant task of telling Rhymes he was on his way to Tampa. A few minutes later he had a far less pleasant task when Reid Brignac asked if he could talk to him.

Brignac was twenty-six and had spent a good deal of time playing shortstop for the Rays in 2010 and 2011. He was a slick fielder, and he had become quite popular in Tampa Bay. In the media room in Port Charlotte, where the Rays hold spring training, there was a photograph on the wall of a woman wearing a sash across her chest that said, "Miss North Florida." She was throwing out the first pitch at a Rays game, having been invited because she was dating the starting shortstop at the time—Brignac.

But Brignac couldn't hit enough to hold on to his spot, especially in a lineup that was hurting at the start of the season because of injuries. He had a career batting average of .228, and the Rays decided to move Sean Rodriguez ahead of him in the pecking order.

Brignac was still on the opening-day roster, but when the Rays—in their constant search for more offense off the bench—claimed Brandon Allen off waivers from Oakland two weeks later, Brignac was sent down to Durham. In early August he was hitting only .227, so when the Rays came looking for more offense, it was Rhymes who got the call.

Discouraged, Brignac went to see his manager. The conversation lasted forty-five minutes—which is about forty minutes longer than most player-manager meetings last.

"I told him there was no doubting the fact that he was a major-league shortstop," Montoyo said. "He knew that. But he also knew that he needed to hit more, that he needed to work on finding a way to be an effective hitter in the major leagues. Teams can't afford to have outs in their lineup. He knew that too. Really, he just needed to vent. I let him vent.

"I told him to take a day off, take a deep breath, and come back ready to play. I always tell the guys it's a lot less hot in August when you're playing well than when you're playing poorly. Reid knows that; he's a pro. This is a cranky time of year for everyone—especially if you think you shouldn't be here."

He shrugged. "Of course around here, that's just about every-one."

––––––––––

"Everyone" isn't just the players, or even the managers and coaches in Triple-A. It is *everyone:* umpires, broadcasters, beat writers, groundskeepers. For them, the road to the majors is even more difficult because they aren't judged on hard numbers.

Umpires are judged by checkers assigned by Major League Baseball who watch them work and make subjective decisions on how they handle a game. Broadcasters almost always need someone important to like them—and their work. It can be a general manager, a director of broadcasting, or someone else in the business who *knows* the general manager or the director of broadcasting.

The toughest jump may be for the guys who take care of the fields at the Triple-A level. "Usually, someone has to die or get fired—or both," Scott Strickland said as he scanned the skies one afternoon in Durham, watching to see if the predicted thunderstorm that he had just warned Montoyo about might be closing in. "Typically, one job a year at the big-league level, either as the head groundskeeper or the number-one assistant, might open up."

Strickland was only thirty, but he had been in charge of the grounds crew at Durham Bulls Athletic Park for nine years, having been hired while he was finishing up as a student in the turf program at North Carolina State. He had grown up in Winston-Salem, the son of two Wake Forest graduates, but had become fascinated with turf management as an American Legion baseball player in high school.

"Our coach was in charge of the field, and he completely killed the grass," he said. "I was part of the group that worked trying to put it back together or at least get it up and running. I just found the whole thing cool. I enjoyed the learning process—what to do, what not to do. So I decided to try to train to do it for a living."

Many people who go to turf-training school aspire to run golf courses. Strickland, a former baseball player and a big baseball fan, always wanted to work in baseball. When he got the chance to start his career at the Triple-A level, he jumped at it. Nine years later he still enjoyed the job. He had a staff of six—most big-league teams have sixteen—and was in charge not only of the field but also of the weather. When the weather was hot—which it almost always was in July and August—the players blamed him. When it rained, management blamed him. Even worse, if he *said* it was going to rain and it didn't, *everyone* blamed him.

All of which Strickland took in good humor. Although he had applied for major-league jobs and received nothing but rave reviews (other than his weather reports) from everyone he had worked for and with, he'd had only one close call with a big-league job.

"Actually, that one wasn't as close as I thought it was—at least as close as I thought it was for a few minutes," he said. "I had a few good minutes before I realized someone had made a mistake."

Strickland had applied for the job as superintendent of grounds for the Milwaukee Brewers. As he pointed out, it had taken the death of Gary VandenBerg, who had worked for the team for thirty years and had been in charge of the grounds crew for twenty, to create an opening. A few days before Christmas, Strickland had just gotten back from lunch when his phone rang. When he saw a 414 area code come up on the caller ID, he tried not to get excited.

That thought didn't last very long.

The call was from the Brewers' office. A very pleasant-sounding woman told Strickland that he was one of the finalists for the job and she wanted to set up the logistics for his trip to Milwaukee. Strickland would probably have walked the 938 miles if that's what he had been told was required of him.

Strickland isn't exactly certain when the conversation went bad, but he knows what was said that caused his heart to sink. "I'm sure Patrick has already spoken to you," the woman said, referencing the person Strickland would be talking to when he got to Milwaukee.

"No," Strickland answered. "Actually, he hasn't spoken to me."

"He hasn't?"

"No."

There was a pause on the other end of the line. At that moment, Strickland's gut told him something was wrong.

"Look, maybe you want to do some checking and then call me back," he said.

"Um, yes. Maybe I should do that."

It didn't take very long for the phone to ring again. There had been a mistake. The person whom Patrick had spoken to who was supposed to fly to Milwaukee was Justin Scott—the assistant groundskeeper for the Kansas City Royals—not Scott Strickland, the head groundskeeper for the Durham Bulls.

"She was very embarrassed and apologetic," Strickland said. "I sort of wish they'd faked it and let me fly out there just so I'd have the experience of doing the interview even if I wasn't going to get the job."

He smiled. "I guess I can claim I was a finalist for the job—even if it was only for about five minutes."

———

There are a handful of people each year who don't mind spending time in Triple-A. They are major leaguers on rehab assignments. The reason they don't mind it is simple. "It means you're headed in the right direction, that you're on your way back to playing," said Sam Fuld, who arrived for a rehab assignment in Durham in mid-July. He'd hurt his wrist the previous September, and it had required surgery in April after the pain had returned during spring training.

"Of course in the back of your mind there's always that tiny bit of fear that when your rehab time is up"—it can be up to twenty days by rule—"they might just say, 'Well, go ahead and stay down there for a while.'"

Fuld knew he wasn't in any real danger of having that happen, although on occasion it did happen to players. He would end up spending nine days in Durham before being recalled to Tampa.

There was irony in the fact that Fuld's time in Durham overlapped with Evan Longoria's rehab assignment there, and that Durham played the Charlotte Knights shortly after Fuld arrived.

Fuld, Longoria, and the Knights' Dan Johnson had been involved in one of the most extraordinary nights in baseball history the previous September. Longoria had hit two home runs, including the game winner, on the last night of the regular season to put the Rays into the playoffs. In between those two home runs, which came in the eighth and twelfth innings, Johnson had hit a game-tying home run with two outs in the ninth inning—pinch-hitting for Fuld.

"I like to point out that I started the rally by walking with the bases loaded in the eighth," Fuld said, grinning. "I was pissed when [manager] Joe [Maddon] took me out for Dan. Afterward, I told him I would have homered twenty rows deeper if he'd let me hit."

This from someone with four major-league home runs.

It had taken Fuld a good long while, though, to think of himself as a full-fledged major leaguer. "Actually, there's part of me that still thinks like a minor leaguer," he said, relaxing after a grueling workout in late afternoon heat. "I spent so long in Triple-A, went back and forth so many times, that part of me still feels like this is a very natural place to be."

He smiled. "Then again, I remember when I was in Triple-A, I always looked at rehab guys and thought how lucky they were. It always seemed to me that the toughest thing that could happen to a major leaguer was having their fillet overcooked at a restaurant. To some degree, I still think there's a lot of truth in that."

Fuld had more than earned his fillet—regardless of how it was cooked. He liked to joke about the fact that he was a one-of-a-kind baseball player. "To start with, I'm pretty sure I'm the only Jewish/type-one diabetic in baseball," he said. "Throw in the fact that my dad's a college dean [College of Liberal Arts, University of New Hampshire] and my mom is a state senator [D-N.H.] and I think I'm pretty safe in saying I'm unique."

Fuld was diagnosed with diabetes at the age of ten, and it has been a driving force in his life ever since.

"I was lucky that I was diagnosed when the stigma of having it if you were an athlete was being erased," he said. "Ron Santo [the Cubs' Hall of Fame third baseman] hid the fact that he had it for years, because he was afraid he might not get a chance if people knew he had it.

"It's always been obstacles that fueled me. When I was younger, people said I was too small—that fueled me. I remember my senior year in college one scout told me the general feeling was that I was too small and I had the 'issue' of being a diabetic, so teams would shy away from me. That fueled me too."

There was never any doubt that Fuld was going to college, regardless of how good a baseball player he was in high school. He lists himself at five feet ten and 175 pounds, but no one in baseball buys those numbers. He might be five nine (at best), and his weight probably hovers around 160. "I have the right to round up," he said, grinning.

He went to Exeter, where he met his future wife, Sarah (who played lacrosse at Princeton), and then to Stanford, where he graduated with a major in economics. Fascinated by numbers, especially as they relate to baseball, he has worked (slowly) toward a master's in statistics.

"I grew up in an academic-minded home, I think it's fair to say that," he said. "The question was always where I'd go to college, not if. Stanford had great baseball and great academics, although I think some people questioned whether I was good enough to play there."

He was plenty good enough, starting for four years and graduating as Stanford's all-time leader in runs scored. The Cubs drafted him in the twenty-fourth round after his junior year and then in the tenth round in 2004 after his senior year. The start of his pro career was delayed when he tore the labrum in his shoulder diving for a ball late in his senior season.

Even so, he moved quickly through the minor leagues, never hitting *worse* than .287 at any level, consistently stealing bases while playing an often spectacular outfield. His first call-up came in September 2007, but Cubs manager Lou Piniella used him strictly as a defensive replacement the first couple of weeks he was in the majors—so much so that his teammates hung a sign that said MOONLIGHT GRAHAM in his locker.

The next three years were frustrating for Fuld. Everyone in baseball seemed to think he was ready to contribute in the majors—except the Cubs. They kept sending him down to Iowa—*not* to the "Field of Dreams," where Moonlight Graham made his brief comeback as a player, but to Iowa City. Just when he was starting to wonder if he was ever going to get a real chance to play in the majors, he was one of five players dealt to Tampa Bay by the Cubs in a deal that sent starting pitcher Matt Garza to Chicago.

"I had gotten frustrated," Fuld said. "I felt stuck because the Cubs had contract obligations to guys who I thought I could play better than. One year I thought I had totally outplayed Reed Johnson, but he was making $3 million a year; I was making the minimum. If someone was going down, it was me.

"In a way, though, it helped me when I got to Tampa. I was out of [minor-league] options, so if they sent me down, they'd probably lose me. It also probably helped me focus a little more too—especially given a new chance to play."

Fuld not only made the Rays out of camp in 2011; he became a cult figure in Tampa within a month. His penchant for running into walls and making remarkable plays in the outfield got him on You-Tube often, and he had a game in Fenway Park—not that far from where he'd grown up—in which he had two doubles, a triple, and a homer. He blew his chance for the cycle in his last at-bat when he stretched a single into a double with his teammates screaming at him to stop at first base.

"Couldn't do it," he said. "It just wouldn't be me."

Once he became a major leaguer—someone people would listen to—Fuld saw part of his role to be a spokesman on behalf of diabetics. He talks often to other baseball players who deal with the disease, as well as to kids, largely to emphasize that while diabetes is part of one's life, it doesn't have to have a negative effect on one's life.

"I point out that it gave me discipline I might not have had otherwise," he said. "Everyone has things they have to overcome in life . . . this is mine. But I mean, seriously, do I have anything to complain about? I play baseball for a living; I have a wife, two beautiful kids. Are you kidding?"

That doesn't mean that he doesn't constantly monitor his blood sugar. "Ten minutes doesn't go by where I don't think about it," he said. "I make a play in the outfield, I'm on the bases, as soon as I get in the dugout, I check. After all these years, it's innate, part of who I am. I even tell people part of the reason I'm spacey is that I'm thinking about my levels. Sometimes that's true; other times I'm just using it as a crutch for spacing out."

Six times a day he uses a glucometer to prick his finger. His teammates tease him about it, which, he says, is a good thing. "In a baseball clubhouse anything that makes you different makes you a target," he said. "It's actually a good thing. I'm Jewish and I'm a diabetic, so that's two things that stand out."

He's also smart and educated. "Yeah, that too, I guess," he said. "Sometimes I dumb things down a little. At least that's what I tell the guys."

———

More often than not, rehab assignments cause headaches for managers and—to a lesser degree—players. Although every player in an organization is technically in the charge of the major-league team, those who are designated to a minor-league team are, for the most part, left in the hands of their manager. Pitchers being rested in case of a call-up are the one notable exception to that rule.

Montoyo had a simple approach when it came to rehab players: help only if asked; otherwise they're in the hands of the major-league-level decision makers.

He made one exception to his don't-mess-with-the-rehab-guys rule in 2012. Seeing Fuld working out by himself one day in searing late afternoon heat while the rest of the team was enjoying the cool of the clubhouse, he walked out to the warning track where Fuld was running.

"Sam, are you sure you aren't overdoing it?" he asked.

"I'm fine," Fuld said. "Need the work."

"It's really hot," Montoyo said.

"I know," Fuld said. "Isn't it great?"

Montoyo left him to his work.

Evan Longoria's arrival in Durham a few days later was another level of the don't-mess rule. Longoria was, by far, the biggest star in the Tampa organization. He arrived in Durham on July 25 to rehab after being out for almost three months with a partial tear in his left hamstring. Montoyo knew that all decisions on when he would play or not play would come from Tampa. Which was fine with him.

"You have to be really careful with the rehab guys," he said. "The last thing you want to do is ask them to do something they aren't ready to do and hurt themselves again." He laughed. "We had Matt Joyce down here in early July on rehab, and one night he's on first and he takes off for second on his own trying to steal the base. He's out by a mile, and then a few innings later he has to come out of the game. I let the front office know that night that he was running on his own. I certainly didn't send him."

As it turned out, Joyce, who was rehabbing a strained oblique muscle, had tweaked his back. Instead of doing two days of rehab and being activated in Tampa, as was the plan, he was on the DL for another eleven days. That's why Triple-A managers leave all rehab decisions to the guys making the big bucks.

Longoria had initially been slated to spend four or five days in Durham as a DH before returning to Tampa, where the team desperately needed his bat in the lineup. The notion that he would play third base again in 2012 had pretty much been given up on. As it turned out, he would need postseason surgery on the hamstring, surgery that would—the Rays hoped—get him to spring training completely healthy in February 2013. Fortunately, it did just that.

The Longoria who showed up in Durham could barely run at anything faster than a moderate walking pace. What the Rays wanted to see was whether he could hit—and the answer was yes. A week after he arrived, Montoyo got word that Longoria might sit out a game on a Sunday evening against Gwinnett. When Longoria arrived at the ballpark, he told Montoyo that he had consulted with Rays' trainer Ron Porterfield in Tampa and the decision was that he would play that night.

Which he did. In the first inning, he hit a majestic fly ball that looked as if it were going to be a long home run to left field. Except that the ball hit at the very top of the Blue Monster and kicked back into play. For some reason, Longoria hobbled around first and tried for a double, even though he would have needed a limo and a police escort to have any chance to beat the throw to second. He was out by at least twenty feet.

Two innings later he again crushed the ball, this time between left and center fields. Healthy, Longoria would have no doubt turned second and thought about trying for third. This time he played it smart and pulled up at first.

"God knows I only want him going one base at a time," Montoyo said later. "Imagine what would have happened if he'd been hurt trying to get to second in the first inning." He rolled his eyes. "Come to think of it, I'd rather *not* imagine it."

Longoria had played in Durham before—though not for long. He had been the No. 3 overall pick in the 2006 draft and had moved rapidly through the Rays' farm system, showing up in Durham late in the 2007 season—Montoyo's first year as manager. "As soon as I saw him, I knew he wasn't going to be around for more than a few weeks," he said, laughing.

Longoria actually began the 2008 season in Durham—another example of a major-league team planning on not calling up a star young player until June, thus giving the team an extra year before the player would be eligible for arbitration.

"I think they were probably thinking about not starting my arbitration clock," Longoria said. "I honestly thought it would be June before I got called up. Then I got a text from Jason Bartlett saying that Willy Aybar was hurt, that he had pulled a hamstring, and the word was they were going to call me up.

"We [Durham] had started the season on the road and come back here for the home opener. I was in the lineup and had just finished BP when Charlie came out and waved me into his office. The thought crossed my mind, but I didn't let myself think it. I sat down, and he just said, 'You're going up. Congratulations.'"

Longoria paused as he told the story and looked around. He was sitting in Montoyo's office in the exact same spot—perhaps the same chair—that he had been sitting in four years and four months earlier, when he had first found out he was going to the big leagues.

"I was actually a little nervous to come back down here," he said. "Let's face it, I'm not making $2,400 a month the way I was when I was last here. I'm not really a member of the team, although if I can get a few hits, that's bonus. But I'm here to get ABs and make sure the hamstring feels a little better every day."

He was staying at the upscale Washington Duke hotel, a few miles from the ballpark. The team pays per diem for a player on rehab that includes his hotel expenses. At this point in his life, Longoria had no trouble paying the difference between the per diem and the tab at the Washington Duke.

Even though ten months had passed since that remarkable September night, Longoria was still being glorified—justifiably—for his role in the Rays' historic victory in their 2011 season finale. Going into the last night of the regular season, the Rays had—astoundingly— tied the Boston Red Sox for the wild card spot in the American League, after being eight games behind earlier in the month.

But they trailed the Yankees 7–0 in the eighth inning while, in Baltimore, the Red Sox had a 3–2 lead going into the ninth inning. It looked as if Tampa Bay's late-season rally would fall one game short.

And then, in what felt like a blink of an eye, everything changed. The Rays scored six runs in the eighth, highlighted by a three-run Longoria home run, to close the gap to 7–6. They then tied the game with two outs in the ninth inning on a home run by little-used pinch hitter Dan Johnson, who had spent most of the season in Durham.

On the game went, into the tenth, eleventh, and twelfth innings. Because there had been a rain delay of an hour and twenty-four minutes in Baltimore, the Red Sox and Orioles were still playing. While the Yankees were batting in the twelfth inning, the Red Sox sent in their lights-out closer, Jonathan Papelbon, to finish the game in Baltimore in the ninth. Papelbon quickly got two outs. In Tampa, the

Rays were scoreboard watching—staring obsessively would be more accurate—figuring they had to win to create a one-game playoff the next day.

"We had actually been thinking that all night," Longoria said. "To us it was a must-win game to stay alive and play [the Red Sox] the next day. When we were down 7–0, it looked pretty bleak since they were winning. When we tied it, we had hope—but we were still thinking we were playing to stay tied with them. I don't think the thought crossed anyone's mind that we could win and advance right then and there."

The clock struck midnight with both games still going on: the Rays were in the process of escaping a first-and-second-no-one-out jam in the top of the twelfth, and Papelbon was trying to get the final out in Baltimore.

Papelbon never succeeded. Chris Davis doubled. Seconds later Nolan Reimold also doubled, and suddenly—stunningly—the score was tied and the winning run was on second base. Less than a minute later, the winning run, in the person of Reimold, was sliding across the plate after Robert Andino hit a bloop to left field that Carl Crawford couldn't reach before it dropped. Crawford's weak throw home was nowhere close, and in a shocking turnaround the Orioles were celebrating as if *they* had won the wild card while the Red Sox trudged to their dugout knowing they now needed the Yankees to win to keep their season alive.

It was 12:02 when Reimold scored to give the Orioles the win. At 12:04 the score was posted inside Tropicana Field, and the crowd went crazy. Longoria had just stepped into the batter's box with one out in the bottom of the twelfth.

"I had to step out for a second to gather myself because seeing that score go up was kind of a shock," he said. "I needed a minute to take a deep breath."

He used it well. On a 2-2 count, Yankee reliever Scott Proctor threw a fastball on the inside part of the plate, and Longoria crushed it on a rope down the line, headed toward the low barrier in left field. It looked a lot like the shot Mark McGwire had hit in 1998 for his historic and steroid-aided sixty-second home run. The ball just cleared the fence as pandemonium broke loose in Tampa.

"It was all a little surreal the way everything happened so fast in that last inning," Longoria said ten months later. "It was one of those things that will be tough to repeat. People still stop me in the street to talk about it, and it's still cool to me."

On this sultry evening in Durham, Longoria was a long way from that home run, but he was even farther from where he had been in his previous lifetime in Durham at $2,400 a month.

Not long after the 2012 season ended, just a few weeks after his twenty-seventh birthday, Longoria signed a contract extension that guaranteed he would be with the Rays at least through 2022 and would be paid at least $136 million.

In short, if he ever landed back in Durham on rehab, he could rent out not just one suite of the Washington Duke—but the entire hotel.

24

Slice of Life

CHARLOTTE

Evan Longoria's walk-off home run was one of those baseball moments that will be replayed for years to prove just how dramatic the game can be at its very best.

But it wouldn't have happened if not for Dan Johnson. And, in truth, what Johnson did was far more stunning than what Longoria did. Longoria is a star, a multimillion-dollar player. If you were casting the hero of a baseball movie, he would have Longoria's profile.

Not so much Dan Johnson.

While Longoria was being given the royal treatment in Durham, Johnson was playing two and a half hours down I-85 in Triple-A Charlotte. Actually, he was playing two miles into South Carolina, just off I-77 in Fort Mill, South Carolina, which was where Knights Stadium was located.

"Right now that night in Tampa feels like it was a long time ago," Johnson said shortly after batting practice one evening. "I really believed going into this season that if I stayed healthy I'd be playing in Chicago. Well, I've stayed healthy . . ."

But staying healthy had not gotten him a roster spot with the White Sox, the team he had signed with after being released by the Rays. And so, he found himself playing every day, as he had hoped—but in Charlotte, not as he had hoped. The only games he had missed

had been when manager Joel Skinner rested him, kicking and screaming because he hated missing even one day in the lineup.

"Look at that wind," he said, sitting in the dugout in Norfolk on
a warm August afternoon on one of the 7 days (of 144) that he wasn't
on Skinner's lineup card. "Blowing straight out to right field. Perfect
night for me and I'm going to be watching."

He had spent some time in Skinner's office earlier that afternoon
pleading his case. Skinner wasn't budging. The Knights were comfortably in first place, and he wanted to keep all his players fresh for the
August stretch run and the September playoffs. That said, Skinner
was hoping Johnson wouldn't be around for the playoffs.

"He's been good every day," he said. "He could definitely help in
Chicago in September. If nothing else, his history says he's a guy you
want around when the games get tense."

Johnson's history as a clutch hitter was remarkable—all the more
so because he had been hounded by injuries almost from the time he
first made it to the major leagues in 2005.

Until then, his career had stayed on a consistent upward curve.
He had grown up in Blaine, Minnesota, a town of about twenty thou-
sand people, where hockey was far more popular than baseball. But
Johnson had always wanted to be a baseball player.

"I played hockey, liked hockey, wasn't bad at hockey," he said.
"But I remember telling my first-grade teacher I wanted to be a baseball player. It was just what I always wanted to do."

Even though the baseball season wasn't very long in Blaine, Johnson was good enough to be recruited by a number of Division I schools.
At one point he thought about going to Iowa State but made a last-
second decision to go to Butler. He was an all-conference player as a
freshman but left after one year to transfer to Iowa Western Community College.

"Too much academics at Butler," he said, smiling. "Being honest,
I knew I wanted to play baseball, and at Butler you spend a lot of time
in class and studying. I wanted to focus more on baseball."

After a year at Iowa Western, he transferred to Nebraska, where he played well enough to be drafted in the seventh round by the Oakland Athletics. In 2005, after a sizzling start at Sacramento, he got called to the majors, where he was the starting first baseman for most of the season, hitting .275 with fifteen home runs and fifty-eight RBIs. He went into 2006 penciled in as the starting first baseman.

That was when the injury bug bit him. Or, more specifically, got in his eyes. He was cleaning out his locker at the end of spring training when he found an old tube of suntan lotion. "I was carrying a bunch of stuff into the training room to dump, and I didn't realize it was open. Some of it got into my right eye. I didn't know it at the time, but it chemically burned the eye. After a while I realized my tear ducts were affected—I couldn't cry. I could still see well enough to hit an occasional fastball, but that was about it."

He was hitting .237 when he got sent down to Sacramento, and it wasn't until after the season that he went to the Arizona Eye Institute and got a proper diagnosis. That allowed him to report to spring training in 2007 completely healthy. It didn't last. Late in a spring training game he got his foot stepped on at first base, and when he twisted in pain, he tore the labrum in his hip. Back to the disabled list. He came back to have a reasonably good season—eighteen home runs, sixty-two runs batted in—but a year later the A's re-acquired Frank Thomas, who could only play first base or DH—which left Johnson as the odd man out. The A's released him in April, and the Rays signed him and sent him to Durham, where he spent most of the season.

At the end of that year his agent came to him with an offer: a Japanese team was willing to pay him $1.2 million—which was almost four times the money he was making on a split contract with the Rays and more than double what he had made in Oakland.

"I jumped at it," he said. "All I asked was, 'When do I leave?' That's the kind of money that changes your life."

Some American players thrive in Japan. Johnson wasn't one of them. He thought the strike zone was too big and felt as if umpires went out of their way to make it even larger when he was at the plate.

"Late in the season one of the umpires told my interpreter that I was just now at the point where I had paid my dues, so they were going to be fair to me.

"I hit twenty-four home runs, but I struck out a lot. It also seemed like I would suddenly be on the bench when I got close to numbers where incentive bonuses kicked in. My family enjoyed it there. I just didn't enjoy the baseball very much. By the end of the season I knew I wanted to come home—regardless of the money."

He re-signed with the Rays for 2010, knowing he would be sent to Durham at the start of the season. Aided, no doubt, by a smaller strike zone, he was having a monster season when he was called up to the Rays in August. In ninety-eight games in Durham he hit thirty home runs, drove in ninety-five runs, and was hitting .303 when the call back to the majors finally came. Although he didn't hit for average down the stretch, he continued to hit for power, hitting seven home runs and driving in twenty-three runs in the last six weeks.

His return to good health, and his combined thirty-seven home runs and 118 RBIs in the majors and minors earned him a one-year $1 million contract with the Rays for 2011. The Rays had lost Carlos Peña, their starting first baseman, to the Cubs in free agency, and it looked as if there would be plenty of playing time for Johnson.

"It was all set up for me—finally," said Johnson, who was thirty-one on opening day of the 2011 season. "I was healthy, I had a good contract with the potential to get a better one, and I was finally solidified in the lineup."

The season started well. On April 8, Johnson hit a three-run, eighth-inning home run with the Rays trailing the White Sox 7–6 that proved to be the game winner. That was a continuation of his knack for getting big hits in big spots. In 2008, shortly after being called up to the Rays, he had hit a walk-off home run in a pivotal September game against the Red Sox. He had done the same thing against the same team late in 2010 after that season's call-up from Durham.

But the good start—and the good health—didn't last. Six days after the home run against the White Sox, he was hit in the hand by a ninety-six-mile-an-hour fastball thrown by Twins closer Matt Capps. "He nailed me with it," Johnson said. "It really squared me up. But I figured it would just be sore for a couple of days and that would be it. Nothing was broken."

The injury appeared to be just what Johnson had thought— a painful bruise and nothing more. Johnson kept playing. But he had no power, and as his batting average slipped, he got anxious at the plate. His ability to draw walks and not swing at bad pitches had always been a strength. Now he wasn't walking very often (he went from walking once every thirteen at-bats to once every twenty-one at-bats), and his batting average dropped like a stone.

"I wanted to play through it," Johnson said. "The doctor told me I'd gotten hit on a nerve and it was kind of a use-it-or-lose-it deal. I could play or I could have major surgery and hope it got fixed. I wanted to play. But I literally couldn't control my hand when it was on the bat. It just wasn't strong enough."

He was sent down to Durham in May, and things didn't improve. "It got to the point where I couldn't carry groceries in from the car," he said. "So I went for another MRI."

This time he was told that the hand would heal on its own but it could be a couple of months or it could be a couple of years. "That was scary," he said. "I was in the twilight zone."

As the summer wore on, the hand began to feel better. He managed to hit thirteen home runs in Durham and was a September call-up to Tampa. By then, Casey Kotchman had established himself as the starting first baseman, and Johnson was used sparingly as a pinch hitter. That was his role on the last night of the season with the Rays tied with the Red Sox for the wild card spot.

Sam Fuld had pinch-hit for catcher Kelly Shoppach in the bottom of the eighth and drawn a two-out, bases-loaded walk to cut the Yankees' lead to 7–1. "At the time I didn't think much of it," Fuld said. "I mean, we were still so far behind, but at least we had a chance right there to cut into the margin."

By the end of the inning, Longoria had hit his three-run home run, and the margin was down to 7–6. As the Rays came to bat in the bottom of the ninth, manager Joe Maddon told Johnson he would bat fifth in the inning if the Rays could get that far.

"I went up to the [indoor batting] cage to get some swings and get loose," he said. "I wasn't there for very long when one of the security guys came in and said, 'Hey, Dan, you're up.'"

Yankees reliever Cory Wade had needed only eight pitches to retire Ben Zobrist on a fly ball and Kotchman on a weak grounder to third. Down to his last out, Maddon decided to push all his chips in and bring up a power hitter, Johnson, to hit for a line-drive hitter, Fuld.

Johnson sprinted down the runway, grabbed a bat, and walked into the cauldron of noise that Tropicana Field was at that moment. Because the Trop is, without question, major-league baseball's worst venue, the Rays almost never sell out—even in a pennant race—and this game was no exception. A crowd of 29,518 was in the ballpark, but they were all now on their feet believing that if Johnson, who was hitting .108 for the season in the major leagues, didn't get on base, the Rays' season would be over since the Red Sox were still winning in Baltimore at that moment.

Johnson had not hit a major-league home run since the three-run shot against the White Sox on April 8. He was comforted somewhat by the sight of Wade on the mound. "I'd played with him in the minors during the season," he said. "I knew he liked to throw his changeup as an out pitch, and I figured at some point I would see one."

Wade had been in Durham until the Rays had released him in June and he had signed with the Yankees, who had sent him to Scranton/Wilkes-Barre until calling him up in September.

The count went to 2-2. The noise was overwhelming. Johnson almost didn't hear it.

"I'm not sure why, but when I get in situations like that, a kind of calm comes over me," he said. "That's the way I had felt in those other situations when I'd hit walk-off homers—very calm."

On the next pitch, Johnson was convinced that Wade would try to get him out with a changeup. He guessed right. Wade threw a changeup high in the zone but on the outside of the plate, or maybe a little bit outside. Johnson swung at it anyway.

"I figured I would hit it hard and, in all likelihood, it would go foul. Ninety-nine times out of a hundred if you swing at a changeup away you're going to pull it foul."

This was the hundredth time. The ball was hooking as it headed in the direction of the right-field stands, and Johnson, watching it, was convinced it would go foul. It didn't—crashing into the foul pole as everyone in the ballpark stared at it in disbelief. Stunned, Johnson rounded the bases and was pummeled by his teammates when he reached home plate.

"I had my jersey torn off; I was pounded, hit, punched; I think I was black-and-blue by the time I got to the dugout," he said. "It was the best feeling I've ever had."

Three innings later, Longoria's home run ended the game. Although most of the postgame and postseason attention was focused on Longoria, Johnson became something of a cult figure and won a number of awards for the most dramatic moment of the 2011 season.

That didn't mean he had a place to play in 2012. Baseball is not a sentimental sport—especially when it comes to front-office decisions. Kotchman, who had hit .306 after taking the first-base job when Johnson was sent down, signed with the Indians—getting the kind of contract ($3 million) that Johnson had hoped he would get for 2012. The Rays, still uncertain about Johnson's hand, decided to bring back Carlos Peña, who had hit twenty-eight home runs in Chicago. That left the hero of September 28 looking for a job before Christmas.

He finally signed a split contract with the White Sox, who were looking for some insurance at first base and at DH after Adam Dunn had been through one of the most miserable seasons any legitimate player had ever had in baseball history. After averaging forty home runs for the previous eight seasons, Dunn had signed with the White Sox prior to 2011 for four years and $56 million. He had hit .159 for the year and—uninjured—had hit only eleven home runs. Not knowing what to expect from Dunn, the White Sox signed Johnson.

"I had a good spring," Johnson said. "My hand was finally okay, and I had my power back. I really thought I was going to be on the club as a first baseman and a DH."

He thought that until he got the call into first-year manager Robin Ventura's office. Ventura told him he was being sent to Charlotte. He was stunned.

"I vented; I let him know how I felt," Johnson said. "I told him I thought the question was whether I was healthy or not and I thought I'd shown them that I was healthy. He nodded and explained to me what they were thinking and gave me the line you always hear: 'If anything happens . . .'" He paused. "Robin's a good guy. I probably let it out the way I did in part because I was frustrated, but also because I wanted him to know I still had the drive."

Going to the minor-league camp was difficult. It wasn't just the crowded room or the stares he got from young players who had seen replays of his home run dozens of times. It was finding himself, at the age of thirty-two, being told he *had* to wear sunglasses in the outfield during batting practice; he had to be clean shaven at all times; his uniform had to be neat and tucked in at all times. Many teams— not all—insist on their minor leaguers being clean shaven and neatly dressed.

"I understand that, especially in camp, you aren't trying to win games, you're trying to teach young players how to win," Johnson said. "I'm not a young player who is learning anymore. It was difficult because of that . . . and because I didn't think I belonged there."

He had put aside his frustration and had played well throughout the spring and summer in Charlotte. He was used to playing on winning teams—at both the major-league and the minor-league levels— and he brought that approach to the Knights' clubhouse.

"The only thing that's tough is giving him a day off," Skinner said. "He doesn't want one. To him, every day is a chance to win a game and show people what he can do."

That was why Johnson kept after Skinner on that August day in Norfolk when he decided to rest him.

"If I was really upset about it, I'd go in and close the door," Johnson said. "Would I rather play? Of course I would. The only thing worse than playing in Triple-A is *not* playing in Triple-A. The only way for me to get another chance is to show people I can still play the game, still hit the ball." He stood up, picked up the bat that he'd been holding, and took a stance. "I can't show them I can still play sitting in the dugout."

On September 1, Johnson was called up to the White Sox. The next night, playing in place of Dunn, he came to the plate against Detroit's Max Scherzer for his first major-league at-bat since The Home Run almost a year earlier. He popped out to short left field but singled later in the game. He played sparingly throughout the month as the White Sox failed to hold on to their division lead against the onrushing Tigers.

On the last day of the season, with the pennant race over, Ventura gave Johnson another start. He hit three home runs, drove in five runs, and finished his major-league season hitting .364 in just twenty-two at-bats.

On November 30, the White Sox, feeling safe after a solid comeback season by Dunn, released him.

It was time—again—to try to find a job. There are no guarantees in baseball—even for heroes.

25

Podsednik

HOT STREAK

Scott Podsednik could certainly attest to the lack of guarantees in baseball. After all, he had been a World Series hero in Chicago in 2005 ... and was released two years later. He had played superbly in Phillies camp in spring training in 2012 ... and had been sent to Lehigh Valley. He had played poorly there and been traded to Pawtucket, and on May 23—six weeks after thinking his baseball career might be over—he walked into the visiting clubhouse in Baltimore, checked manager Bobby Valentine's lineup card, and saw his name penciled into the eighth spot in the batting order, starting and playing right field.

"I've heard guys who have been in the majors for a while and then gone down say that getting back is as gratifying as the first time you've been there, and I know now that's true," he said. "The thing is, when it happened, even though I hadn't played well at Lehigh Valley, I felt I deserved it and that I was good enough to still contribute.

"I wasn't nervous, because I felt like I belonged up there. I was excited but not nervous."

When he had gotten the call from Pawtucket to join the team in Baltimore, Podsednik had been out of the big leagues for a year and a half—since September 2010—when he had hurt his foot playing for the Dodgers. After he had spent all of 2011 either in the minors or hurt, and started 2012 at home thinking about retiring, to be back in the majors at the age of thirty-six was no small thing.

"You do appreciate things as you get older," he said. "It took me a while to get to the majors the first time around, and longer to become an everyday player. I've had a lot of injuries I've had to fight through. I just didn't want to walk away bitter. If I had quit without going to Lehigh Valley, or if I'd quit while I was there and not playing well, I would have gone out as one of those bitter guys in Triple-A who told people he could still play but couldn't prove it. Now at least I get a chance to find out if I'm right—that I can still play major-league ball."

Podsednik was in the majors because the Red Sox' starting outfield had been hammered by injuries: Jacoby Ellsbury and Carl Crawford were on the sixty-day disabled list, and Cody Ross had just broken a foot, leading to Podsednik's call-up. Podsednik knew that all of them were going to have places in the lineup waiting for them when healthy. That wasn't his concern. Proving to the Red Sox—or someone else watching—that he belonged in the majors was his concern.

Which is exactly what he did. On his first day back in a major-league lineup, Podsednik homered in a 6–5 Red Sox victory. A day later he was leading off. The next four weeks brought back memories of his best days in Chicago. Seeing that he could still steal a base, Valentine often moved him to the leadoff spot, slotting him in the lineup in the outfield wherever he fit best on a given day.

After nineteen games in Boston, Podsednik was hitting an eye-popping .387 and had stolen six bases—putting him on pace to steal about fifty if he were to play an entire season. On the Red Sox, fifty stolen bases is often considered a good *decade*.

But the injury bug bit yet again.

On June 17—Father's Day—the Red Sox played a Sunday night game in Chicago against the Cubs. Podsednik led off the game with a single to center field and scored a moment later on a Dustin Pedroia double. But in the third inning, running out a ground ball to shortstop, he felt something pull in his groin on the left side. He said nothing about it because the last thing he wanted was to come out of a game. He hoped it was just a tweak and it would loosen up as the evening wore on.

It didn't. In the fifth, Podsednik came up with one out and a runner on first base and hit a hard ground ball to second base. Trying to bust out of the batter's box to avoid a double play, he realized he couldn't push off on the leg at all. He could barely jog to first base, allowing the Cubs to complete an easy double play. Seeing that he was hurt, Valentine sent Daniel Nava to play center field in his place in the bottom of the inning.

The next day the Boston media reported the groin pull as "mild" and quoted Podsednik as saying, "I just tweaked it. Nothing serious. I'll be fine."

There is no such thing as a mild groin strain—especially for a player whose game is dependent on his legs. Two days later, Podsednik went on the disabled list just as Cody Ross was coming off it. Ellsbury and Crawford weren't too far away from playing, so Podsednik knew his future in Boston was suddenly in doubt—regardless of his batting average or his play.

"It was discouraging," Podsednik said. "In a lot of ways it's been the story of my career. If you check, you'll see that whenever I'm healthy, I produce. The only thing that's really stopped me is getting hurt." He smiled. "Unfortunately, that's happened a lot. In this case, the timing couldn't have been much worse."

Podsednik was ready to come off the DL on July 6, nineteen days after his injury. By then, Ross was back in the lineup and Nava was playing well. Ellsbury was rehabbing and would be back in Boston within a week; Crawford wasn't far behind. And so Podsednik was reactivated and sent immediately back to Pawtucket. This time, though, he wasn't as discouraged as he had been at the end of spring training.

"They knew what I could do," he said. "Scouts had seen what I could do. The trading deadline was only a few weeks away. I took the approach that there was a good chance something would happen, either in Boston or with someone else, by the end of July. I wasn't happy to go back, but I told myself it wasn't going to be long. I just had to show people I was healthy—again."

Podsednik played solidly in Pawtucket, hitting .281 and stealing four more bases in twenty-five games. His theory turned out to be right: something did happen by the end of July. On the thirty-first, just prior to the trading deadline, the Red Sox traded him along with pitcher Matt Albers to Arizona for Craig Breslow, a relief pitcher they thought could help their bullpen.

Podsednik was ready to get on a plane and head to Phoenix when he got a call from his agent, Ryan Gleichowski. "They want you to report to Reno," he said. "They want you in Triple-A."

This was one of those baseball trades that made little sense. Basically, the two teams had swapped relievers. Podsednik had been thrown into the deal for no apparent reason except perhaps that the Red Sox figured with their outfield now healthy he was no longer needed.

When Gleichowski told Podsednik the Diamondbacks wanted him in Reno, his reaction was quick and it was firm: "No. I'm not going out there to play in Triple-A."

Since he had been in the majors during the season and the contract he had signed with the Phillies allowed him to opt out if he was in the minors anytime after June 1, he wasn't violating his contract by refusing to report.

Gleichowski asked Podsednik what he wanted him to do. "Call around, see what's out there," Podsednik told him. "I'll wait here."

He still had the apartment he had rented in Boston. Lisa and the kids had been with him in June and July. On August 2, at Podsednik's request, the Diamondbacks released him.

The family headed back to Boston and waited to see if the phone would ring.

26

Ron Johnson

REAL LIFE GETS SERIOUS

Dan Johnson did get back into the lineup in Norfolk, the day after Charlotte manager Joel Skinner insisted that he sit out. As he sat and watched from the dugout that evening, his team cruised to a 12–3 win that was often cringe-worthy for the home team.

The Tides were brutal. They gave up one run when catcher Luis Exposito could not successfully throw the ball back to his pitcher. The throw ticked off the glove of Pedro Viola while Charlotte runners on second and third each moved up a base.

"That's it," the Tides' Dave Rosenfield said as he watched his team fail to execute a catcher-to-pitcher toss. "It's time to go home."

Sadly for Rosenfield and the Tides, it was only the fifth inning.

The next day, it rained most of the morning and afternoon in Norfolk. It was a get-away day, both teams needing to travel as soon as the five o'clock game was over. The Knights had a relatively easy three-hour trip to Durham. The Tides had to travel 543 miles to get to Gwinnett—which would take almost nine hours.

"Everything goes well, we get in about six in the morning," Tides manager Ron Johnson said. He shrugged and repeated his Triple-A mantra: "If you don't like it, play better and get out of the minor leagues."

Johnson was an expert on life in the minor leagues. He had left Fresno State in 1978 to sign with the Kansas City Royals after being drafted in the twenty-fourth round and had spent most of the past thirty-four years in the minors. Three times during his playing career he'd made it to the majors. In 1982 he was in Kansas City for eight games. A year later, he was back for nine more games. The following year, after being traded to Montreal, he made it to the Expos for five games. In all, he played in twenty-two games and had twelve hits in forty-six at-bats for a .261 career average. He also drove in two runs.

"I guess you could say I'm in the twilight of a mediocre career," he said, laughing—something he does often. "Honestly, I'm quite proud of the fact that I made it to the majors even if it wasn't for very long."

Johnson had been a football star in high school and could have played Division I college football but chose baseball instead. At fifty-six, he still has the look of an old football player. He was six feet three, 215 pounds during his playing days but is probably closer to 240 now. A large tattoo juts out from under his uniform jersey, and he's the kind of person who comes straight at you—which makes him the perfect manager to work for Rosenfield, who is exactly the same way.

"There's no BS at all in RJ," said Rosenfield. "It makes life a lot simpler for everyone when someone is like that—especially down here."

Johnson made the transition from player to minor-league manager bumpily after he quit playing prior to the 1986 season. He was living in Florida, working for his then wife's father in his carpet store, and hating every minute of it. "Fish out of water," he said. "Absolutely wasn't for me."

Since he was living not far from where the Royals trained, Johnson showed up one day at training camp to see some old friends from his playing days. He ran into John Schuerholz, then the Royals' general manager, and, on a whim, asked him if there might be a job for him in the Royals' front office.

Schuerholz told him no, there wasn't anything open and that he saw him more as a coach than as a front-office person. He recommended he call John Boles, who was then the Royals' farm director, and let him know he might be interested in a job. Boles didn't have anything open but told Johnson he'd keep him in mind. Thinking he had struck out, Johnson went back to work for his father-in-law. A couple of months later, Boles called. He was coming to town to see the Royals' Class A team play. Maybe they could get together.

"They'd lost their hitting coach," Johnson said. "John offered it to me. The next day I was in uniform."

He's been in uniform ever since. He coached for six years before getting his first managing job, with the same Class A Royals team where he had been first hired to coach. The team was based in what was then known as Baseball City, Florida—just outside Orlando. He had moved up to the Triple-A job in Omaha before Allard Baird, who had become the Royals' assistant general manager, cleaned house prior to the 2000 season. After eight years managing Royals minor leaguers, the last two in Omaha, Johnson was among those cleaned out.

He hooked on with the Red Sox as the manager at Class A Sarasota.

"I felt like I was back to square one," Johnson said. "I thought the whole thing was unfair. There I was a step away from the majors, and all of a sudden I'm back in the Florida State League, where they play every afternoon in hundred-degree heat in front of five fans.

"I'd always had good teams managing for the Royals. They had a lot of young talent in the organization. I'd managed [Carlos] Beltrán and [Johnny] Damon and [Kevin] Appier and a bunch of other good players. So I won a lot. I wasn't doing very much to make them better players, but I was winning—so I thought I was doing a good job.

"About halfway through my first season [working for the Red Sox] in Sarasota, Dave Jauss [who was then the Red Sox' minor-league field coordinator] called to say he was in town and let's go out to eat. I remember we went out and ate wings and he totally blew me up. I was expecting to get a woe-is-you talk, and he basically looked me in the eye and said, 'You've been terrible.'"

Johnson laughed. "We all think we're unique in baseball—like no one else has ever been fired. Hey, we *all* get fired. That's the norm. I wasn't doing the things I needed to do as a minor-league manager, especially at that level, where teaching and developing is so important. I can honestly say it wasn't until then that I felt like I had any idea what it takes to be a good minor-league manager."

Lesson learned—without getting fired—Johnson began climbing the ladder again, this time with a different approach to the job. By 2005 he was in Pawtucket, and after five solid seasons there he got the call he had often thought would never come: The Red Sox had an opening on their staff because Brad Mills had been hired to manage in Houston. Terry Francona offered him the job as first-base coach in 2010.

"Dream come true," Johnson said. "Let's face it, there's no comparison between life in the minors and life in the big leagues."

And then the dream became a nightmare.

———

Most baseball fans now know the basics of the story: On August 1, 2010, the Red Sox were hosting the Detroit Tigers on a Sunday afternoon in Fenway Park. The Red Sox won a tight 4–3 game, and as they came up the runway, traveling secretary Jack McCormick was in his usual spot, just outside the clubhouse, waiting for Terry Francona and the coaches.

Baseball is so much about ritual. McCormick's postgame ritual after a win was to stand by the door and give the manager and his coaches a high five as they walked past him. Francona was the first person to realize something was wrong when he put up his hand for his high five and McCormick looked right through him. A moment later, Johnson arrived and saw that McCormick was holding a phone in his hand. He could tell by the expression on his face that something was terribly wrong.

"I remember thinking, 'I hope that phone isn't for me,'" Johnson said two years later, the memory still clearly vivid. "Before I could even say, 'John, what's wrong?' he handed the phone to me and said, 'Call Daphane. Right now.'"

Ron and Daphane Johnson have now been together for twenty-five years. They met when Johnson, a country music buff, was giving dancing lessons in a country music bar near where he lived in Tennessee. Daphane came in one night, and, as Johnson puts it, "We got to two-stepping and the rest is history."

They have a total of five children, two from Daphane's first marriage and three of their own. That afternoon, the two youngest children, Cheyanne, who was fourteen, and Bridget, who was eleven days away from turning eleven, were riding their horses from their farm to a neighbor's house to go swimming. Both girls were outstanding riders—all the Johnsons are expert riders. They were rounding a curve on Cooper Road, right near a sign put there by those who live in the area that says, PLEASE DRIVE SLOW, WE LOVE OUR CHILDREN, when they had to cross the road.

Cheyanne made it across safely. Bridget did not. A car came around the curve traveling, according to the police report, at forty-two miles per hour—the speed limit was thirty-five. According to what the driver told police, he didn't see Bridget because he was distracted by Cheyanne. He hit Bridget head-on, sending her and the horse flying.

What happened in the next few minutes is difficult for Johnson to describe even now. Bridget's left leg was severed. As she lay on the road in a pool of blood, another neighbor, who was not that far behind the driver who hit Bridget, jumped from his car and worked to stanch the bleeding while Cheyanne called her mother. Paramedics were called in, and seventeen minutes later Bridget was in a helicopter en route to Vanderbilt University Children's Hospital.

Ron Johnson knew none of this because he was on the field in Boston and his cell phone was in his locker. Unable to reach anyone with the game going on, Daphane finally called the Red Sox' switchboard, explained who she was, and was put through to McCormick.

When his wife told him what had happened, Johnson asked her one question: "Is she going to live?"

"I don't know" was the honest answer.

He told Francona and general manager Theo Epstein what had happened, and they had McCormick arrange to get him to the airport and on a plane as soon as possible. Francona later said that when Johnson told him what had occurred, he almost became physically ill.

McCormick had Johnson on a flight out of Logan Airport within an hour. The problem was he had to go through Detroit to get to Nashville. There was no other way. Naturally, Johnson got stuck in Detroit. "They had the plane there but no pilots," he said. "I was, to put it mildly, a complete wreck."

The airport was virtually empty on a Sunday night, and he sat in a small coffee shop waiting for the flight. There was no news from Nashville except that Bridget was in surgery. While he sipped on some coffee, a man came up to him looking, Johnson said, "as if he was straight out of the '70s."

"Are you okay?" the man asked. "You look terrible."

Johnson told him briefly what was going on.

"He looked me in the eye and said, 'Your daughter's going to be okay.' Then he asked for my cell number because he said Rick Allen was a good friend of his and he wanted to put him in touch with me. I had no idea who Rick Allen was, but the guy seemed like a good guy, so I gave him the number."

The guy in the coffee shop turned out to be Donny Clark, a close friend of Allen—the Def Leppard drummer who had lost an arm in a car accident in 1984 and had continued his career playing with one arm. Once he got to Nashville, Johnson forgot about the encounter and was baffled by the texts he kept receiving from someone named Rick. When he finally remembered the guy in the airport, he asked his teenage son Christian if he had any idea who Rick Allen was.

"Of course he was amazed that I had no idea who he was," Johnson said. "What do you think the chances are of my running into Donny Clark that way at that moment?"

It was two in the morning before Johnson made it to the hospital. Bridget was out of surgery but was asleep. "We went in and Daphane said, 'Bridget, Daddy's here,' and her eyes flickered open," Johnson said softly.

His daughter's first words that night stayed with him: "Daddy, don't go."

"Honey, I'm not leaving, I'm not walking out of this hospital until you do" was his answer.

He didn't leave the hospital for the next thirty-four days. Every night Daphane would go to get some sleep in a hotel across the street (that the Red Sox paid for), and Johnson slept in a chair next to his daughter's bed. "I didn't ever want her to wake up alone," he said.

The most difficult moment of Bridget's hospital stay might have come when Ron and Daphane had to tell her that her horse had died in the aftermath of the accident. "She dealt with so much physical pain," Johnson said, eyes welling again. "The emotional pain of losing the horse was, without doubt, the toughest thing she dealt with."

The Red Sox, led by Kevin Youkilis, who had played for Johnson at Pawtucket and still credits him with helping make him a major leaguer, raised money to help Johnson deal with all the expenses that were still to come. Other baseball teams—including the Yankees— literally passed the hat in their clubhouses to raise money. Cards, texts, letters, poured in from all over.

The doctors couldn't save Bridget's leg below the knee but told her she would ride horses again and could be fitted for a prosthetic in a few months. To this day, Johnson chokes up when he talks about the outpouring that came from the Red Sox and all of baseball.

The only time his voice hardens is when he talks about the man whose car hit his daughter.

"It was an accident, I understand that," he said, the words coming more slowly as he spoke. "The police never explained to me why there was no sobriety test at the scene. I thought that was standard in that kind of situation. I have no idea if he was drinking or not.

"What I do know is that he never called, he never asked to come and see Bridget. One card—he sent one card—and that was it. After she came home, still nothing. He lives so close I can see his house from my barn. For a long time I had trouble letting go of that. It took a lot of talk and a lot of counseling to get to the point where I could just say to myself, 'Let him live in his own personal hell, we've moved on.'

"I've done that now. Bridget is doing great. Her prosthetic has been great, she's back riding horses regularly, she's just a terrific and happy kid. It was a horrible, awful thing we lived through, but we lived through it. Most important, she lived through it."

Johnson can't talk enough about the way the Red Sox treated him in the aftermath of the accident—not only financially, but with constant moral and emotional support. He didn't return to the team for the rest of the 2010 season, and Theo Epstein told him if he wanted to take 2011 off with full pay, that was fine with him and with the club.

Johnson chose to go back to work in 2011. Bridget was back in school and doing fine, and he was a baseball guy. For most of the season, the Red Sox appeared to be a lock for the playoffs. Then came the collapse that set up the home runs by Dan Johnson and Evan Longoria that sealed Boston's fate on the last night of the season.

Two days later, Terry Francona—who had managed the Red Sox to two World Series titles in eight seasons and had helped break the Red Sox' dreaded "Curse of the Bambino" in 2004—"resigned." He and the team had agreed that the option on his contract for 2012 would not be picked up.

Johnson knew his days in Boston were numbered even before Francona was let go. "You go into the last month of the season with an eight-game lead and don't make the playoffs, heads are going to roll, especially in a market like Boston," he said. "Once Tito [Francona] left, I was pretty certain it was just a matter of time for me."

The time was six days. After what he had been through the year before, getting fired hardly seemed catastrophic to Johnson. Disappointing certainly—he'd been in the Red Sox organization for twelve years—but hardly something he couldn't handle. He went home and thought about taking a season off from the game to spend more time with his family.

That notion lasted about six weeks. In early November, soon after Dan Duquette had been named as the new general manager of the Baltimore Orioles, Johnson's phone rang. It was Duquette, who had hired Johnson to manage in the Red Sox' system when he had been the general manager there in 2000. Now he wanted to know if Johnson would like to manage in Norfolk.

It meant going back to the minor leagues—to the long bus trips, the roadside motels, and the 4:00 a.m. wake-ups to deal with airport security for a commercial flight. But Johnson didn't have to think about it twice. "I'm in," he said.

The 2012 season had been hectic, especially since four of the five pitchers who had been in the Orioles' rotation at the start of the season had been sent to Norfolk during the season—not because of rehab assignments, but because they hadn't pitched well enough.

"Buck and I have a routine," Johnson said, talking about Orioles manager Buck Showalter, who almost always called him directly when he was thinking about a call-up or sending someone down. "He calls and says, 'RJ, you got a minute?' I just say, 'What do you need?' and then he asks me what I think. We're usually on the same page, but every once in a while he wants to try something different. I don't argue. He's the boss."

In the background, as Johnson talked about Showalter, his office television was tuned to the game between the Orioles and the Tigers that was going on in Detroit. Johnson was watching with more than passing interest at that moment. Wei-Yin Chen, the Orioles' starter that afternoon, had been jumped on for five runs in the first inning.

"He comes out early, and Buck has to stretch the bullpen out; he's going to be on the phone in a couple of hours looking for a pitcher," Johnson said. "The good news is whoever it is will get out of the bus trip to Gwinnett."

He looked away from the game for a moment and saw Joel Skinner, the Charlotte manager, poking his head inside the door.

"What do you think, they gonna bang it?" Skinner asked.

"Bang it" is baseball slang for calling a game off. It had been raining steadily all day with no apparent end in sight three hours before game time.

"If they do, it won't be until the last possible moment," Johnson said. "I wish they'd do it right now so we could get on the road to Gwinnett."

Skinner made a face. "Nine hours from here, right?"

"We can make it in a little less if we're lucky," Johnson said. "The good news is we've got a great bus. Makes life a lot easier."

He offered Skinner a seat. Managers at the major-league level rarely socialize with one another beyond the occasional conversation around the batting cage. On the minor-league level it is more relaxed. It may have to do with a feeling of shared suffering.

Skinner wanted to be certain that Johnson understood he hadn't been trying to embarrass Johnson's team the night before in spite of the final score. Johnson waved him off. "I get it," he said. "I know you aren't taking extra bases or stealing on me with that kind of lead."

Johnson shook his head. "It's tough, though, down here sometimes. The other night I cost one of my guys a run on his ERA when we had a big lead. Guy gets to first on a bleeder, might even have been an error, but they called it a hit. We're up 13–1, I think, so I'm not holding the guy at first base and he takes off—steals second. Next guy hits a roller through the middle for a hit, and they get a run. I know what happened, but the big club doesn't. I felt badly about it."

In the minors, players and managers *do* worry about every individual statistic because it not only can make a difference in how the team views someone but can help or hurt a player in negotiating a contract.

A few weeks earlier, the Durham Bulls had been hosting the Rochester Red Wings in about as routine a July game as can be played at the Triple-A level. In the sixth inning, Henry Wrigley, who had started the season in Double-A Montgomery before being promoted to Durham in May, singled. Wrigley, who was about to turn twenty-six, was at Triple-A for the first time and had been making the most of his chance, hitting .343 since his call-up.

He took a long lead off first base, and pitcher Brendan Wise threw over. Wrigley took off for second, and first baseman Chris Parmelee made a bad throw that couldn't be handled by shortstop Pedro Florimón. The ball went off his glove, and Wrigley slid in safely.

Brent Belvin, the official scorer, looked at the play live and then on a replay and decided that Wrigley would have been out if Parmelee's throw had been accurate. So he gave Parmelee an error and charged Wrigley with a caught stealing. Both players would have been much happier if he had credited Wrigley with a stolen base, but Belvin didn't think that was the right thing to do.

The next evening, Wrigley sat in the Bulls' dugout complaining—half kidding, half serious—about the ruling. "I thought I was there before the throw," he said to a group of listeners including, most importantly, Bulls PR director Zach Weber. "That extra bag [steal] could make a difference when I'm negotiating my contract next year. It could be worth a couple of thousand dollars."

He was smiling when he said it, and everyone listening laughed at the exaggeration. But Weber had been around enough players to know it wasn't just a casual joke. "If you want, I can ask Brent to take another look at it," he said to Wrigley.

"Yeah, that would be good," Wrigley said. "Because if I'm there and you have to assume a perfect throw and tag, I should get the bag."

"That's right, you should," Durham radio play-by-play man Patrick Kinas said. "It's worth checking."

Belvin did look at the replay again later that evening. He saw the same thing he saw the night before: the throw arriving well ahead of Wrigley but off-line. He told Weber he couldn't change the ruling. The easiest thing for an official scorer to do is to rule in favor of the player—especially someone on the home team whom he may have to deal with in the future. The good ones aren't influenced by that.

Wrigley's caught stealing stood. So did Parmelee's error. The error apparently didn't bother the Twins. They called Parmelee up to the majors the next day. Wrigley finished the season with one caught stealing and zero stolen bases. Apparently, he was right—he could have used the extra bag.

———

About an hour after Joel Skinner left Ron Johnson's office, the rain in Norfolk began to slacken. By game time a crowd of 3,801—about half of what the Tides would normally draw on a Sunday evening—had found its way into the ballpark, and the rain had stopped. In all, it wasn't an uncomfortable evening. The game-time temperature was a balmy seventy-six degrees with a comfortable breeze.

The Tides beat the Knights 5–4 in a game played in a brisk two hours and thirty-two minutes. By 9:30, they were on their bus en route to Gwinnett, meaning they would be at their hotel by about 6:30 in the morning.

The Tides were now two games over .500 and still in contention for a wild card berth in the IL playoffs. All that said, Johnson— and Skinner—would have been just as happy if the game had been banged. Skinner had a long way to travel before he slept; Johnson had much longer to travel. After what he had lived through, nine hours on a "great bus" was fine with him.

27

Maine and Schwinden

COMEBACKS

There are no favorites in Triple-A baseball. No one sits around in March picking the teams that will win the International League North, South, and West Division titles. It isn't just that winning is not the top priority in the minor leagues; it's that there's no way of projecting what a roster is going to look like in August. In all likelihood, if a team plays well in April and May, some of its key players won't be with the team by June. And, if the major-league team has injuries, a Triple-A team's best players are going to be in the big leagues, and no one is going to bat an eye worrying about how that will affect the Triple-A club's chances of winning.

"If you think about it, you don't want your team to be stable," said Wally Backman, the manager in 2012 of the Buffalo Bisons. "I want to see my guys moving up—preferably not because of injury or poor performance; but it's a fact of baseball life that those things happen."

Backman's roster certainly wasn't stable. By mid-August he'd had twenty-two players called up to the New York Mets at some point during the season. In Norfolk, Ron Johnson occasionally had trouble recognizing all his pitchers because they were shuttling back and forth to Baltimore so often. Durham's roster seemed to change daily too, as the Rays searched for more hitting and healthy bodies with their disabled list overflowing with important players.

If there was one team in the league that would have been voted

Least Likely to Succeed at the start of the season it was the Scranton/ Wilkes-Barre Yankees.

This was unusual because the Yankees had traditionally signed a lot of veterans for their Triple-A team, even though they were often higher priced, for two reasons: those with more experience were most likely to be ready for the major leagues if needed, and George Steinbrenner, when he was still "The Boss," had always wanted his minorleague teams to have good records, regardless of cost—even if no one working for him thought it was important. In fact, Steinbrenner often threw tantrums over poor spring training performances.

Hal Steinbrenner had succeeded his father as the man in charge of the Yankees even before George's death in July 2010, and Hal was far more interested in the financial bottom line than the baseball bottom line. His father had already ceded most of the final baseball decisions to Brian Cashman by then, and Hal Steinbrenner continued to leave those decisions to Cashman. Like most baseball people, Cashman saw the minor leagues as a place to develop players for the major-league team. If, along the way, you won some games, that was fine too.

Which is why Cashman hadn't objected to the notion of leaving the Scranton/Wilkes-Barre team homeless in 2012 while the stadium in Scranton was being renovated. Once his plan to have the team play home games in Newark fell through, he knew he was asking manager Dave Miley to do the impossible by keeping the team competitive while constantly on the road—and also meeting the many demands of the major-league team.

"I know it's been tough on the players," Miley said, staring at his phone one evening as if he knew it was going to ring at any moment. "But in a way it's made us closer than most Triple-A teams because we're always on the road. That's where teams tend to pull closer together—on the road."

When the league reached its All-Star break—which was the same week as the major-league break—the Indianapolis Indians were 56-34 and had an eleven-game lead over Columbus in the West. Charlotte was 50-42 and led Norfolk by three games in the South. In the

North—which had six teams as opposed to the other divisions, which had four teams apiece—Lehigh Valley was 52-39 with Pawtucket at 51-41 and Scranton/Wilkes-Barre right behind at 49-43.

"If Dave Miley's not the Manager of the Year, there ought to be an investigation," Pawtucket manager Arnie Beyeler said. "Being competitive is remarkable. Being in contention is unbelievable."

Miley did have a number of veterans on the team, including Jack Cust, who had hit 25 or more home runs for three straight major-league seasons from 2007 to 2009; Russell Branyan, who had hit 194 home runs in the big-leagues; Chris Dickerson, who had spent a good deal of time with the Yankees; and Kosuke Fukudome, who had come to the Cubs as a heralded star and had been a regular in both Chicago and Cleveland before finding his way to the Yankees' system.

The starting pitcher for the Yankees (who would change their name to RailRiders prior to the 2013 season) in the team's last game before the All-Star break was John Maine.

Maine was, if nothing else, a familiar name to New York baseball fans—specifically New York Mets fans. Only a few years earlier, he had appeared to be a cornerstone of the Mets' staff, only to disappear after a series of shoulder injuries and a couple of run-ins with the team's management.

Maine was not, by any stretch, the prototype personality seen in most baseball clubhouses. Even though he had been a high school star while growing up in Fredericksburg, Virginia, he had no interest in turning pro after graduating. To him baseball was a means to pay for college, and he was delighted to get a scholarship to UNC Charlotte, where he majored in biomechanical engineering.

But he was too talented a pitcher for scouts not to notice. By his junior year he knew he was going to be drafted, and since he had completed all his course work and needed only to finish labs to get his degree, he decided to give baseball a shot when the Baltimore Orioles drafted him in the sixth round of the 2002 draft.

"I was twenty-one," he said. "I told myself I'd give it four years at the most. If I wasn't in the major leagues by the time I was twenty-five, I'd be done."

He beat his deadline by two years, making it to the Orioles when he was twenty-three. But his career didn't really take off until two years later after he had been traded by the Orioles to the Mets as a throw-in part of a deal in which the Orioles traded a once-solid reliever (Jorge Julio) for a once-solid starter (Kris Benson). The deal ended up being a steal for the Mets—because of Maine, the throw-in.

Benson, who had been the No. 1 pick in the entire draft in 1996, pitched one year in Baltimore after the trade, won eleven games with an ERA of 4.82, and then didn't pitch for the next two years. He won two more games after that, before retiring after a series of injuries.

The key to the trade, or so the Mets thought, was Julio, who had been the Orioles' closer at one point and had been a dominating relief pitcher at different points in his career. Maine, who had started eight games for the Orioles in 2005, was added to the deal only after word had leaked that the Mets were going to trade Benson straight up for Julio. That didn't sound like enough for Benson, so the Mets convinced the Orioles to send Maine along too. He was ticketed for Norfolk (then the Mets' Triple-A team) at the start of the season, a pitcher who might step in if someone in the rotation got hurt.

That was how he first got to the majors that year: Brian Bannister got hurt and couldn't take a start in early May, and Maine was called up to take his place. He didn't pitch very well, and he hurt the middle finger on his pitching hand in the process, which landed him on the disabled list. He went back to Norfolk after that, only to be called up again in early July because the Mets, even in the midst of their best season in years, were constantly looking for a fifth starter.

Maine pitched well enough in his return on July 3 to stick with the team. Orlando Hernández, one of the Mets' three aging starters (the team had Tom Glavine, Pedro Martinez, and Hernández on the roster that season), was slated to start a game on July 29, but it looked as if it might be delayed by rain, so the Mets decided to give him the night off and start Maine.

Maine responded with a four-hit shutout against the Houston Astros, and he went on to pitch twenty-six straight scoreless innings. When both Hernández and Martinez were hurt just prior to the start of the playoffs, Maine ended up starting game one of the division series against the Dodgers. He gave up one run in four and one-third innings of a game the Mets won, and he also pitched games two and six of the League Championship Series against the Cardinals—beating Chris Carpenter in game six to extend the series to seven games.

"It all happened very fast," Maine said. "I mean, halfway through the season I was pitching in Triple-A, and then I'm starting against the Cy Young Award winner [Carpenter] in game six of the LCS. I went from the guy who watched everyone else in the clubhouse get interviewed to being one of the guys everyone was interviewing."

Maine was able to handle it. He was honest and unspoiled, someone who hadn't been in the spotlight enough to resent it or to fall back on clichés. When the 2007 season began, he was the Mets' No. 3 starter, and he went 4-0 in the month of April with a 1.35 ERA. That won him the National League Pitcher of the Month award. He became a fixture in a corner of the Mets' Shea Stadium clubhouse playing chess with relief pitcher Aaron Heilman, outfielder Damion Easley, or—most often—outfielder Shawn Green.

Chess-playing baseball players are slightly less unusual than an overweight jockey, but there aren't many of them. The 2007 Mets had four chess players in their clubhouse, which may have accounted—at least in part—for their approach to the pennant race, which, when the team ended up a game out of first place, was labeled by critics as too cerebral and lacking in emotion.

Maine certainly couldn't be blamed for the team's late-season collapse. On the second-to-last day of the season he pitched seven and two-thirds innings of one-hit ball against the Marlins (the only hit was a roller to third in the eighth inning) and kept the Mets tied for first place with the Phillies. It was Glavine, the future Hall of Famer, who got knocked out in the first inning the next afternoon, sealing the Mets' fate.

Maine finished the season 15-10 with an ERA of 3.91. Since he was a year short of arbitration, the Mets signed him for only $450,000 for 2008. Maine was 10-8 in early August that year when he was put on the DL with a strained rotator cuff. It turned out he had a bone spur in his pitching shoulder, which doctors removed after the season was over. At the time the injury appeared to be just a blip, and the Mets signed him for $2.6 million the next year rather than go to arbitration.

The injury wasn't just a blip, though. It was the start of a trend. The doctors had to do the surgery twice because the spur was so big they didn't get all of it the first time. Even then, Maine never felt right the next season. He missed most of the second half of 2009 because of "arm fatigue," the euphemism the Mets came up with to describe his on-again, off-again appearances on the mound.

"My velocity was down about ten miles an hour," he said. "It hurt. I'd get a [cortisone] shot and pitch, it would wear off, I'd sit awhile, get another shot, and try to pitch again. I was miserable."

Maine had pitched too well for the Mets simply to give up on him. Hoping he would be healthy again in 2010, they gave him another one-year contract, this one for $3.3 million. But Maine wasn't the pitcher he had been in 2006 and 2007 or during the first four months of the 2008 season. By mid-May his ERA was over six runs a game, and as he warmed up for a start in Washington on May 20, pitching coach Dan Warthen was convinced something was wrong with him. He asked Maine if he was okay, and Maine said he felt fine.

When Maine walked to the mound to pitch in the bottom of the first inning, he looked out to the left-field bullpen and saw long reliever Raúl Valdés warming up. "That really unnerved me," he said. "I mean, if they didn't think I could throw, scratch me. I thought I could pitch when I warmed up and told Dan that. I pitched to one batter [a five-pitch walk] and I look up and here comes Dan signaling to the bullpen. I couldn't believe it. Of all the ups and downs I've had in baseball, that night might have been the most disappointing."

Maine came out after pitching to that one batter. After the game Warthen said that Maine wasn't always up-front about how his arm felt, and went so far as to say he was dishonest about how his arm felt at times. Most teams value someone who tries to play through pain.

The Mets, who have a history of insisting that players are "day-to-day," only to see them go on the disabled list for long stints, apparently didn't want Maine to try to take the ball if he was less than 100 percent.

A month later, Maine underwent surgery on his shoulder again. His Mets career was over. He signed with the Colorado Rockies during the off-season and was sent to Colorado Springs at the start of the season.

"I was awful," he said. "I went to spring training thinking I had a chance to get a job [with the Rockies], and really, being honest, I wasn't good enough for Triple-A. I remember when it hit me. I had two outs one night and I gave up hits to the No. 7 and 8 hitters in the lineup. They probably should have come out and gotten me then, but they let me pitch to the No. 9 hitter. He hit a three-run home run.

"*Then* they came and got me. I was so angry at myself and so frustrated I just decided that was it, I was done.

"The year before, when I was trying to rehab in St. Lucie [where the Mets' minor-league complex is located] after the surgery, it kind of hit me that the game was going along just fine without me. I began to wonder if it wasn't time to think about finding a way to get along without the game. I was getting close to thirty, and I'd initially said I wouldn't pitch in the minors beyond twenty-five. Well, I'm way past twenty-five . . . and there I am back in the minors and getting shelled. It was time to go home and decide what to do next."

———

Maine had pitched forty-six innings in Colorado Springs to an ERA of 7.43, walking thirty-seven batters. In that last start, the home run had climaxed an outing in which he gave up eight runs in four and two-thirds innings.

He went home to Charlotte, where he and his wife, Kristi, lived during the off-season (they had met in college), and began playing coed softball with some of his friends. Late in the summer, just for the heck of it, he began throwing to one of his friends and realized that, for the first time in three years, he could throw a fastball without shoulder pain. It was Kristi who encouraged him to take one more shot—if only to find out what it might feel like to pitch with a healthy shoulder.

Maine signed with the Red Sox early in 2012 prior to spring training, knowing he probably wouldn't be 100 percent in April because he hadn't pitched at all since the previous June. When it got to be May and he was still in extended spring training in Fort Myers, he got impatient.

"I'm thirty years old and I'm down there with a bunch of eighteen-year-olds," he said. "Plus, I thought I was ready to at least try it in Triple-A."

He asked for his release, went home again, and waited for the phone to ring. It was a month later when the Yankees called. They were willing to send him to Scranton/Wilkes-Barre after a short stint to get his arm stretched out in extended spring training at their minor-league base in Tampa. Maine agreed, even after being warned that because the Yankees were currently a team without a stadium, he wouldn't be pitching any home games when he got to Triple-A.

"It's funny because we've got a lot of older guys on this team," he said. "I think that's one reason why we've dealt pretty well with being on the road all the time. We're all here because we decided to be here. I could be at home, figuring out what I want to do next. I'm pretty sure I'll have options ... and there are a lot of guys on this team who are the same way. We all believe we still have some baseball left in us, so we've chosen to be here. I have no complaints. I wanted a chance to prove I could be a starting pitcher again, and they've given it to me."

Maine had started slowly but had pitched better as the season wore on. "I am getting better," he said. "I think I know what it takes to pitch in the majors, and, being honest, I'm probably not there yet." He smiled. "Not that I'd tell them that if they called me up."

His ERA at the All-Star break was over 7.00. By mid-August the ERA was under 5.00, and he was giving up less than a hit per inning—usually a good sign for a pitcher. "I'd like to put myself in a position where I can be someplace next spring with a legitimate chance to make someone's rotation," he said. "I don't think that's out of the question at this point.

"If nothing else, I'm proof of how fast things can change. In '06, I'm pitching game six of the NLCS. Five years later, I'm playing coed softball. And now, a year after that, I honestly believe I can pitch in the big leagues again."

He was sitting on an equipment chest outside the visiting clubhouse in Lehigh Valley. There simply wasn't enough room inside to sit and talk comfortably, so he had walked outside and found the equipment chest to sit on.

He stood up and looked at his cell phone for the time. "I've got to go," he said apologetically. "I've got the bucket today."

Each day during batting practice one starting pitcher who is not throwing a bullpen session is assigned to gather up the baseballs that have ended up in the infield and outfield and return them to the mound for the batting practice pitcher to reuse. And so John Maine, who had stood on the mound at Shea Stadium in October 2006 with fifty thousand fans hanging on every pitch as he tried to get the Mets to within one game of the World Series, headed down the tunnel at Coca-Cola Field in Allentown, Pennsylvania, to find the bucket.

The next night he pitched seven shutout innings, allowing three hits, striking out five, and walking one. He had not pitched in the major leagues since 2010. He walked off the mound that night believing he would pitch there again.

———

Chris Schwinden's hopes were not all that different from John Maine's. He hadn't pitched in any coed softball leagues, but he had spent the month of June wandering the minor leagues for (almost) forty days and forty nights.

And then, finally, he had returned to Buffalo. Which is where he found happiness once again—although not without some scar tissue picked up along the way. The jokes about all his SkyMiles were fine—even welcome after his thirty-five-day odyssey through four organizations.

But he couldn't help but doubt himself at least a little bit after being waived out of four organizations—even if one had taken him back. "I had a lot of downtime each time I was waived," he said. "What happened to me made it kind of tough to like this business. And it was certainly a reminder that this is a business, if I didn't know it already.

"I mean, to some extent, it's almost as if teams *do* see you as agate—just a name being moved around a board somewhere. I wondered a few times whether this was what I was supposed to be doing. Then I'd say to myself, 'Well, teams keep picking you up, so you can't be all *that* bad.'

"The negative can overpower you. I actually wondered on a few occasions, 'Who did I piss off? Why has this been happening? Was it somehow planned?' There were so many different scenarios it was hard to grasp. All I knew was I felt awful."

Being back in Buffalo was like being given a new lease on life—even if Schwinden was somewhat sobered by the previous five weeks. It also caused him to rethink who he was as a pitcher.

"You can't spend your life with one foot in Triple-A and one foot in the big leagues," he said. "That's where I think I had gotten to. I was good enough to be called up when an extra arm was needed, but I wasn't *really* good enough to pitch in the majors. I needed to get better. What I was producing just wasn't good enough."

He went to work with Bisons pitching coach Mark Brewer to see if he could develop another pitch—other than his fastball—to get batters out with on a consistent basis. They spent a lot of time working on his changeup, specifically changing his release point.

"I started to release it just a tad later than I had been," he said. "I think it's given the pitch some later movement than it used to have, made it a little tougher on the batters. All of a sudden, once I got comfortable with it, I've been able to strike batters out with it. That means I can mix my pitches up more and things have really clicked for me."

Once he settled back into the rotation, Schwinden began to pitch well on a regular basis—so well that some thought he might get another call to New York before the end of the season.

"I doubt it," he said, sitting in the dugout one afternoon. "I'm pitching better, but they've got some young guys throwing very well who I know they want to take a look at this season. I get that. The key for me now is to keep pitching well and be in a position where I can go to spring training next year and show them I've got something I didn't have in the past. That's what I'm going to need to be a major-league pitcher."

He smiled. "It's nice to be back to the point where I can think that way. In June, I wasn't sure I could still be a minor-league pitcher.

"I'm still not old for baseball [he would turn twenty-six in September], but I'm not young either. I know the Mets have younger guys than me who they are counting on for the future. I just have to keep working to get better if I want to be in their plans.

"The minor leagues are a weird place to be. The guys in your clubhouse are your best friends. You come to depend on them. But the other pitchers, even though you work together and you support one another every day, are your competition. You had better be gunning for them . . . because they're going to be gunning for you. Not in your face, but you better be aware of it anyway."

He sighed. "This is a hard life, it's simple as that. But there's a reason people tell you that if you don't like it, the only thing to do is get better. It's the truth."

28

One At-Bat in Eight Years

Every minor-league baseball season is filled with promotions, ranging from monkeys riding collie dogs to George Jetson Night to firefighters rappelling into the outfield carrying that night's game ball. Not to mention Whack an Intern.

But the most unusual pregame or in-game ceremony of the 2012 season had to be the one that took place in Allentown on June 15.

That was the night the IronPigs honored the starting center fielder—for the Durham Bulls.

"I told him he had to be the only player in minor-league history who was honored while playing on the road," Durham manager Charlie Montoyo said. "Usually, that kind of thing only happens to guys who are going to the Hall of Fame."

Rich Thompson isn't going to the Hall of Fame—unless they create one for guys who never give up. He first got to the major leagues in 2004, making the Kansas City Royals out of spring training as a defensive replacement and pinch runner. He was up for three weeks before being sent back to the minors, and he got one at-bat while in the majors. He grounded into a double play.

"It was a cold day in Cleveland, and I figured the first pitch was probably going to be as good as any I would see," he said. "I actually hit the ball pretty hard, but I hit it in the direction of Omar Vizquel, which wasn't a very good idea." Given that Vizquel won eleven Gold Gloves playing shortstop, that analysis was no doubt accurate.

Eight years later, that was still Thompson's only major-league at-bat. That was one more at-bat than Moonlight Graham had gotten during his major-league career that had been made famous by the movie *Field of Dreams*.

Graham wasn't the only major leaguer to play one game without an at-bat. Since 1901, there have been thirty-seven players like him—although he was the only one ever played by Burt Lancaster in a movie. Thompson was one of 176 non-pitchers to have exactly one plate appearance but was the only player in the group whose one time at the plate had resulted in a double play.

"Not exactly the legacy you'd want," he said with a smile. "But I would rather have ended my career with that one at-bat than without ever having been there."

That was what Thompson told himself and anyone who asked as he wandered from one baseball organization to another in search of a home. Like every kid who dreamed of playing baseball for a living, he never envisioned eleven different minor-league stops and fourteen seasons riding buses from one small town to another and then one midsize town to another.

"When I played Little League, I just figured all of us would be in the major leagues someday," he said, laughing at the memory. "Then, when I tried out for my JV team as a freshman in high school, I got cut. That was a clue, I guess. Two of my friends also got cut, and one of their dads called and got us on another team so we could keep playing."

It was speed that got Thompson into big-time baseball, and it is speed, even now at the age of thirty-four, that has kept him in the game. He went to baseball camps at both Princeton and James Madison, and it was his time in the sixty-yard dash more than anything that caught the attention of the coaches. He chose JMU because it had a better baseball program. "If I'd been going to college for academics, I'd have gone to Princeton," he said. "But I wasn't."

He majored in finance at JMU and was a very good college

player. It was while playing in the Cape Cod League in the summer of 1999 that he attracted the attention of pro scouts. A year later, the Toronto Blue Jays drafted him in the sixth round, and he began the climb through the minors that most players make in order to get to the majors.

He reached Triple-A for the second time in 2003 and was traded at mid-season from the Jays to the Pirates, which meant he was sent from Syracuse to Nashville. That winter the San Diego Padres selected him in the Rule 5 Draft and then traded him to Kansas City. A player taken in the Rule 5 Draft is, in effect, being given a major-league tryout. If he is not on the big-league roster of his new team during the next season, he must be sent back to the organization from which he was drafted.

The Royals wanted Thompson for a very specific reason: they had two players on their roster, Juan Gonzalez and Matt Stairs, who couldn't run at all and were liabilities defensively.

Thompson's job was to pinch-run for one late in a close game or, if both were in the lineup, meaning one had to play the field, take over defensively in the later innings if the Royals had a lead.

That's what he did during the first month of the 2004 season, getting his one at-bat in a game in which the Royals were leading Cleveland, 15–5. The Indians had completely thrown in the towel on the game, and backup catcher Tim Laker was pitching, playing the role that Craig Albernaz was sometimes asked to play by Charlie Montoyo in Durham. That was the at-bat that led to Thompson's hitting into a double play. So, when the Royals sent Thompson back to the Pirates—and on to Nashville—at the end of the month, he still hadn't faced a true major-league pitcher in a major-league game.

Thompson wandered the next four years. His problem was simple: he didn't hit with power, and his batting average, always solid at the minor-league level, was never quite good enough to allow him to be a big-league leadoff hitter on a regular basis.

At six feet two and a lean 185 pounds, Thompson rarely hit home runs—he had hit thirty-four in 5,217 minor-league at-bats through the end of the 2012 season—so he almost had to be a .300 hitter to be taken seriously by major-league scouts. His minor-league career batting average of .281 was respectable but not brilliant.

"There really is a very small margin of error between the majors and minors," he said. "It's the old Crash Davis speech about one extra hit a week. There's something to that. But it's also about opportunity. A lot of times I've been in organizations where someone was penciled in ahead of me because of a contract or because they were a prospect. I get it. That's the way it is. You just have to hope at some point you get another chance."

Thompson went from Pittsburgh to Arizona and Boston without ever getting another sniff at the majors. When the Red Sox released him in April 2008, he wondered if he might be finished. He was twenty-nine, and, like it or not, he had become a career minor leaguer. By then, he was taking online classes to become a CPA, so the notion of baseball being over saddened him but didn't panic him.

Twelve days after the Red Sox released him, the Phillies called. They were looking for an outfielder for their new Triple-A team in Allentown. Having grown up in central Pennsylvania, Thompson was familiar with the Lehigh valley. Even if he hadn't been, he would have taken the deal.

The IronPigs were his eleventh minor-league team. Remarkably, he had finally found a home—not the one he had dreamed about, but a home nonetheless. At the end of each season (four of them) he became a free agent before re-signing with the Phillies and returning to Allentown.

Very few minor leaguers become fan favorites. If they play well, they usually move up to the next level. Most minor-league fans go to the games for the overall experience—the promotions, the atmosphere, the mascots—and to see baseball up close at a relatively inexpensive price. The most expensive ticket in an International League park is $15. Those are the club seats that in a major-league park cost anywhere from $250 to more than $1,000 (yes, for one game) depending on the city you are in. Box seats typically sell for $10 (compared with $75 to $200 at the big-league level), and general admission in most parks is $5 to $7. Parking ranges from free to as much as $3. Most major-league teams charge a minimum of $15 to park anywhere close to the ballpark, and if you want to drive your car to a game at Yankee Stadium and park in an official stadium lot, it will cost you $45. That's before you've bought a single ticket or anything to eat.

Only rarely do fans come to a Triple-A park to see specific players. The exceptions are a young star passing through—like Bryce Harper at Syracuse in April 2012—or an already established star who is in town for a few days on rehab: Evan Longoria in Durham; Orioles second baseman Brian Roberts in Norfolk; Kevin Youkilis in Pawtucket.

The appearance of a star on rehab in a minor-league town can create major headaches for team officials. In May, the Rays signed Hideki Matsui, the onetime Yankee who had been the MVP of the 2009 World Series, and sent him to Durham to try to get into baseball shape. At the same time, Daisuke Matsuzaka, who had been a superstar in Japan before joining the Red Sox, was in Pawtucket on a rehab assignment after having undergone Tommy John surgery a year earlier.

The worlds collided in Durham on May 17, with Matsuzaka pitching for Pawtucket and Matsui batting cleanup for Durham. The good news for the Bulls was that they sold 10,064 tickets to the game after the first two games of the series had drawn a *total* of 9,061. The bad news was that there was absolutely no place to put all the Japanese media at the game.

On a normal night, there might be ten people in the Bulls' press box. It can comfortably seat about fifteen. That would leave five empty spots for non-regulars. The only problem was that there were close to fifty members of the Japanese media there to cover the two Japanese stars.

"We just put them anywhere we could find empty space," said Zach Weber, who was the Bulls' PR director. "There was no way to find seats for all of them."

The Bulls won the game 5–0. Matsuzaka, who had cost the Red Sox more than $100 million in salary and transfer fees and had won forty-nine games in five years, gave up two home runs pitching for Pawtucket. Jim Paduch, who started for the Bulls, pitched six shutout innings. He was twenty-nine, had spent much of his career playing independent league ball, and was costing the Bulls about $8,000 a month. It is probably safe to say that not a single member of the media was there that night to see him pitch. He looked like the $100 million pitcher.

Matsui was 0 for 3.

Those nights were the exceptional ones—fans and media flocking to a Triple-A park because of who was going to be on the field.

But Rich Thompson became a different kind of exception in Allentown. To begin with, he was a very good Triple-A player. He was a consistent, if not spectacular, .270 to .280 hitter each year, and he was a threat to steal whenever he got on base at a time in baseball when stealing had become a lost art at all levels. He stole 138 bases in four seasons, played an excellent center field, and was always available whenever the team did any kind of event in the community.

He and his wife, Teresa, had started a family by then, and they felt very comfortable living in the Lehigh valley. In a league that had few players who could be described as fan favorites, Thompson became exactly that.

"The funny thing is I never thought I'd play baseball this long," he said. "And I certainly never thought I'd play it in the minor leagues this long. I've always understood that I'm lucky to still be playing. One bad year, maybe even less than that, and I could be out of baseball. I've been sent down to Double-A a couple of times, so I always knew where I stood in the pecking order.

"Obviously, if I didn't love it, I wouldn't still be doing it. I have three children now and a mortgage, and I started 2012 making $15,500 a month for a six-month season. That's not a bad living, but it isn't going to mean I can retire or take it easy whenever I stop playing." He smiled. "If I can get a month in the majors and get paid at that rate, maybe I can buy a nice car. But the idea that I'm going to play ten years in the majors and not need to work when I stop playing went away a long time ago."

Thompson began 2012 once again at Lehigh Valley. He had passed his CPA exam during the winter and was extremely proud of the fact that he had needed to take the test only once to pass it. "The stat I heard was that only 42 percent pass the first time," he said. "I wanted to get it done the first time."

On the morning of May 16 he was having breakfast at home. The IronPigs had gotten home from a long road trip a day earlier, and he was happy to be back with Teresa and their three children—aged seven, five, and two. His cell phone rang, and he saw that it was manager Ryne Sandberg. Like most players, Thompson's first reaction was, "Uh-oh."

Sandberg had called Thompson on only three other occasions. "It was either to tell me he was giving me a day off because he liked to let guys know before they got to the park or to tell me I was going on the phantom DL."

The "phantom DL" is a minor-league term for the seven-day disabled list that players are sometimes put on when their team needs a roster spot either to send someone down (players on rehab don't count) or to bring someone up a level. It is usually a veteran like Thompson who is put on the phantom DL when needed.

This time the call was different. Always to the point, Sandberg said, "Rich, you've been traded to Tampa Bay. They want you in Tampa tonight. Congratulations."

Thompson was stunned. Scott Podsednik had been traded to the Red Sox a few days earlier, so it seemed unlikely that Lehigh Valley would move another outfielder at that moment—unless an injury in Philadelphia forced a call-up. He'd been traded and *not* to Durham but to the major-league team. By lunchtime he was on a plane, and he was at Tropicana Field that evening before the Rays game against the Red Sox.

With the Rays leading 2–1 in the eighth and trying to build an insurance run, manager Joe Maddon sent Thompson in to pinch-run for the painfully slow Luke Scott. Thompson didn't steal a base, but he did induce Red Sox reliever Franklin Morales into a balk—which was just as good. He didn't score, ending the inning on third base, but the Rays held on to win anyway.

The next night Maddon had him in the lineup—batting ninth

and playing center field. After striking out in the third, Thompson came up again in the bottom of the fourth, with Boston leading 3–1 and Sean Rodriguez on second base. Facing Red Sox star rookie Félix Doubront, Thompson lined a 1-1 fastball to center field for an RBI single.

At the age of thirty-three, he had his first major-league hit—and RBI. His teammates all came to the top step of the dugout to applaud him. It had been 2,645 days since his first at-bat in Cleveland. In that time he had been to the plate in the minor leagues 3,711 times.

"I didn't feel vindicated or validated by it," he said. "But I knew the road I had taken to get to that moment, and it was very gratifying to get there, no doubt. Everyone was great about it. I did get a little bit choked up thinking about what it had taken to get back. I wasn't sobbing or anything, but I was a little choked up."

He didn't lose his focus, though, stealing both second base and third base. That meant in one inning he had gotten his first hit, his first RBI, and his second and third stolen bases—he'd stolen one as a pinch runner in Kansas City. After the game, Tampa Bay clubhouse manager Chris Westmoreland made sure he got the baseball that had been recovered from the Red Sox after the hit.

Thompson stayed in Tampa for three weeks. When Desmond Jennings came off the DL on June 5, he was optioned to Durham. Which is why he was in a Bulls uniform when the team traveled to Allentown on June 15. That was the day the IronPigs decided to honor him by giving him a cake and a jersey.

Four days after the modest ceremony in Allentown, Thompson was back in the big leagues. This time his stay lasted three days. Once again a player coming off the disabled list—Jeff Keppinger—was the reason he was sent back down. To some, it might sound like a waste of time to get called up to the majors for three days. For Thompson, it was worth almost $8,000 in prorated major-league pay, no small thing since he had taken a pay cut when he was traded by the Phillies to the Rays.

As an IronPig, Thompson was being paid $15,500 a month—one of the higher salaries in the minor leagues. The Rays capped their minor leaguers at $13,000 a month, which meant the trade would cost Thompson about $8,000 in minor-league pay during the remainder of 2012. Fortunately, the twenty days he had spent in Tampa from mid-May to early June had been worth about $55,000, meaning his 2012 salary would be into six figures.

When he returned to Durham he rented a town house, figuring that was where he would be for the rest of the summer.

"I'll be thirty-four next year," he said. "I think I can still play, so if someone will have me, I'll keep playing." He smiled. "I've got plenty of years ahead of me as a CPA. In that business, you never win, you just do your job and hope you don't lose anything. It can't possibly be as much fun as this is—I can't imagine any job being as much fun as the one I've got right now."

And, unlike Moonlight Graham, he did get that second chance in the big leagues.

29

Elarton

FIGHTING FATHER TIME

For Scott Elarton, the summer in Allentown was turning out to be long and hot.

Which had nothing to do with the weather—although it was also very warm.

On May 16, after he had pitched six innings of three-hit shutout baseball against the Indianapolis Indians, Elarton had a record of 5-1 and an ERA of 2.06. In the meantime, the Phillies' pitching staff was struggling: Joel Piñeiro and Dontrelle Willis, the other veterans invited to training camp as starting pitching insurance, had both been released. Cliff Lee had gone on the DL in April. Vance Worley followed—on the day that Elarton dropped his ERA to 2.06. Less than two weeks later Roy Halladay was on the shelf.

On three occasions, the calls to Lehigh Valley came—but not for Elarton. "This is not a business built for the elderly," he said one afternoon with a smile. "That's true in more ways than one."

Elarton pitched well enough to win against Gwinnett on June 7—giving up one run and four hits in six innings—but got a no-decision when the bullpen gave up a 1–0 lead soon after he left. His next start didn't come until seven days later because of a rainout on June 12 and a rare off day on the thirteenth. Maybe it was working on six days' rest instead of four, or maybe it was just a bad night. Either way, Elarton was hit hard by the Durham Bulls: he allowed seven earned runs—including two home runs—and didn't get out of the fourth inning. That started a string of seven starts in which Elarton gave up five runs or more every time out except once. By July 17, just after the All-Star break, his ERA had soared to 5.60, and he had dropped seven straight decisions. Any thoughts of a call-up to Philadelphia were in the past.

"There's a lot that goes into pitching well, including good luck, and a lot that goes into pitching poorly, including bad luck," he said with a wan grin. "I've had seasons where I felt like all the breaks I got were good: I'd make a bad pitch, and someone would foul it off. I'd get a call when I needed it or an out when I needed it. I had really good run support.

"This year it's felt the opposite a lot of the time. A broken bat becomes a hit. I throw a pitch that I think is strike three, I don't get the call, and the next pitch becomes a key hit. I can't complain—that's just the way baseball is sometimes. You figure that out as you get older. I haven't been good enough the last couple of months, that's the bottom line."

Elarton knew that part of his problem was that his legs weren't as strong as they had been when he was younger. He had worked out hard to prepare in the off-season, but not having pitched regularly for almost four years and having to work harder at thirty-six to make good pitches than when he was twenty-six had taken their toll. He kept grinding, believing that what he had been doing in March, April, and May was still buried someplace inside him.

Sure enough, on July 22 against Columbus, his pitches had bite again. He pitched six innings and gave up two runs. His next two starts were equally good—although he didn't get wins in any of them. During that three-game stretch he pitched to an ERA of 2.55, and his ERA for the season dropped by more than half a run. Then came a bad outing against Rochester in which he gave up six runs and three home runs and came out in the sixth inning.

"I wasn't discouraged by that," he said. "I wasn't happy, but you have starts like that. I just wanted to come back and pitch well in Buffalo the next time out."

He did. But he might have been trying just a little too hard. With one out in the fifth inning, he felt a tweak in his leg while throwing a pitch. His legs had been sore, but he hadn't paid attention, just figuring it was normal late-season soreness that any thirty-six-year-old pitcher was bound to feel. He threw one more pitch and induced a ground ball to first base—which, as it turned out, was the worst thing that could have happened at that moment.

As he ran to cover first base, Elarton felt a sharp pain in the back of his leg, and he knew right away he'd done something to his hamstring. He made the play and then looked into the dugout for help.

"I told them I had to come out," he said. "Funny thing is I'd never done that before in my life. I remember a few years ago I got hurt during a game and I decided I was going to tough it out. No way was I going to ask out. There was a man on third base, and I was intentionally walking the batter to set up a double play. I threw the first intentional-walk pitch to the backstop."

He smiled. "After that I didn't have to ask out. They came and got me. This time I knew to get out before I made it worse."

He ended up getting tagged with the loss that night to drop his record to 5-11. It was his tenth straight loss since the night in mid-May when he had been pitching so well and wondered if he was going to get the call to Philadelphia. Now, in August, May was a distant memory. His biggest concern at that moment was simple: he didn't want to end the season on the disabled list or without pitching again. There were less than three weeks left to play.

"The good news was it wasn't my arm, and I knew it wasn't that bad," he said. "If you tear something down there, you can feel it. I knew I had to be careful with it, but I also knew it was just a strain. I wanted to get back on the mound before the season was over."

By now, Elarton knew for certain he wasn't going to see the major leagues in 2012. "If they called in September, I certainly wouldn't turn them down," he said, laughing. "But I know they aren't calling."

On August 28, having missed just one turn because of the hamstring, Elarton was back on the mound. The IronPigs were still mathematically in playoff contention, trying to chase the Pawtucket Red

Sox down for the wild card spot, so this was one of those rare Triple-A games where the outcome has serious meaning for everyone on the team.

The opponent was Scranton/Wilkes-Barre. The game was in Allentown, but it was technically a Yankees home game. That didn't really matter to Elarton. He gave up two runs on three hits in the second inning but settled down and pitched solidly for five innings, not surrendering another hit. He ended the fifth inning by striking out Ronnier Mustelier. Sandberg had decided that eighty-two pitches was enough for him after the missed start.

With Juan Morillo warming up in the bullpen to replace Elarton, the IronPigs scored two runs in the top of the sixth to take a 3–2 lead. Morillo pitched two shutout innings. Then Joe Savery, who twice had been called to the Phillies early in the season when Elarton thought he might get the call, pitched a scoreless eighth. Jake Diekman finished the job in the ninth, and the IronPigs had a 3–2 victory—giving Elarton his first win in more than three months.

That was nice. What was nicer was that he had pitched pain-free. The hamstring had felt fine. Sandberg told him he would get one more start—on September 3, the last day of the season. Elarton's family had gone home to Colorado while he was working his way back from the hamstring injury. By the weekend, the IronPigs knew they weren't going to make the playoffs, that their Labor Day game against the Buffalo Bisons would be their finale.

Elarton's car was packed and ready for the trip. "It's 1,575 miles from here," he said on the season's final Sunday. "As soon as the game's over on Monday, I head down the road. The kids have told me I better be home in time to pick them up from school on Wednesday."

He was ready to go home. He was not, however, ready to stay home. "I want to play next year," he said. "I'm not sure about a lot of things. But I'm sure about that."

30

Voices of the Minors

Having managed in the International League for six years, Charlie Montoyo is familiar with just about everything and everyone associated with the league.

Including the umpires.

"They're no different than the rest of us down here," Montoyo said one morning in early August. "This time of year, they get a little cranky. It's hot, they've been on the road all year, and they're wondering how they're doing. They're not like us—they don't have standings to tell them if they're doing well. They have to wait to hear."

While it was certainly difficult for umpires to make the jump from Triple-A to the majors, at least they knew that openings would occur and there was a chance they might be next in line to fill them. There were seventy full-time major-league umpires, and even though it seemed as if some of them never retired, they did, in fact, retire—usually by the age of sixty.

Not so with broadcasters.

Getting a major-league broadcasting job isn't quite as difficult as getting appointed to the Supreme Court, but once someone gets there, he isn't likely to leave unless he's dragged to the door—usually kicking and screaming. For those sitting on the doorstep but not inside the door, that can be remarkably frustrating.

"What's frustrating about it is you never know what it is that will get you hired or what it is that isn't getting you hired," said Steve Hyder, who had been doing play-by-play for the Pawtucket Red Sox for nine years. "Umpires, at least, have some kind of evaluation system even if it's subjective. For us, it's a question of a job opening and then having someone in a decision-making position who happens to like your work."

The PawSox have a great tradition of being a stepping-stone to major-league jobs for broadcasters: Gary Cohen had been hired by the Mets in 1988 after two seasons in Pawtucket; Don Orsillo had moved up to the Red Sox in 2001; Dave Flemming had been hired by the Giants in 2004; Andy Freed moved on to Tampa in 2005; and Dave Jageler was hired in Washington in 2006 after one season in Pawtucket. All five of those men still work for the big-league teams that hired them.

The PawSox are one of a handful of Triple-A teams that use more than one radio play-by-play man. Traditionally, Triple-A radio is handled by one play-by-play man, perhaps supplemented by an ex-player who does color. In Pawtucket there have been two play-by-play men for years.

After Jageler's departure in 2006, Hyder worked with Dan Hoard in Pawtucket. Twice he had been a finalist for major-league jobs: in 2005 when the new Washington Nationals were hiring and that same year in Oakland. He hadn't gotten either job but had thought his time was bound to come.

"I grew up in Rhode Island and I went to UMass, so this area has been my home for a lot of my life," he said. "When I got the job here in 2004, I felt like I was in the front row of Red Sox Nation and the timing couldn't have been better. For the most part, I loved the job. I loved knowing the guys who came through here like Dustin [Pedroia], [Kevin] Youkilis, and Jacoby [Ellsbury]. I always felt part of it, even in a small way, and I loved that."

Two things happened in 2011 that forced Hyder to rethink his life. First, he had a heart attack. He had just turned fifty, and he knew that the job had taken a toll on him through the years. It had already affected his personal life—he'd been divorced twice. Now it was affecting his health.

"The minor-league life isn't easy, especially as you get older," he said. "The players are young, and they don't plan to be around very long. Even the ones who are still playing in their thirties are relatively young. It's not a fluke that you don't see a lot of managers and coaches who do this at this level for very long. The travel wears on you. Working 144 games in 152 days wears on you."

And being one step away from the big money and from living the major-league life also wears on you—especially after years and years in the job. Some make their peace with it. Howard Kellman has been doing play-by-play for the Indianapolis Indians since 1974 and is a beloved and respected figure in Indianapolis. The same is true in Toledo of Jim Weber, who grew up there, started with the Mud Hens in 1975, and has never left his hometown.

They are exceptions to the rule. Most Triple-A broadcasters are exactly like the players: they grow up dreaming of being in the big leagues.

Matt Swierad has been broadcasting minor-league baseball for twenty-three years—ever since he graduated from Jacksonville University with a degree in history. He spent seven years in the Class A South Atlantic League before landing the job in Charlotte in 1998. He was only thirty-one at the time and was on the path he wanted to be to get to the major leagues.

Seven years later, Swierad was still in Charlotte and beginning to wonder if the major leagues were just a pipe dream. Then came an unexpected—if temporary—opportunity. Jerry Coleman, who had been doing play-by-play for the San Diego Padres forever, was being inducted into the Hall of Fame. The Padres needed someone to fill in for the three games that Coleman would miss during Hall of Fame weekend and put out a notice that anyone interested in the three-day job could send in an application.

Swierad almost didn't bother. "I figured there was no chance, that someone who had an in with someone out there would probably get it," he said. "My wife finally convinced me that I should at least give it a shot."

The Knights were in Buffalo on a long road trip and had gotten to the hotel early one morning to find that they couldn't check into their rooms right away—a frequent occurrence of Triple-A travel. When they finally got in their rooms, Swierad walked over to a nearby food court to get some lunch.

He was sitting down to eat when the phone rang.

"At first I didn't even want to answer it," he said. "I was tired, frustrated by a long trip, and hungry. But I picked it up, and it was the guy who was in charge of the search for Jerry's replacement. He told me they had picked me and asked if I still wanted to come out and do the three games.

"I hung up the phone and just started to cry. I was sitting in a food court in Buffalo, and I'd just found out I was going to the major leagues. I didn't care that it was only for three games. I'd done it."

Hyder hadn't gotten that break or had that moment. He worked the second half of the 2011 season wondering if perhaps it was time to get off the road, to find something different to do with his life.

Then his friend Hoard was hired to become the play-by-play voice of the Cincinnati Bengals. Hyder wondered if moving up to the No. 1 slot combined with feeling better physically would put more life into his step—and his broadcasts—in 2012.

Except that he didn't move up to the No. 1 slot. The PawSox hired Aaron Goldsmith, who had been working for the Texas Rangers' Double-A team in Frisco, Texas, and announced he would be their No. 1 voice with Hyder remaining in the No. 2 slot. Goldsmith was twenty-eight. Hyder got the message.

"Nothing against the kid," he said, referring to Goldsmith. "It's not his fault. I just thought I deserved the chance to be the No. 1 guy. They felt differently. If I said that didn't hurt, I'd be lying to you.

"I didn't want to make an emotional decision when they made the announcement. I decided to go back and work and see how I felt—physically and mentally. Opening day I knew I was done. I just didn't have the feeling I needed to have to do the job as well as I possibly could. The enthusiasm wasn't there. I knew it was time—past time—for me to go."

It made for a bittersweet summer. He told no one in the organization of his intention to leave and felt fortunate that the PawSox were having a good season. For broadcasters, the fate of the team day to day is very important because having players move on to the major leagues and succeed doesn't make the games they are working any more fun. A winning team is always more fun to be around than a losing team. From day one, even with all the turnover created by a spate of Red Sox injuries that made the clubhouse feel like a baseball halfway house with players coming and going, the team was in contention in the IL North.

That made the season a lot more fun for Hyder. It also made the thought of leaving that much more difficult to take.

31

The Endless Month

There are many things not to like about minor-league life—especially for those who have been in the big leagues. Most of the differences are apparent: salary, mode of travel, hotels, per diem, clubhouses, even the quality of the postgame meal—same food, as many players point out, different taste.

Which leads players to the one thing they would all wish to change first and foremost: noise.

They miss the noise, the sounds, the electricity of a major-league park. "It's not anybody's fault," said Buddy Carlyle, sitting in the dugout on a hot, humid afternoon in Gwinnett. "It just can't be the same. Even if you have a sellout and there's eight or nine thousand people, that's not close to the same as forty thousand. And if you're playing in a half-full minor-league stadium, there are nights when you swear you can hear the crickets."

This was a problem for Carlyle and the rest of his teammates in Gwinnett. Coolray Field (named for a heating and air-conditioning company) was a sparkling three-year-old stadium with pretty backdrops outside the outfield fences and all the modern amenities. The Braves had moved their Triple-A team there in 2009 after being unable to get a deal done with the city of Richmond to renovate the Diamond, the creaky (though charming) park where the Richmond

Braves had played since 1985 after moving to Richmond nineteen years earlier.

The move to Gwinnett made sense in many ways. After all, having your Triple-A team 34 miles from your home ballpark certainly made things easier than having it 535 miles away. What's more, Gwinnett County was willing to pay for the construction *and* the maintenance of a brand-new 10,475-seat stadium that was three miles from the I-85 corridor.

There was just one problem: if a baseball fan is thirty-four miles—or less—from a major-league park, he isn't likely to make a regular habit of going to a minor-league park. The most successful minor-league teams are almost always those that aren't too close to a major-league stadium.

"It isn't as if fans *won't* come here, they do," said Dave Brundage, who had managed the team in Richmond for two years and then made the move to Gwinnett. "But instead of coming here ten or fifteen times a year, they might come here four or five and go to Turner [Field] a half-dozen times. It's tough to compete with a team when everyone knows your best players are going to play for them and not for you."

Even the first season the G-Braves, as they were called (they'd been the R-Braves in Richmond), had trouble drawing fans. They averaged 5,965 per game, which ranked them twelfth in the fourteen-team league. By 2012, with the novelty of a Triple-A club having worn off, the average had dropped to 4,680 a game. Only the Charlotte Knights—whose stadium was almost twenty miles from downtown on a heavily traveled road—drew fewer fans in 2012 than the G-Braves.

Which is why August, a difficult month in any minor-league town, was especially tough in Gwinnett. The weather was uncomfortable most nights, the team was struggling, and the crickets could frequently be heard long before the seventh-inning stretch.

The Braves were in last place in the IL South, the weather (of course) was hot, hotter, and hottest, and there were nights when it felt as if there were more crickets in the ballpark than fans. This was one of those nights—early August, the first day of school in the county—

and a crowd of 1,881 that looked more like 881 would be in the ball-park, even though it was a pretty summer night.

"It's this time of year when playing baseball is a job," said Car-lyle as he looked around the empty park prior to that night's game. "I've been doing this for seventeen years now. I've played in Japan and Korea, I've played in the majors and in the minors. I've thought my career was over and gotten another chance. I think I appreciate how lucky I am to play the game—or, more specifically, to still be playing the game.

"But you get home at four o'clock in the morning and then you're back at the ballpark mid-afternoon, and you know the place is going to be empty when the game starts, and it does get to be a grind. Then again, every job has tough days."

He smiled. "I guess when you've flown those major-league char-ters, sitting in the middle seat when you fly and getting a small salad and a cookie is a little bit more difficult than if you haven't flown them."

Carlyle had flown or ridden in just about every kind of plane or bus imaginable since the day he decided to bypass college as an eighteen-year-old kid in Bellevue, Nebraska, and sign with the Reds for a $270,000 bonus as a second-round draft pick.

"That money felt like $270 *billion* at the time," he said, laughing. "I figured, this is it, I'm set for life, I never have to earn another dol-lar beyond this. I also never counted on what it was going to feel like at that age going from living at home with my parents to playing in Princeton, West Virginia, two weeks after I signed. That's the thing about the decision you make coming out of high school to sign: life on a college campus is considerably different than life in the low minor leagues."

Carlyle had made it to the majors in 1999 at the age of twenty-one, called up to the San Diego Padres (the Reds had traded him there the previous year) for seven starts. That was when the odys-sey began. The Padres traded him to Japan, which didn't bother him then, because he was young and he and his wife, Jessica, had no kids and thought the travel would be fun. Then it was back to pitch in the minors for the Royals and the Yankees before he made it back to the Dodgers briefly in 2005. He pitched ten games in relief before an appendectomy shut him down.

More travel followed. He signed with the Marlins, who sold him to a team in Korea. Since he wasn't yet arbitration eligible, having not yet spent three years in the majors, off he went. That winter, Roger McDowell, who had been his pitching coach in Las Vegas when he had been with the Dodgers, had taken the job as the Braves' pitching coach, and he recommended that they sign Carlyle. It was that year— 2007—that his life settled down a little and he began to have some success at the major-league level.

He pitched well in Richmond to start the season and was called up to the Braves in May. He ended up getting twenty big-league starts and won the second game of his major-league career—the first had come in San Diego in 1999—in June. He went on to finish 8-7 with a high (5.21) ERA. A year later the Braves made him a reliever, and he had his best year, pitching to a 3.59 ERA. Finally, it seemed, at the age of thirty, he was an established major-league pitcher.

"Pitching for Bobby [Cox] was the best experience I've ever had as a baseball player," he said. "It was like being managed by your grandfather. He made you feel as if he cared about you that much every day. And he always knew the right thing to say.

"One night I'm out there and just getting crushed. Everything is a line drive. Bobby comes out to get me, and as I hand him the ball, he says, 'The umps just didn't give you anything tonight.' I knew the umps had nothing to do with me getting lit up, but it made me feel better. Those two years were a lot of fun. I felt as if I belonged."

And then life intervened. The next spring, after starting the season with the Braves, Carlyle began to feel weak and started having dizzy spells. His weight dropped very suddenly—twenty pounds in a little more than a week. He went in for tests and was diagnosed with type 1 diabetes—just as Sam Fuld had been diagnosed at the age of ten. Being diagnosed at thirty-one when you are the father of two small children was a little bit different.

"To call it a life-changing event is a vast understatement," he said, smiling. "To begin with, I felt awful for a good long while. Then, when you get into a regimen with insulin shots and monitoring your [sugar] levels all the time, it becomes part of your day. But you're aware of it all the time. It isn't like you go a day or two or even a few hours and then think, 'Oh, I better check my level.'

Carlyle actually managed to come back and pitch in the majors before the end of the 2009 season, a true feel-good story. Of course major-league baseball teams don't care much about feel-good stories; they care about winning. Carlyle wasn't offered a contract for 2010 and landed back in Japan for another year. This time, with two young children (seven and four years old), it wasn't as easy as the first time around.

"It had become a job," he said. "That was the first time I remember thinking to myself, 'Life is short, but this season is very long.'"

He came home and bought a house in Atlanta. He had made $425,000 pitching for the Braves in 2009 and almost as much in Japan. Jessica had a job as an English teacher and a basketball coach at a local high school, so it made sense. He signed with the Yankees, made it up briefly, but was released in August. He decided to take one more shot—or so he thought—when the Braves offered him a minor-league contract for 2012.

"I'm thirty-four, and I still believe I can pitch in the majors again or I wouldn't be here," he said. "The good news is I can make the commute from here to Atlanta most of the time and not be away from my kids except when we're on the road. Sometimes, though, I just accept the fact that I can't make it back. We got home at four o'clock this morning; we have a game tonight, so I went and slept at [fellow pitcher] Peter Moylan's house. A couple of times I've just slept in the clubhouse because it was easier."

He sighed. "That's when I feel old. That's when I wonder what happened to the teenage kid with all those hopes back in West Virginia in the summer of 1996.

"The thing about baseball is, in the end, there are no excuses. It's great when your manager says the umps didn't give you anything, but you know better and so does he. The numbers don't lie in this game.

They might lie when a bloop becomes a hit or a line drive becomes an out, but over the long haul they don't lie.

"I've been around long enough to know you have to be careful who you talk to down here. Negativity can get contagious very quickly, especially when the team is struggling and it's a million degrees out and there's no one in the stands. It can happen in a second.

"The Braves gave me a second life as a baseball player when they signed me in '07. I'm proud that I've fought through the diabetes to be here. I know it's not a pipe dream to think I could be in Atlanta pitching the ninth inning tomorrow. You keep grinding, taking the ball, and getting outs, anything can happen.

"I used to be a guy who whenever someone else went up I'd beat my head against the 'why-not-me' wall. I'm long past that. I've packed enough cars going in both directions to not worry about it anymore."

He smiled again. "You know what I've learned through all the years and all the moves? The stroller never fits in the car when you've packed everything else. I've left a lot of strollers behind in a lot of different places."

———

J. C. Boscan had been luckier than Carlyle. He hadn't had to leave nearly as many strollers behind. He was two years younger than Carlyle but was in his sixteenth season in baseball since he had signed his first contract with the Braves as a sixteen-year-old coming out of Venezuela.

"I still remember the day I flew to Florida after I had signed," he said. "My mother cried at the airport. I think she was proud of me, but she was also worried about her little boy."

Her little boy wasn't that little. Boscan—Jean Carlos—was six feet two and a solid 190 pounds by the time he was fourteen. He was already being scouted at that point because international players can be signed by major-league teams at sixteen. "I was big and strong," he said. "I could throw and I could hit. The scouts were there all the time. If I could have signed at fourteen, I would have."

He was sixteen when the Braves offered him $210,000 to sign.

He used the money to buy a car for himself and a farm for his parents. He went to play rookie ball in the summer of 1997 for the Braves' Gulf Coast League rookie-ball team in Orlando. Unlike Charlie Montoyo, who learned to speak English watching baseball and *Bewitched* on TV, Boscan learned from his teammates.

"Never been much of a watcher of baseball," he said. "I just like to play. There weren't that many Latin players in the game back then, and a lot of my teammates were older [as in eighteen or nineteen] and they took care of me. They made sure I learned to speak English correctly."

Boscan speaks English now as if he grew up in Minnesota, not Maracaibo. There is barely the hint of an accent. Learning English, as it turned out, was a lot easier than learning how to hit breaking pitches with any consistency as he moved up the minor-league ladder.

"I had a good year in 2004," he said. "I was only twenty-four, so I hadn't been discouraged. I was in Triple-A, and at the end of the season they sent me to the Instructional League and said, 'Keep playing because you're going to get called up.' Only I didn't get called up.

"The next year, things began to go backward. I was a free agent at the end of the year, and I thought I needed to go someplace else where they didn't just see me as an organization guy. I signed in Milwaukee, and it was a disaster. I played badly—couldn't hit at all. Ended up back in Double-A."

He tried another change of scenery for 2007, signing with the Reds. The results were largely the same. More time in Double-A— and very little playing time there. He was, at best, stuck in neutral and was looked at as an old twenty-seven because he had been around for ten years.

"I told my wife I thought I might be done," he said. "I knew I had to show someone it was worth taking a chance to sign me. I didn't even have a job in winter-league ball in Venezuela. I had hit rock bottom."

Boscan called Phil Regan, the former relief pitcher and major-league pitching coach who had been managing in Venezuela for years. He had played for Regan in the past, and Regan was now managing the team in Margarita. Boscan was blunt when he called. "I need a job," he said. Regan told him he had one for him.

He had playing time for him too, and Boscan, who had almost always hit well in winter ball, did so again. Midway through the winter season he got a call from Rolando Petit, the scout who had signed him to his first contract as a sixteen-year-old.

"I've got a [minor-league] Braves contract for you to sign," he said. "Do you want it?"

"I think I said yes before he finished the sentence," Boscan said.

Just as they had done for Buddy Carlyle, the Braves gave Boscan a second life.

He spent most of 2008 in Double-A but was more laid-back than he had been in the past.

"I had a different attitude," he said. "I stopped being frustrated that I wasn't in the major leagues." He shook his head. "Don't get me wrong, I still prayed I would get the chance, but I stopped thinking of myself as a failure because I hadn't gotten there."

Coincidence or not, he began to hit better—perhaps because he was more relaxed at the plate and not squeezing the sawdust out of the bat the way he had in previous years. By 2009 he was back in Triple-A and made the All-Star team. Which led to the scene in the Gwinnett clubhouse in 2010 when the call to the majors finally came.

"Brundy [Brundage] tells people he didn't mess with me at all because he saw the look on my face when I went in," he said, a smile creasing his face as he sat in the almost-empty clubhouse where his best baseball moment had taken place. "Actually, for a minute he did. The first thing he said when I sat down was, 'JC, you've been playing a long time, haven't you?' For a split second I panicked because I thought he was going to tell me I should feel good about my career but this was the end.

"Then he said, 'Have you ever been to the big leagues?'

"That's when I thought maybe this was it because he knew I'd never been. *Everyone* knew I'd never been. That was when he said, 'I was going to mess with you, but I can't,' and he told me I was going up. I'll never forget the words: 'This is your day.' I'm sure I was crying by the time he finished the sentence."

When Boscan got to Atlanta the next day, the first thing he did was take a picture of his uniform hanging in his locker.

"I'd had a major-league uniform in the big-league locker room in spring training," he said. "But that was different. In spring training, you're a visitor. This time I felt like I really belonged."

He was along for the ride as the Braves tried to get Cox to the playoffs one final time that September. He got to bat only once—and walked. That meant he had an on-base percentage in the majors of 1.000, but technically he did not have an at-bat, just a plate appearance.

A year later the Braves brought him back for another September cameo, and in the heat of another pennant race he got to the plate nine times and got his first three major-league hits.

"Because I'm a catcher, I feel like I'll get chances longer than most guys," he said. "But regardless of what happens the rest of my career, I will never—*never*—forget the day I got called up.

"I remember it minute to minute. If I played down here for another ten years, that memory will never change."

It wasn't just Boscan's best moment. "Because I've done this awhile, I've had the chance to send quite a few guys up, many for the first time," Brundage said. "But that moment with JC, the look on his face when he realized what I was telling him, and, to be honest, the way his teammates looked when we went out into the clubhouse . . ." He paused. "Never seen anything quite like it. Doubt I ever will again.

"Hot nights in August during a long season like this one, you think back to that moment and you smile. And you remember why you have a great job."

32

Slice of Life

On July 21, 2012, John Lannan made it back to the big leagues. It had been three and a half months since Davey Johnson had found Lannan in the tunnel during the Washington Nationals exhibition game with the Red Sox and had to tell him he was being exiled to Syracuse.

Now Lannan was back. His chance came because a rainout earlier in the season had forced the Nationals and the Atlanta Braves to play a day-night doubleheader in Washington, as part of what had become a crucial four-game series.

His start that night became even more crucial after the way the series began. On Friday night, the Nationals had a 9–0 lead after five innings (with ace Stephen Strasburg on the mound) and somehow found a way to lose 10–9 in eleven innings. The next afternoon, they were shut out 4–0, shut down for six innings by Ben Sheets—another pitcher trying to restart his major-league career. Suddenly what had once been a comfortable lead in the National League East was down to one and a half games with Lannan, a Triple-A pitcher all season, scheduled to pitch in the night game.

"I loved getting the ball in that situation," Lannan said later. "If you don't love it, then you need to find another job."

Easy to say, not so easy to get that job done. But Lannan did just that. He gave up two runs in the first inning and nothing afterward, leaving the game after seven innings with a 3–2 lead that became a 5–2 Nationals victory. After the game his teammates gave him a Gatorade shower as he did a postgame TV interview.

Then Johnson called him into the same office where he had given him the news that he was being sent down in April and told him he'd done a great job and that the team would call him when he was needed again. He was on a plane back to Syracuse the next morning and had dinner by himself that night sitting at the bar of a Pizzeria Uno.

Welcome back to Triple-A.

Thirteen days after his win over Atlanta, Lannan got the same call from Washington. This time the day-night doubleheader was against the Miami Marlins due to another early season rainout. Lannan pitched in the afternoon game. He gave up three runs in six innings and got another win, this time 8–3, and another plane ticket back to Syracuse.

"By then, I had stopped second-guessing or even first-guessing what they were going to do," he said. "I knew as long as all five starters were healthy up there, I was going to be in Syracuse. They had made their decision in April, and all of them had pitched well."

That wasn't exactly true. Ross Detwiler, who had beaten Lannan out for the fifth starting spot, had pitched well. But Edwin Jackson, whom the Nationals had thrown $11 million at during the winter in large part because they were conned by his agent, Scott Boras, had been decidedly mediocre. Boras had persuaded team owner Ted Lerner to sign Jackson as backup for Stephen Strasburg—another Boras client.

Boras had already convinced Nationals general manager Mike Rizzo that he should shut Strasburg down after he had pitched 160 innings in 2012, even if he was healthy, to make *sure* he had no recurrence of the elbow problems that had led to Tommy John surgery in 2010. Then he talked the owner into spending $11 million on Jackson to fill a role that Lannan could have filled as well or better.

As upset as he had been in April when he'd been demoted, Lannan was resigned to his fate by August. He went back to Syracuse and continued to work with pitching coach Greg Booker on his delivery. In his last two Triple-A starts of the season he pitched shutouts. Then, with the Nationals getting ready to shut Strasburg down in early September, he was finally called back to the big leagues for good at the end of August.

He was very happy to be back in the major leagues for a stint that lasted more than twenty-four hours. It had been a long summer in Syracuse.

———

If there is one person in the International League who does not crave a call from the major leagues, it is Randy Mobley.

Mobley has spent his entire life in the state of Ohio and his entire adult life working in the minor leagues. He grew up in Hamilton—about thirty miles north of Cincinnati; got his academic degrees at Otterbein College (sixteen miles northeast of Columbus) and at Ohio State (an MBA). While there, he worked as an intern for the Columbus Clippers and then was hired for a job in the International League office, which was then in Grove City (ten miles southwest of Columbus). After he became the league president in 1990, he moved the office back to Columbus.

There is no truth to the rumor that he has never been outside the state of Ohio.

"If you describe me as a midwestern kid, though," he said, "that would certainly be accurate."

Mobley is fifty-four and looks younger than that, perhaps because he's completely satisfied with his life. He and his deputy, Chris Sprague, run a two-man league office, and there are very few people in the league who have any complaints with the way the two of them keep the league's engine running.

"I've been very lucky," he said on a comfortable summer night in Columbus (where else?) as he looked around an almost-full Huntington Park. "I grew up in this league, got to run this league when I was very young [thirty-two], and I still love what I'm doing because the job changes so much from year to year. It's never boring."

Mobley has certainly seen change since he first worked for the Clippers more than thirty years ago. Back then, they played in Cooper Stadium, on the outskirts of town, right off I-70. The ballpark had been around forever, as the home first of the old Columbus Red Birds and then of the Columbus Senators before the Clippers came to town in 1977 (after the city had gone six years without a Triple-A team).

"This ballpark, all the parks that have been built in the last few years, is symbolic of how far we've come in the minor leagues," Mobley said. "What you saw in *Bull Durham* really doesn't exist anymore. In fact, I don't think you can refer to us as 'the bush leagues' anymore either. This isn't the major leagues, but it's a long way from being the bush leagues."

Huntington is the prototype of the modern minor-league park. It is in downtown Columbus, with parts of the city skyline serving as a backdrop. It is named for a bank, which paid $23 million for twelve years for the naming rights when the stadium opened in 2009. Its capacity is 10,100, but because of the grassy areas beyond the outfield fences the one-game attendance record is 12,517. It has all the modern amenities, corporate boxes, and corporate-named "porches" beyond the outfield fences. Franklin County built the ballpark for $70 million and maintains it. The clubhouses, especially the home clubhouse, would be considered quite acceptable as visiting clubhouses in most major-league parks.

The fact that the Clippers' clubhouse comfortably fits a Ping-Pong table is a perfect example of how far minor-league life has come in terms of comfort level.

"It's still a place where no one wants to stay very long, for obvious reasons," Mobley said. "The financial differences for ballplayers, for umpires, for broadcasters, are still huge. But getting sent back down isn't quite the culture shock it used to be in the old days."

Mobley played a major role in the realignment of the minor leagues that occurred in 1998, leading to what exists now. Where there had once been three leagues in Triple-A—the International League, the American Association, and the Pacific Coast League—there are now two: the IL and the PCL, which combined, for all intents and purposes, to swallow the AA in that 1998 shake-up.

Since 2006 the two leagues have staged a one-game "National

Championship" between their respective champions. The game is basically meant to be a showcase for Triple-A players who have had good seasons, although, as Mobley points out, it is also worth some extra money for the players: $2,000 per player to the winning team and $1,000 per player to the losing team. For men making somewhere between $8,000 and $15,000 a month on a six-month-a-year job, that isn't a bad one-game bonus.

"I'm one of those lucky people who found a niche early that I'm completely comfortable with," Mobley said. "My family [he has two grown children] grew up here, and I enjoy the people I work with. I guess I'm the one minor leaguer who has no aspirations of ever becoming a big leaguer."

Just don't call him a bush leaguer.

33

Tomko and Lindsey

IT'S NEVER OVER TILL...

Brett Tomko was back in uniform . . . again.

He had gone home after David Bell had given him the news that the Reds were releasing him from Louisville and wondered if he had finally reached the end of the line as a baseball player. Louisville had been his twenty-fifth stop in his eighteen years as a professional pitcher—ten in the majors; fifteen in the minors. Maybe that was the final number. Maybe it was time to jump off the carousel.

Or maybe not.

He had been home in Phoenix for a week with Julia and the twins, who were now a month shy of turning three, when the phone rang. It was Joe Longo, his agent. The Arizona Diamondbacks were interested in signing him for the rest of the season. Tomko wasn't too surprised to hear that the call had come from the Diamondbacks: he knew that David Bell would put in a good word for him with his brother Mike, who was their farm director.

Even so, when Longo said "Arizona," for a split second Tomko thought the perfect storm had landed in his backyard: not only was he being offered a job, but the Diamondbacks were right there in Phoenix. He could live in his own home and pitch again.

Then he came back to reality. The Diamondbacks' offer was to go to Mobile, Alabama—which was 1,640 miles from his backyard—and, beyond that, in the Double-A Southern League. That was the offer: BayBears or bust. Tomko sighed, packed again, and got on a plane to fly to Alabama.

He still believed he could pitch—as he had told Bell before leaving Louisville—and, sure enough, given the ball in Mobile, he had two good outings in a row. He even got a couple of wins, something that hadn't happened in Louisville even on those nights when he had pitched well. The Diamondbacks noticed, and on August 24 they moved him up to Reno—which was in contention for the PCL playoffs.

"It all happened very quickly," Tomko said. "On August 1, I was in Louisville pitching for a last-place team. The next day I'm released. Three weeks later I've been to Mobile and I'm in Reno pitching for a team where the games actually kind of matter. The stadium was full, which was nice too. The important thing was I was still playing baseball."

He was playing in the twenty-seventh city of his career.

Tomko wasn't expecting the Diamondbacks to call him up in September. He still believed he could help, just as he believed he could have helped the Reds. But he was thirty-nine, and he had been released less than a month earlier. He knew his chances for a call-up were somewhere between slim and none, and slim rarely shows up in Triple-A in late August.

So he put his head down and kept grinding. He got two starts in Reno before the playoffs began. They were a lot like his starts in Louisville: reasonably good, but not as good as Tomko would have liked. Still, he was on the playoff roster when the Aces began the postseason against Sacramento—a team that Tomko, not surprisingly, had pitched for in the past.

"Let's face it, there aren't a lot of places where I *haven't* pitched," he joked.

The first-round playoff series was a best of five with no off days, meaning each team would need five starting pitchers unless one of the managers decided to start someone on three days' rest. That was, generally speaking, frowned upon in the minors, even in postseason. Aces manager Brett Butler let Tomko know that if there was a fifth and deciding game, he would go with his No. 5 starter and not bring back game-one starter Charles Brewer on short rest.

Which meant, if the series came down to a fifth game, Tomko would have the ball.

He was still in the game.

————

There are two kinds of Augusts in major-league baseball. There are the Augusts when a team is in contention and the ballpark is full or close to full every day. It may be hot, but you almost don't notice, because the games are important and the electricity in the building fills you with adrenaline.

"When you take the field at home and you hear the crowd, the only thing you feel at that moment is the rush," said Nate McLouth, who had gone from unemployed in early June to starting in left field in Baltimore in early August. The Orioles were contending for the first time in fifteen years, and even though the fans were only just beginning to notice, the feeling in Camden Yards each night was different than it had been the previous fourteen Augusts.

Then, the Orioles had been going through the other kind of August. The kind where you drag into the ballpark in the middle of the afternoon—or, worse, the middle of the morning for day games—and stay in the air-conditioned clubhouse until the last possible moment. During Augusts like that, you tell yourself there's still a lot to play for: your future, your pride, and those who loyally show up night after night even when the team is going nowhere.

Still, it is tough to take the field to the sounds of silence. It isn't fun, for example, to be a New York Met and play in a ballpark technically called "Citi Field" but dubbed by New York radio talk show host Steve Somers "Citi Morgue."

"The only good thing about a season like that is you find out a lot about guys," said Tony La Russa, who had managed through very few of those seasons during thirty-three years as a major-league manager. "The guy who still comes to play, even when it doesn't matter, is the guy you want to keep around. The guy who has already mentally packed it in, you probably don't want."

He smiled. "Of course they're all in the big leagues, making big-league money, living the big-league life. It isn't exactly all bad."

It is a lot better than August in Triple-A, regardless of a team's record. Charlie Montoyo's mantra that he kept repeating to his players: "It's a lot less hot in August when you're winning than when you're losing," was true—up to a certain point.

Montoyo had been through five Triple-A Augusts as the manager of a contending team. He preferred that to the August he was living through in 2012, with a team that was under .500 and would be packing its bags to go home as soon as the season ended on September 3.

"You come to the park every day, and you give your best effort," Montoyo said. "You have to do that for your players. Some of them are going to be September call-ups. They're all fighting for that chance. That's really what they've got left to play for now. That and making sure they have a job next year."

That's what John Lindsey was playing for in August. He hadn't had a job with a major-league team at the start of 2012 and had gotten to Toledo (via Laguna, Mexico) only in June. The Mud Hens weren't in contention either, and Lindsey was about 99 percent certain he wasn't going to be a September call-up to the Tigers. Most of the time when an older player gets a September call-up, it is to a non-contending team that wants to reward him with a month in the majors. The Tigers were fighting for their lives in the American League Central, and their late-season needs were more about relief pitchers and defense.

Lindsey couldn't pitch, and he wasn't especially good playing defense. He knew his season would end in Toledo. The larger question had become where he might be in 2013.

"I think the good thing about the last couple months is that I've proven I can still hit and I can still hit with some power," he said. "I don't think there's any doubt the work that I did last off-season, the weight I lost, have added time to my career. I would hope that someone will want to give me a job next year."

Lindsey had become the Mud Hens' everyday DH, hitting cleanup more often than not. He had responded with fifteen home runs and forty-seven RBIs once he had joined the team, in only sixty-five games. If you did the math on those numbers over a full Triple-A season that meant Lindsey would hit about thirty-three home runs and drive in 105 runs. Those were numbers that would get people's attention.

Lindsey had something else going for him, even though he would turn thirty-six in the off-season.

"If you had a clubhouse full of John Lindseys, managing would be the easiest job in the world," said Phil Nevin, Lindsey's manager the second half of 2012. "He's the first guy here every day. He does exactly what you ask him to, and he's just the kind of example you want for younger players to be around.

"That can be an issue at Triple-A. Sometimes you have older guys moping around, constantly pissed off at their lot in life. John's just the opposite."

Of course there were reasons for that. Lindsey had spent twenty-two days in the major leagues . . . and a total of eighteen years in the minors. In spite of Tony La Russa's theory that it took about ten days for a player to develop a "major-league attitude," he wasn't even close to having one. He had spent so much time on the other side—the vision problems that had slowed his development, the years in independent ball, and the half season in Mexico—that he was grateful to be in Toledo.

"I've probably enjoyed this season as much as any in my career," he said. "Part of it is that when spring training began, I didn't know if I'd be playing anywhere. I knew I wanted to try to play, but I wasn't sure I'd get a chance—especially this close to the big leagues. If I can get a contract before spring training and go to camp with a chance to show people what I can still do . . ." His face twisted into a smile. "Of course no one knows better than I do how much easier that is said than done."

Even so, Lindsey knew he was back to being just an accident away. That was a long way from Laguna.

34

Slice of Life

SYRACUSE

Zach Duke knew as well as anyone in baseball the truth of "being an accident away."

He had been burning up the International League in 2005 as a twenty-two-year-old phenom when the phone call had come from Pittsburgh. Oliver Pérez, one of the Pirates' starting pitchers, had broken his big toe kicking over a laundry cart in the clubhouse during a post-start fit of temper. The Pirates needed someone to take his place, and they wanted the young lefty, who had a 12-3 record with a 2.32 ERA at the end of June, to be that person.

"The funny thing about my career is how quickly the highs and the lows have come," Duke said with a laugh. "I started out as a non-prospect [drafted in the twentieth round by the Pirates in 2001] and then became a hot prospect and then, suddenly, someone they were kind of building their future around."

He shook his head. "And then a crash to earth."

There weren't very many players still stuck in Triple-A in August 2012 who were not counting the days until the end of the season. Duke was a rare exception. He was happy to be on the roster of the Syracuse Chiefs and, more important, happy to feel as if he could pitch successfully again.

"When you get released, it really doesn't matter how they phrase it or what they tell you," he said. "The bottom line is you've been fired.

You aren't good enough to do your job. That's a terrible feeling. Going home to your partner and saying, 'I've been fired, I'm out of work,' is about as low as you can get professionally."

Duke had gone through that experience in March 2012, when the Houston Astros had released him. "The worst part of it was they were absolutely right to do what they did," he said. "I deserved it."

His release, on March 27, came less than three years after he had been a National League All-Star. It came two years after the Pirates had paid him $4.3 million to be an important part of their rotation.

"It was a quick climb and a long fall," he said. "I'll say this much: I've learned a lot about baseball and about myself during the fall."

Duke had grown up in Waco, Texas, and was considered a prospect in part because he was left-handed and in part because he had almost uncanny control for a teenager. But he wasn't a flamethrower. He was more like Tom Glavine (one of his boyhood heroes), someone who could spot his pitches with remarkable consistency. That was good enough to get him drafted but not enough to make anyone think he was destined to be an All-Star.

"It really changed when I was in Single-A ball in Hickory [North Carolina] in '03," he said. "I found a routine that worked for me. I wasn't technically perfect by any means; in fact I probably threw across my body too much. But I could stand on the mound and know exactly—I mean exactly—where just about every pitch I threw was going to go. I felt like I could do it in my sleep."

He wasn't sleepwalking when he pitched to a 1.46 ERA in two minor-league towns in 2004. That earned him a spot in Indianapolis in 2005, a quick rise for any pitcher but remarkable for someone whose fastball rarely touched ninety.

Two important things happened in Indianapolis: he continued to pitch lights out, making the call when Pérez threw his tantrum the easiest decision the Pirates could possibly make. And he met a Butler University journalism/theater major named Kristin Gross.

"She was the on-field MC for all the various promotions," Duke said. "I asked her out three times. She said no three times. Finally, she said yes and stood me up. I asked her what the deal was, and she said no way did she want to date a baseball player. I finally said, 'Look, have dinner with me one time, and if we don't have fun, I promise I'll leave you alone.'"

She said yes . . . and she didn't date a baseball player for that long, because she ended up marrying him. By then he was a star.

Duke pitched in Pérez's place on July 2 and struck out nine Milwaukee Brewers but left with the game tied and ended up with a no-decision. His next five starts were not no-decisions, they were all wins—making him the second Pirates pitcher *ever* to start his career with a 5-0 record. His ERA for the month of July was 0.87 and included a 3–0 shutout of the Cubs when his opponent was Greg Maddux.

"It was dizzying," Duke said. "Remember, I was two years removed from pitching in low Class A, and now I'm an important part of the Pirates' rotation. At that point, it all seemed very easy."

He finished that season 8-2 with an ERA of 1.81. The Pirates were a bad team—they had just completed their thirteenth straight season with a losing record. Duke and Ian Snell, another young pitcher, became their poster boys for 2006. It was a lot to handle—especially on a team that still didn't have enough players to compete seriously.

Duke didn't pitch poorly the next few seasons, even though he had losing records. But he wasn't as dominating as he had been as a rookie.

"Part of it was just the normal hitters-adjusting-to-a-new-pitcher thing that happens. But somewhere along the line I lost that routine I had. I was trying to copy it, copy myself basically, but I wasn't doing it. When I struggled, like most people do, I tried to change things, and that wasn't the right thing to do. It wasn't as if I pitched really horribly; I just didn't pitch as well as I had when I first came up."

In 2009, Duke's salary in his first year of arbitration soared to $2.2 million. Even though his final record that season was 11-16 (with another bad team), he was a workhorse—pitching 213 innings. He also made the All-Star team as the Pirates' lone (required) representative.

"I still remember looking around that clubhouse saying, 'What am I doing in here with *these* guys?'" he said, laughing. "I took a lot of pictures and a lot of videos just so I could prove later on that I'd actually been there."

A year later his salary almost doubled to $4.3 million, but he didn't pitch as well. His ERA by season's end was 5.72, and rather than continue to pay him big money without knowing what they were getting, the Pirates traded him to Arizona during the off-season.

It was there that the injury bug began to bite him: he had broken a bone in his foot the previous season, and he rushed through his rehab to be ready for spring training in 2011 with a new team.

"I thought they were right on the verge of doing something good," he said. "I'd been with a losing team for a long time, and I was excited about potentially being with a winner. I wanted a taste of winning. The break was between the fourth and fifth metatarsals, and I probably came back too fast . . . I had trouble pushing off on the foot.

"It's not as if I throw all that hard to begin with," he said. "Then I got hit with a line drive during spring training, and that set me back too. I had no endurance. My velocity dropped, and my ERA went up. Bad combination. I went from starting to being the second lefty out of the bullpen. I hadn't pitched in relief my entire pro career. I wasn't awful. But I wasn't very good either."

He signed a two-way minor-league/major-league contract with the Astros for 2012, thinking he might have a chance to claim a spot in their rotation. But from the moment he reported to camp, nothing went right.

"They were looking for something to make me the pitcher I had been," he said. "Every day it seemed like a different coach was telling me to try something different. Move here, move there. Try this delivery. I really wanted to say, 'Hey, lay off.' But I wasn't in a position to do that.

"When they released me, based on my performance, I had no argument with it."

He and Kristin sat down after he got home. Maybe, Zach said, it was time to move on to the next thing. She had a better idea: Why don't you contact Tony Beasley?

Beasley had been Duke's manager in both Hickory at Single-A and Altoona in Double-A and had been the Pirates' third-base coach in 2008 and 2009. Now he was managing the Washington Nationals' Triple-A team in Syracuse. Duke sent him a text.

Within a couple of hours, the team had been in touch with his agent to offer him a minor-league contract to go play for Syracuse.

"Somebody wanted me . . . that was the best part of it," Duke said. "People hadn't exactly been lining up in the winter before I signed with the Astros, so I wondered if someone would want me after I got released. That's the great thing about sports: it only takes one person to believe in you."

There was a bonus to signing with the Nationals: their minor-league roving pitching instructor was Spin Williams—who had been with the Pirates when Duke was there. "Spin had seen me when I was at my best," Duke said. "I decided I needed one set of eyes on me and that maybe I should try to go back to doing exactly what I was doing when I was at my best with the Pirates."

Duke got in touch with Kevin Roach, the Pirates' video coordinator, and asked if he could find some video of him dating to 2005. Roach sent it to Williams, and Duke reported to the Nationals' extended minor-league camp in Viera, Florida.

"Spin looked at the video and so did I," Duke said. "Then we started working in front of a mirror, literally trying to replicate what I'd been doing. Everyone pitches differently. What works for one guy doesn't work for another. You can't teach someone perfect technique, because there's a human factor involved. No two guys are built the same or pitch the same.

"I went back to pitching the way I pitched best. I had to find out where to stand on the rubber again and realize it was okay to throw a little bit across my body. It came back fairly quickly once I started back down the road."

After a few weeks, Duke was ready to report to Syracuse. He continued to work with Chiefs pitching coach Greg Booker, and Williams stopped in occasionally to check on him. The self-confidence came back.

"I needed to reconfirm in my brain that this was the best way for me to pitch," he said. "I needed to trust what I was doing again. I'd lost trust in myself."

He smiled. "I feel like I've restarted my career. I'd gotten beaten down. I wondered if this was what I should be doing. Now I feel like it is." He paused. "Of course if it wasn't what I should be doing, I'd have no idea what else I could do. This *is* what I do."

By mid-August there was no doubt that the Chiefs' two best pitchers were John Lannan and Zach Duke. They were close in age—Duke twenty-nine, Lannan about to turn twenty-eight—but Lannan was being paid $5 million in 2012 and had successfully started—and won—games in the majors twice that summer. Duke was guaranteed $100,000 on the minor-league side of his contract and hadn't been in the majors all year.

Lannan knew he was going to be called up September 1—especially since the Nationals would need an extra starter when Stephen Strasburg was shut down.

Duke could only hope.

"The key, though, is that I *have* hope," he said. "That's a long way from where I was in March."

35

Lollo

A BAD CALL

Mark Lollo had also come a long way since March. But he wasn't convinced he had gone in the right direction.

As the International League season wound down, Lollo had gotten both good news and bad news: The good news was that he would be the crew chief for both a first-round playoff series and the Governors' Cup finals. That was a nice honor and a pretty strong indication of what International League president Randy Mobley thought of his work.

The bad news was he hadn't been called back to the majors. By September, all the big-league umps had taken their vacations, and only an injury might get an umpire a call-up game. If that happened, Lollo knew it would be one of the guys clearly ahead of him on the list who, by now, had considerably more major-league experience than he did.

On August 29, Lollo was in Gwinnett. Hurricane Isaac had been pounding the Southeast and the Gulf Coast, and Lollo was on the phone with Mobley discussing contingency plans if the doubleheader that had been scheduled in Gwinnett that day (to make up for a rainout the night before) could not be played.

Once they had made their plans, Mobley asked Lollo how he was doing. He was, naturally, aware of the fact that Lollo had gotten called up for only two games because he had to rework umpiring schedules whenever someone went up.

Lollo admitted he was a little bit nervous. It was still only his second year, but he wondered if his going in the wrong direction was coincidence or if it meant something. That was when Mobley offered help.

"You want me to see what I can find out?" Mobley said.

Lollo thought about it for a moment. "Sure, that would be fine," he finally answered. "I'd appreciate it."

Two days later he had gotten the surprise phone call from Cris Jones, his supervisor. Lollo knew that Jones had watched him work five times during the season, and he told him he had comments based on those games. Nervously, Lollo told Jones he was eager to hear them.

"Not now," Jones told him. "We [the umpiring supervisors] have meetings over the weekend, and I'll talk to you about it more thoroughly next week."

Lollo pressed Jones. "I'd like to know what you think now," he said.

Jones sighed and said okay.

"To be honest with you, Mark, you're at the bottom of the [call-up] list," he said.

Lollo had known he wasn't in the top ten based on assignments and had suspected he might not even be in the third group of five.

"So I'm in the bottom tier," he said.

"No," Jones said. "You *are* the bottom. You're rated last. Eighteen out of eighteen. Based on the observations we've done this year, you are not where we want you to be."

That stung. Lollo didn't think it was right or fair. "I felt like I'd had a very good season," he said. "Now I'm being told that, based on five games, I'm on the bottom rung."

There was more.

The supervisors had concerns about his weight and what it might mean in the future. There was also the issue of time off: Two years earlier in the Arizona Fall League, Lollo had missed two days after the death of an uncle with whom he had been close. He had also missed two weeks in the fall of 2011 while his second child was being born.

"There are concerns about your commitment," Jones said. "The amount of time you've missed throws up a red flag."

"Commitment?" Lollo said, starting to get angry. "Because I missed some Fall League games to see my child born? Because I missed two days to go to my uncle's funeral, you question my commitment?"

"I thought it was more than two days," Jones said. "Maybe our records are wrong."

"Two days," Lollo said. "That's it."

"Maybe we got bad information on that."

Lollo asked Jones if his rating was based strictly on Jones's opinions or if there was a consensus.

"Mark, one opinion isn't going to keep you out or get you in," Jones said. "That's not the way it works."

Lollo almost didn't want to ask the next question.

"Am I going to be released?" he finally asked.

There was a long pause. "It's a possibility," Jones answered.

Lollo felt the air go out of him. He had been concerned about not being called up more often, but he hadn't really thought there was a possibility he was going to be out of a job.

When Lollo said nothing, Jones went into what Lollo later called "the farewell spiel."

"He talked about how this was the toughest part of the job and how far I had come to be where I was. Everything you would expect. It was the old 'really love you, you're fired' speech.

"I was stunned. All of a sudden it hit me that I was going to be looking for a job, a full-time job, very soon. I wasn't going to be an umpire anymore. I wasn't going to the big leagues. He'd just told me my dream was dead.

"It hurt. It was sad, very sad. But there was some sense of relief. At least I *knew*. I had to start making plans, had to figure out where and how to start my life over at the age of thirty."

He smiled. "The only good thing was I knew my wife was going to be thrilled. I would be home, a full-time husband and father. I tried to picture her doing cartwheels when I told her so I could cheer myself up.

"Umpiring is never an easy life. If you make it to the big leagues, you can make very good money and live very well. I know I beat the odds: I went from a one-in-a-hundred chance to make the majors full-time to a one-in-three chance. I feel good about the work I did and the people I met.

"I made myself think all those things when I hung up the phone that day. I believe all those things—because they're true."

He paused. "But I'd be lying if I told you it didn't hurt."

36

March to September

The end of the Triple-A season comes quickly. Once August begins, everyone has one eye on the door—knowing it is either going to lead to a September call-up (chances being about one in six on most teams) or home. Making the playoffs is a mixed blessing: It means extra pay, and it means you've won more often than you've lost. But it also means extra travel when you're tired and playing games that ultimately aren't going to get you closer to the big leagues.

"I hope they call every one of my guys up before the playoffs start," said Dave Miley, the manager at Scranton/Wilkes-Barre. "I'll play with whoever they leave me. I know they'd all rather be on a major-league bench someplace than down here playing postseason."

Miley's wish was almost granted. On the night of August 31, after his team had played a "home" game in Pawtucket, came word that six of Miley's players were September call-ups. They were all out of Pawtucket headed for Yankee Stadium within a couple of hours of getting word. Miley, who was going to be the runaway choice for IL Manager of the Year (after his team won the North Division by five games over the PawSox), was left to re-create his roster in four days before the playoffs began.

"Couldn't be happier for all of them," he said.

The happiest among the six players called up had to be Chris Dickerson, who had started the season very angry—not just because he hadn't made the team, but because he had been taken off the forty-man roster when he was sent down early in spring training. He had spent most of the season quietly seething about his fate but had played good enough baseball to force the Yankees to put him back on the forty-man so they could call him up. Teams don't like moving players onto their forty-man roster before September unless they have to, because the player who is removed has to go through waivers, meaning any other team can claim him. The Yankees decided he could help in September when rosters expanded, so he was moved to the forty-man so he could be called up.

"The only answer to what they did," he said one night in July, "is to hit .316."

Which is what he was hitting for Scranton/Wilkes-Barre at that moment.

The Scranton six all made it to Yankee Stadium in time for a Saturday afternoon game against the Baltimore Orioles, who were making life miserable for the Yankees by hanging right with them in the race for the AL Eastern Division lead. For once, the Yankees didn't have to worry about the Red Sox, who were on their way to a horrific 69-93 season, but the pesky Orioles were right on their heels.

On Sunday morning, Dickerson walked into the clubhouse, checked the lineup, and saw that he was playing center field and batting eighth. Curtis Granderson had tweaked a hamstring the day before, and manager Joe Girardi had told Dickerson before he left the clubhouse there was a possibility he might be in the lineup on Sunday.

"Joe has always done that, given me a heads-up if he thinks he's going to start me," Dickerson said. "He just said to me, 'Be ready,' as I was leaving on Saturday. I was definitely ready."

Dickerson's first major-league at-bat of the 2012 season came in the bottom of the second inning against Orioles right-hander Chris Tillman. Catcher Russell Martin was on first base. The count went to 2-1, and Tillman tried to get a cutter inside on Dickerson's hands.

He failed.

Dickerson, expecting the pitch, got his hands into the hitting zone before the ball could cut all the way through it. "I knew it was gone pretty much as soon as it came off the bat," he said. "I turned on it and got all of it. I would have been surprised if it hadn't gone out."

It did, into the right-center-field bleachers, giving the Yankees a 2–0 lead. Dickerson's feet barely touched the ground as he rounded the bases.

"All the home runs I've hit in my life I've never felt like that," he said. "Not as a kid, not the first one I hit in the majors [in 2008]. There was a rush of adrenaline through my body that was unreal. To come back to that stadium after the year I'd had and the way I'd been treated and hit one out my first time up . . ."

He stopped. "Some things are beyond description. You feel it inside you in a way you can't put into words."

As he rounded the bases on that bright Sunday afternoon, Dickerson was a long way from the lonely nights he had spent in hotel rooms throughout the 2012 season. He was back where he believed he belonged.

———

Scott Elarton was pleased with the fact that he had been able to come back from his hamstring injury (after missing only one start) to get back on the mound and—finally—win his sixth game of 2012. But as he watched the final few days of the season wind down in Lehigh Valley, he felt an almost inescapable sense of melancholy.

"Once we knew we weren't making the playoffs [which happened with two games left in the season], I began thinking that Monday [the last game of the season] might be the last time I ever pitched in a real game," he said. "I mean, I had no idea what 2013 was going to hold for me.

"The fact is, after my good start, I fell off a cliff. You can put it any way you want to, but that's what happened. I've thought about it a lot. I know in mid-May, after I'd pitched so well to start the season, I thought there was a real chance I'd get called up. The opportunity was there because the Phillies had guys hurt. In the end, I guess they decided it wasn't worth taking someone off the forty-man [roster] to put me on it for what might only be a couple of starts.

"I get that, but it was definitely a disappointment. Whether that affected me emotionally, I just don't know. But I wasn't the same pitcher the next couple months. So now I'm looking at turning thirty-seven and knowing teams are going to look at my numbers from this season and aren't going to be bowled over. I know I pitched well a lot of the time, and I believe I can still pitch."

He smiled. "But I may be a little bit biased."

During those final days, Elarton made a point of seeking out some of his teammates, especially the older ones, to spend some time talking about life in baseball, about their experiences and their feelings as they knew their careers were winding down.

"It wasn't one of those 'meaning of life' sort of things, nothing like that," he said. "It was just sitting around with guys like Michael Spidale and Pete Orr, who aren't as old as I am [Spidale was thirty, Orr, thirty-three] but who had been around awhile and knew that there probably weren't that many years left—if any, in my case. It was good for me because it made me realize that in spite of all my ups and downs I'd been very lucky. But it also made me think again about the fact that there comes a time when you are no longer a baseball player, and that's tough to handle for all of us. That's why most of us hang on to it for as long as we possibly can."

———

The last day of the season dawned rainy and bleak. The game was scheduled for one o'clock, and Elarton was in the clubhouse early. His car was packed so he could start driving west as soon as the game was over once he had showered and said his good-byes.

The weather report wasn't good—all-day rain was the forecast. But the IronPigs didn't want to send a sellout crowd home—or whatever portion of that crowd showed up—without doing everything possible to play one more baseball game before closing up shop for the winter.

As he was sitting in the clubhouse, it occurred to Elarton that he really wanted the chance to pitch one more game. He wanted to end the season on a high note—two straight good outings—and show people that he had found whatever it was that had been missing when he had gone over the cliff.

But it was more than that. As the rain continued to come down, it occurred to Elarton once more that this might be his last day in a baseball uniform. He walked out to the dugout and sat alone for a while watching it rain, knowing that the chances of playing weren't good at all.

"They were going to wait as long as they could," he said. "But there was going to come a point where playing was dangerous. It wouldn't make sense to risk someone getting hurt in order to play a meaningless game."

Not meaningless to Elarton, but, in the grand scheme of things, meaningless. He was pondering all that when John Suomi joined him in the dugout. Suomi was a month shy of thirty-two and had been playing in the minor leagues for eleven years. This was his fourth stint with Lehigh Valley and the longest he had ever stuck in Triple-A. He had no idea what his future held beyond that afternoon.

Elarton had already seen what life was like without baseball once, and he had struggled with it—in part because he had felt as if he had walked away in mid-sentence: that his struggles with alcohol and his health had *forced* him to leave before he was ready. Now, four years older, at the end of a season in which he had been healthy both emotionally and physically, he still wasn't sure if he was ready to face the end.

"John and I had a long talk about what your last day in baseball might feel like," Elarton said. "We agreed we didn't want it to feel like this, but maybe this was just reality."

Or, in this case, instead of a career ending with a ground ball to shortstop, it might end with a rainout.

The end came officially just before four o'clock when manager Ryne Sandberg told the players the game had been called off. A man of few words to the end, Sandberg thanked everyone for their hard work during the season and wished them all luck.

"I sat there for about two minutes thinking how disappointed I was that I didn't get to pitch one more time," Elarton said. "And then it was over. I got dressed, said some quick good-byes, and I was probably in the car within fifteen minutes of Ryno finishing up. I had a long way to drive."

He had 1,606 miles to drive to get to Lamar. His goal was to be there in time to pick the kids up from school on Wednesday, as they had requested/ordered him to do. "I stopped in a motel and slept for four hours," he said. "Other than that I just kept on going."

And so, when Kenan and Chloe Elarton walked out of school on Wednesday afternoon, their dad was waiting for them—just as he had promised.

It wasn't a perfect ending to the season, but it was a perfect start to the off-season. Or whatever came next.

———

Chris Schwinden was in Allentown that same final day, sitting in the cramped visitors' clubhouse across the hall from the IronPigs' clubhouse. He felt none of the swirling emotions Elarton did as he waited out the last rain delay of the season.

There were reasons for this: For one thing, he would turn twenty-six on his next birthday, not thirty-seven. For another, he wasn't scheduled to pitch. He had ended his season four days earlier on a satisfying note in Rochester, pitching six strong innings (three earned runs, four hits, and five strikeouts) to get the win.

The victory meant he finished the Buffalo portion of his season with an 8-6 record and an ERA of 2.70. During the thirty-five days he had wandered in the Triple-A desert, he had pitched 22.1 innings and given up twenty earned runs. In 106.1 innings in Buffalo he had given up thirty-two earned runs.

Buffalo, as it turned out, was the promised land.

"Some of it was comfort, some of it was getting my confidence back, some of it was being able to develop my changeup as a strikeout pitch," he said, sitting in the first-base dugout on the other side of the infield from where Elarton would soon come out to ponder the rain and his future. "In the end, though, all it means is I've got something to take with me to spring training next year. I still know I'm not the pitcher I need to be to have success in the majors. Triple-A, yes; the majors, so far, no. I haven't won a game there, and I haven't pitched very well there.

"I need to show them that they can give me the ball every fifth day and expect a quality start out of me. Of course, after this year, I'm going to have to earn my way back up there. I know I've fallen back in the pecking order some, but I think I showed them I still have the potential to be a good pitcher.

"I just need another chance."

He smiled. "I guess that's what everyone says, isn't it? 'Give me one more chance.' Well, I can say it too. I hope I get it."

John Lindsey's season ended on an uptick. He had finished 2011 wondering if it might be time to retire. He finished 2012 convinced he still had a chance to get back to the major leagues one more time.

On the penultimate day of the season, a cool, overcast day in Toledo, he hit a three-run fifth-inning home run off Columbus's Eric Berger with a sellout crowd of 9,831 in the ballpark. Even during a 60-84 season, the people of Toledo flocked to Fifth Third Field right until the end.

The home run led the Mud Hens to what would be their last win of the season, an 8–5 decision over the Clippers. The home run was the fifteenth Lindsey had hit since he had arrived in Toledo in June and Phil Nevin had slotted him into the cleanup spot in the lineup. "The guy can flat out hit," Nevin said. "It would help him if he had a natural position defensively, but at this point in his career he really doesn't. But if you need a bat, he's going to give you one."

The Tigers were healthy for their September stretch run, and

Lindsey didn't harbor any fantasies about a late call-up. But he did believe he had revived his career with the season he'd had—starting out in Mexico and ending with success in Triple-A.

"I had to work my way back into a major-league organization," he said. "No one wanted to sign me in the spring. Now I feel like someone is going to give me a chance in spring training next season. I'd like to get into some exhibition games, show people I can hit major-league pitching, at least put that in their minds even if I don't make a team out of camp.

"A year ago I was close to retiring. Now I feel like I'm not that far from the majors. I honestly believe it can happen again. I'm just going to go back and do what I did last off-season, because I think the weight I took off made my bat quicker and kept me fresher during the season.

"Funny thing is, if they looked at the numbers I had this year and I was going to be twenty-six instead of thirty-six, I'd probably be thought of as a pretty hot prospect. I understand how it works. I have to make sure *not* to think about things like that. They just get in the way. I'll just go someplace and try to keep putting up numbers—wherever I might be.

"At least now I feel confident that I'll get a chance. That's all I've ever asked for in the game—a chance."

Lindsey had earned that—for at least one more year.

———

While Elarton, Lindsey, and Schwinden were nearing the ends of their seasons, there wasn't a lot of suspense to the Triple-A pennant races as the season wound down around the league.

The International League division races were all decided before the final weekend—well before it in both the South and the West. Indianapolis won the West by a whopping fourteen-game margin over Columbus, finishing at 89-55, the league's best record. Charlotte won almost as easily in the South, finishing nine games ahead of Norfolk with an 83-61 mark. In the North, Scranton/Wilkes-Barre stumbled a little down the stretch—the long season of travel perhaps catching up—but still finished a comfortable five games ahead of Pawtucket with a final record of 84-60.

The only real suspense was for the wild card spot, with Pawtucket, Lehigh Valley, and Norfolk still having a shot going into the final week of the season. But the PawSox went on a six-game winning streak during the final week, making it impossible for either Lehigh Valley or Norfolk to close ground. They clinched the last playoff spot with two days left in the season, when thirty-eight-year-old Nelson Figueroa pitched eight shutout innings in a 2–0 win over Scranton/Wilkes-Barre (which was playing its first game without the six September call-ups) to raise his record for the season to 12-5.

That meant the playoffs were set: Charlotte would play Indianapolis, and Pawtucket would play Scranton/Wilkes-Barre. Unlike in the majors, where wild card teams don't play a team from their own division in the first round, the playoff matchups are locked in before the season begins. The North champion was scheduled to play the wild card team regardless of what division that team came from.

Minor-league playoffs, especially at the Triple-A level, don't have the urgency that major-league playoffs have, in large part because teams often strip the Triple-A club of key players before or even during the playoffs if they have a need.

"It isn't as if you don't want to win," Pawtucket manager Arnie Beyeler said. "Of course you want to win. And when you get to hold a championship trophy at any level of baseball, it's a special feeling. But it isn't as if this is what you've been building to all season. It isn't the same kind of climax I would think they feel up in the majors."

The series are all best of five, with a two-three format. That means the wild card team—in this case Pawtucket—gets to play its first two games at home. Again, an advantage more at the Triple-A level than in the majors.

"You get down 2–0 and go home knowing you have to win three, it's going to be tough," Charlotte manager Joel Skinner said. "You shouldn't be feeling let down, but it's human nature. Guys are tired; some are unhappy they aren't in the majors. It's just not as easy to get up one more time when you get in a hole like that."

Scranton/Wilkes-Barre found itself in that sort of hole after losing the opening two games in Pawtucket. Returning to their "home" in Rochester, the Yankees found themselves down 3–1 going to the bottom of the ninth inning of game three. Clearly, it was time to call it a season. Somehow, they rallied one more time. After they had scored a run off Tony Peña Jr., Pawtucket manager Beyeler called in veteran Pedro Beato to try to finish off the Yankees. Beato got the second out of the inning, but with the score 3–2, two men out, and a man on first Melky Mesa turned on a Beato fastball and hit it out of the park for a walk-off, two-run homer, keeping the Yankees' season alive.

That moment was cause for a celebration at home plate because it happened with such stunning swiftness. Mesa was surrounded by the time he reached the plate, and suddenly—or so it seemed—the Yankees had life.

"It's a team that won't die," manager Dave Miley said with a satisfied smile after the game.

At least until the next night. On a cool, cloudy night, with an announced attendance of 442 fans milling around Rochester's Frontier Field, the PawSox shelled Yankees starter Vidal Nuño for seven runs in the second inning and cruised to a 7–1 win from there—Nelson Figueroa again the winning pitcher.

That put the PawSox into the Governors' Cup Series against Charlotte, which had beaten Indianapolis in four games. The teams had split two games in Indy before the Knights, playing in front of crowds not much bigger than the ones in Rochester, won the last two games at home to reach the finals.

The championship series didn't take very long. Again, the PawSox were untouchable at home. By the time the teams got back to Charlotte, the Knights not only were down 2–0 but knew they had to face Figueroa, who had been virtually unhittable the last month of the season after being traded by the Yankees to the Red Sox, meaning he had moved from Scranton/Wilkes-Barre to Pawtucket. A crowd of 1,102 showed up for game three, and the Knights never had a lead. Figueroa was again brilliant, and the PawSox clinched their first Governors' Cup since 1984 with a 4–1 victory.

Figueroa had pitched in parts of nine seasons in the majors and had probably never pitched better than he did during the last six weeks of the 2012 season. But it wasn't enough to merit another call-up.

"It's a nice feeling," Beyeler said of winning the title. "I'm sure we'll all remember that we were a part of this."

On the night the championship was clinched, seven of the twenty-five players in uniform had been playing in Pawtucket on opening day in April. All were excited to win and to have their picture taken with the trophy.

And, if truth were told, they all would rather have been someplace else that night.

———

They would rather have been where Scott Podsednik was: playing in Boston for the Red Sox.

Eight days after he had been told to report to Reno by the Arizona Diamondbacks, Podsednik, having received his release, was still in Boston hoping the phone would ring with the news that someone wanted to sign him to a major-league contract.

It hadn't.

"Finally, I decided it was time to pack up and go home," he said. "We made plane reservations, packed the apartment, and put our car on a truck to be shipped back to Texas. Honestly, I thought maybe it was over."

On the morning the Podsedniks were scheduled to fly out of Boston (August 9), the phone finally rang. It was his agent, Ryan Gleichowski. The Red Sox had decided they wanted to re-sign him for the rest of the season. They were willing to guarantee he would stay in the majors—easier in mid-August since rosters would expand on September 1.

The Red Sox had decided to option Ryan Kalish, who was hitting .229, back to Pawtucket. That left an opening for an outfielder, and they decided that Podsednik was the best option.

"It was great to get the call, but it was a little bit wild," Podsednik said, laughing. "I had to get in the car we had rented and chase down our car—because all my stuff was in it. It was a couple of hours down the road, so I called the guys driving the truck and just told them to pull over and wait until I got there. I caught up to them, got what I needed, and turned around and drove back to Boston."

Lisa and the boys went home as had already been planned. Podsednik got an extension on the apartment lease and headed to Cleveland to meet the team there. The Red Sox were just starting a ten-game road trip to Cleveland, Baltimore, and New York. He was back on the road again—but it was in the major leagues.

"I just felt I had proved that I could still produce in the majors, so what was the point of going back to the minors again?" he said. "And I had decided that if I was going to spend time away from my family, even just on road trips, I was going to do it in the major leagues. I was thirty-six years old. I did my time in Triple-A. I went back there at the start of the year, even though I didn't think I belonged there, and I proved when I got to Boston that I didn't belong there.

"So it was a major-league deal or go home. I was happy not to go home."

And the Red Sox were happy to have him back. He was in and out of the lineup the rest of the season, frequently going in as a defensive replacement on the nights he didn't start. He ended up the season with 199 major-league at-bats, a batting average of .302, and eight steals. Solid numbers, the kind that would make most people think the Red Sox would want him back in 2013.

But the team had been unloading big names and salaries even before the end of the season, retrenching after a 69-93 disaster. Manager Bobby Valentine was fired. The Red Sox decided to go young, not old. Podsednik became a free agent at the end of October.

He had gotten his wish and his chance—finally—in 2012. But there were no guarantees for the future.

37

Lollo and Tomko

ENDING

SEPTEMBER 18, 2012 . . . DURHAM, NORTH CAROLINA

The last day of the minor-league baseball season was a perfect day to play ball—indoors. The rain started in Durham before the sun came up, and by mid-afternoon the entire town looked drowned, with the rain still coming down in sheets.

International League president Randy Mobley forced a smile while standing in the lobby of the hotel that was the headquarters for all those who had come from around the country for the national championship game. The Pacific Coast League champions, the Reno Aces, were set to take on the International League champion, the Pawtucket Red Sox, but the weather was presenting a major challenge.

"They're saying that there might be a window late afternoon into the evening for a few hours," Mobley said. "Maybe we'll get lucky. I know everyone wants to get the game in tonight."

Mobley is one of those people who can look at rain coming down sideways and see the rainbow coming behind it. There was no doubt he was right about one thing: everyone wanted to play that night. No one wanted another twenty-four hours of sitting-around time when the next stop on everyone's itinerary was home.

Mark Lollo was also sitting in the lobby as the rain poured down.

Like almost everyone else, he was happy to be someplace other than his room. He listened to Mobley's weather report and shook his head.

"This whole month has been bittersweet, and today sort of sums it all up," he said. "They haven't officially told me yet that I'm going to be released . . . but I feel pretty certain this is my last game. It was great to be chosen as the crew chief for both playoff series I worked, to work the plate in game one of the championship series. That's a nice feeling, that the people you work for respect what you're doing."

He smiled. "My wife's happy. She can't wait for me to come home and stay home and have a job where I won't be on the road all the time. I can't blame her. It's tough when I'm away for a long time and she's at home with two very young kids."

He took a long pause and glanced in the direction of the window, where the rain was still pelting down. "It's just hard to think that whenever I walk off the field—tonight, tomorrow, whenever we play—that's it. I'm not an umpire anymore. I've thought of myself as an umpire since I was a teenager."

Those who play go through what Lollo was going through, but usually not as abruptly—and rarely when they feel their career should still be on an up curve. Someone who has risen from the lowest level of the minors to spend time in the majors rarely finds himself being told he's *done* at the age of thirty. Players are sent back to the minors, yes, but the option to play and move up again is still there. For an umpire, there is no option. It is up or out. Unless someone in New York decided to overrule Cris Jones's evaluation of him, Lollo knew he was out.

"I'm going to work this game tonight as if it's the last one I'll ever work in my life," he said, forcing a laugh. "Because, in all likelihood, it is."

———

Brett Tomko was taking the same approach.

He knew he probably wasn't going to play in the championship game that night but comforted himself knowing that he had played a role in getting Reno to the championship game. He had pitched the deciding fifth game of Reno's series against Sacramento in the opening round of the PCL playoffs, although he hadn't been certain until the day of the game that he'd be able to make it to the mound.

"I was still sore," he said. "Getting back to 100 percent after a major injury at thirty-nine is a lot harder than when you're twenty-nine. When I took my physical with the Diamondbacks, they found all sorts of stuff in my shoulder left over from the injury in Louisville back in May.

"I thought I might flunk, but they said, 'Hey, you're thirty-nine, you're coming back from an injury, this is normal.' I knew I could go out and pitch, but when I did, I was sore. It was okay in the regular season and I pitched pretty well, but when you get in postseason, you *are* trying to win. And when you're playing a win-or-go-home game, you don't want to walk out there and get blown up and walk off the mound knowing you've cost your team a chance to win the ball game."

Reno manager Brett Butler had played in the majors until he was forty, so he understood the notion of pushing a creaky body to the breaking point. Before game four, with Reno up 2–1 in the series, he called Tomko in to see how he was feeling.

"If we have to play tomorrow, you okay?" he asked.

Tomko thought it was important to be honest with Butler, not just to play the brave soldier, because doing so and getting bombed wouldn't help anyone.

"Brett, I'm not 100 percent," he said. "You know that. I think I'm 80, I really believe that. I think I can give you five or six innings, but if you're worried about me not being totally healthy and you want to go with someone else, I understand."

Butler leaned forward and said softly, "Brett, I'd take you at 50 percent. I mean that. Let's see what happens tonight. Then you tell me how you feel if we have to play."

They had to play. Sacramento won the fourth game 7–1, meaning the deciding fifth game would be the next night. Tomko tossed and turned trying to sleep but woke up knowing he wanted to pitch.

"It was there in my gut, I knew I wanted to go out there," he said. "I knew it might be my last time starting a professional game, and I wanted to battle and just give everything I had left. I believed it would be good enough. If I didn't, I wouldn't have pitched."

He told Butler how he felt when he got to the park. Butler nodded—that was the answer he had wanted.

Tomko got through five innings. He pitched out of a couple of jams, gave up three runs early, but kept the Aces in the game. He got everything he could out of the 80 percent he had. He left down 3–0, but the Aces rallied to win 7–4, and he knew he had helped by keeping the score close until their bats had broken loose.

"It wasn't as if I'd gone out and pitched a three-hit shutout," he said. "But I knew I'd done everything I could, and my teammates knew it too. That was a great feeling."

Butler told him the rotation for the PCL championship series against Omaha would be the same as it had been against Sacramento: if there was a game five, Tomko would be his starter. This time, though, there was no game five; the Aces won the fourth game 8–2 to clinch the series and the Pacific Coast League title, meaning they would play Pawtucket in the national championship game in Durham. Tomko was happy to see his team win, although he wouldn't have minded one more chance to pitch.

Like Elarton, he had become keenly aware of the ticking clock and the fact that he might be spending his last days as a baseball player. "It crossed my mind all the time," Tomko said. "I'd find myself thinking, 'Is this the last time I walk into a clubhouse and put on a uniform? Is this the last time I throw a bullpen? Ride a team bus? Check into a hotel? Pack for a road trip?'

"It was all there, very clearly in my mind. I knew I wanted to see if I could play again in '13, but I also know there aren't a lot of jobs for banged-up forty-year-old pitchers—and I'd be forty [April 7] right around opening day. I wanted to make sure I took everything in because it might be my last chance."

Tomko was thinking those thoughts as he walked through the hotel lobby on the afternoon of the championship game, wondering if the game would be played. "I was thinking it might be my last rain-out," he joked.

The lobby was crowded because it was almost time to leave for the ballpark—but no one was sure if there was a ball game to go to. Tomko ran into Lollo, and the two men stopped to chat for a few minutes. They had developed an interesting relationship during the season—not a friendship, because players and umpires can't be friends, but a relationship.

"I had never had him in a game before this season," Lollo said. "I knew who he was because he'd been around such a long time and had been in the majors for so long. Then I had the plate for a game he pitched in May—just before he got hurt.

"I could tell right away why he'd been so successful. He knew *how* to pitch, how to work a batter. Early in the game, there were some pitches I could tell he wanted that I didn't give him. I have a pretty consistent zone. Good pitchers figure that out. He never reacted like, 'You missed it'; I could just tell when he wanted one—good pitchers push that envelope because the more zone they can get, the tougher it is for the hitter. But he adjusted and pitched a really good game.

"I ran into him later and he said nice things about the way I worked the game and I told him the same. After that, whenever we had Louisville someplace, I'd chat with him a little. They were strug-gling as a team, and a lot of the other guys in the league didn't like working their games very much. [Manager] David Bell got on people a lot, but I got along fine with him too. I liked working their games."

Lollo told Tomko he was glad to see he had found another place to pitch after Louisville had given him his release in early August. Tomko, who knew that Lollo had worked games in the majors, asked him how his season had gone.

"Well, I'm here, which is good," Lollo said. "But I've been told I'm probably going to be released at the end of the season."

Tomko was stunned. He thought Lollo was a good umpire and a good guy. As a player, he never really thought much about umpires either moving up or being moved out.

"It really hit me," he said. "Here I was thinking I might be at the end, but knowing I was going to go home and look at my options. He didn't have any options. They just said, 'You're gone,' and it might be because one guy just didn't like him for some reason. I honestly felt awful after we talked. I kept looking at him all through the game thinking about how unfair it was."

Lollo was working first base because he'd had the plate during the All-Star game, meaning the lead umpire for the PCL, Eric Loveless, would work the plate. Loveless had never made the call-up list, and like Lollo he had been told he wasn't coming back for 2013.

That meant there were three men in the game who knew this was their last night on a baseball field: Loveless, Lollo, and Aces catcher Ryan Budde, who had decided at the age of thirty-three that it was time to move on with his life. Budde had been to the majors four times between 2007 and 2010, playing in twenty-nine games during that time. He had gone 7 for 33 and hit a home run. He had decided that playing on a championship team in a championship game was a good way to go out.

Budde had a choice. The two umpires did not.

———

Steve Hyder had made his choice on opening day of the PawSox season. He had decided not to make a snap decision even after he was passed over for the job as the No. 1 radio voice for the team during the winter. He had wondered even before that happened if he wanted to come back for 2012, after he'd had a heart attack in 2011, not too long after going through a second divorce.

He had walked onto the field before the team's opener at McCoy Stadium on April 5 and felt no buzz. A year earlier he had thought it was his health. Now he felt fine physically but empty emotionally.

"I waited to make a decision because I wanted to see if being healthy would make a difference," he said. "Maybe if I'd gotten the No. 1 job, it would have been different, but I didn't. That hurt. I thought I had earned it. They disagreed. I just decided on opening day this was going to be it. I'm fifty-one. There has to be something else out there for me."

Hyder worked hard throughout the season on his personal journal, hoping he would be able to make a book out of it after his last game. He already had a title: "The Real McCoy."

Now, with the last game of his career looming, Hyder had no intention of turning back, even though he had a good deal of trepidation about starting over.

"I love baseball, and I've loved the job and the relationships I've had," he said. "I wouldn't trade them for anything. But I don't think anyone can stay in the minor leagues full-time in any job for very long. It's too draining and, if you want to move up the way most of us do, too frustrating.

"I'm glad I'm going out as part of a winner. It was fun to see the team win the championship. It's amazing to think sixty-nine different guys wore the uniform during the season and only seven were still left the night they won. I'm happy my last game is going to be the last game of the season for everyone. Makes it a little bit easier to take.

"Even so, when I walk out of the ballpark tonight, I know I'm going to have a melancholy feeling. It would be impossible not to feel that way."

———

As it turned out, Randy Mobley's hopeful weather report was accurate. The rain began to clear at about six o'clock, and the game actually started on time. In spite of the weather, 8,606 fans showed up.

As part of the pregame ceremony, Scotty McCreery, the *American Idol* winner for 2011, who had grown up thirty-one miles from Durham in Garner, North Carolina, was scheduled to throw out the first pitch. Since the Aces were the home team, Brett Butler needed a volunteer to catch for McCreery.

Brett Tomko put his hand up right away.

"I remember I had caught a first pitch a few years earlier when I was in Kansas City from David Cook, the year he won *American Idol*," Tomko said. "I figured, 'What the heck,' it might be the only way I get to see the field. So I told Brett I'd do it."

He caught McCreery's pitch, and soon after, the Aces began teeing off on Nelson Figueroa's pitches. Figueroa had been the PawSox' ace down the stretch and throughout the International League play-offs, but this simply wasn't his night. He was gone after two innings with his team trailing 6–0. The irony was that Pawtucket had a better record (38-26) playing in Bulls Athletic Park than any other visiting team in the International League.

Not on this night. The lead grew to 8–0, and the game crawled along. By now, with the outcome not in any serious doubt, everyone pretty much wanted to go home. The evening had turned out quite pleasant—a cool sixty-nine degrees at game time with almost no wind—but as the sky darkened, clouds could be seen on the horizon, and it was apparent the window for playing baseball wasn't going to be open too much longer.

The rain was starting to come down by the time the PawSox came up in the ninth, trailing 10–3. Even with a seven-run lead, Butler sent Jonathan Albaladejo to pitch the ninth, in part because he thought he deserved to be on the mound for the last out—he had done so forty-two times during the season, twenty-five times in save situations— and in part because there was certainly no reason to rest him. His next outing wouldn't be until March.

Andy LaRoche led off the inning with an infield single. Bryce Brentz struck out. The rain came down harder. No one wanted the season to end in a rain delay. Dan Butler lined a double into the right-center-field gap, and LaRoche was running all the way—perhaps not the best idea with his team down seven. Center fielder A. J. Pollock ran the ball down in the wet outfield and hit shortstop Taylor Harbin with a perfect relay throw. Harbin turned and saw LaRoche rounding third. He fired the ball to Ryan Budde as LaRoche pounded toward the plate.

Because the ball had been hit in the gap, the umpires had rotated positions, with Loveless covering third in case Butler tried to go to third and there was a play there. Lollo came sprinting down from first to cover for Loveless at the plate. As a result it was his call as the ball and LaRoche arrived at almost the same time.

Lollo thought he saw Budde get the tag on LaRoche a split second before LaRoche hit the plate. Except his angle wasn't as good as it might have been if he hadn't had to come down from first base to cover the plate.

"I missed it," he said. "LaRoche said to me, 'He never tagged me,' and I realized too late he was right. If I'd been in a slightly different position, I think I would have seen it, but because I was coming from first, I didn't get the best possible angle. I felt sick about it when I realized too late that I'd missed the call.

"My last call ever—and I missed it."

Everyone agreed it was a tough call to make, especially coming from first, and that the play was hardly a game decider. Two batters later, Che-Hsuan Lin hit a line drive almost directly at left fielder Keon Broxton for the final out, and everyone sprinted for the clubhouses as the sky started to explode with rain. The game had taken three hours and twenty-nine minutes. The Triple-A baseball season ended at 10:37 p.m. as the rain swept through the ballpark.

An hour later, at an after-party thrown by the two leagues, Lollo encountered LaRoche and apologized to him.

LaRoche grinned and patted him on the shoulder. "If you'd called me safe, we'd probably be back at the ballpark right now in a rain delay," he said. "It's not as if we were going to score seven and tie the game. Don't give it another thought."

But Lollo did, even though others echoed LaRoche's sentiment.

"It's hard to get out of my mind," he said. "That was my last call as a professional umpire. It wasn't the way I wanted to go out."

He went out hustling to make a tough call. There's no shame in that. Whether it is your first call or your last call.

Epilogue

McLOUTH

On the night of October 7, almost three weeks after the minor-league season had ended, Nate McLouth jogged from the first-base dugout inside Oriole Park at Camden Yards in the direction of left field, hearing a loud roar as he and his teammates took the field for game one of the American League Division Series against the New York Yankees.

Oriole Park, which had been a mausoleum on many game nights during the previous five seasons, was packed with 47,841 fans, and almost all were on their feet as the Orioles took up their defensive positions.

It occurred to McLouth that he had come a long way from the afternoon in late May when he had sat in Pirates manager Clint Hurdle's office and had been offered a choice: go to the minors or be released.

He had chosen to be released. After a nervous week of waiting, he had gotten the call from the Orioles—who wanted to sign him and send him to Norfolk as potential outfield insurance after Nick Markakis, their starting right fielder, had broken his wrist the same day that the Pirates formally released McLouth.

McLouth had struggled early in Norfolk, but beginning with Cowboy Monkey Rodeo Night in late June, he had gotten hot in the sizzling southeastern Virginia summer weather. The Orioles had called him up on August 4 after he had gone on a power binge, hitting ten home runs and driving in thirty-three runs over a thirty-six-game stretch. They had decided that adding that sort of bat to the speed and defense he brought made him a better backup outfielder than the thirty-four-year-old veteran Endy Chávez.

"I felt that if I could get hot, then I might have a shot to get called up," McLouth said. "I wasn't counting on anything, because if you start thinking that way, you don't do what you have to do to get noticed. I managed to get hot at the right time, and next thing I knew, RJ [manager Ron Johnson] was calling me into the office to tell me I was going up. It was a big deal, especially after the way the spring had gone for me."

McLouth filled in when one of the outfielders needed a night off and, frequently, late in games for defense. That changed on September 8 when Markakis—yes, again—took a C. C. Sabathia pitch on the left hand in the fifth inning of a game against the Yankees in Camden Yards. The hand was broken, and Markakis, as it turned out, was done for the season. The Orioles decided to move Chris Davis, normally a first baseman or a DH, to right field and put McLouth in left field.

Soon after McLouth was moved into the starting lineup, manager Buck Showalter put him in the leadoff spot and he flourished. By season's end he had played in fifty-five games and hit .268 with seven home runs, eighteen RBIs, and twelve stolen bases.

He was in left field and leading off when the Orioles, after making the playoffs for the first time since 1997, met the Texas Rangers in the new one-game, win-or-go-home wild card game. McLouth walked to begin the game and scored the Orioles' first run. In the third, he grounded a single to right to drive in the Orioles' second run. And in the eighth he hit a sacrifice fly to right field to drive in their last run in a 5–1 win.

That win put the Orioles into the division series against the Yankees, and there was McLouth in left field for five straight nights—two in Baltimore and three in New York—in front of packed houses.

"It was a long way from sitting home in Knoxville in June," he said, laughing. "It was, to be honest, what I'd always dreamed of. When I was a productive player with the Pirates, I was on bad teams. Then I went to Atlanta and played on good teams, but I wasn't a productive player. Finally, I was able to put it altogether—be an important part of a good postseason baseball team. It was a great feeling—and it was everything I ever dreamed it might be.

"When I was younger, I'm not sure I would have appreciated it as much. But to get to play in that atmosphere, looking around the ballpark each night, after I'd wondered if I would ever play in the majors again, was an amazing feeling."

The Orioles lost the series in five games, but it wasn't because of McLouth. He hit .318 for the series, including a home run and three RBIs. While the loss was disappointing, McLouth, at thirty, had reestablished himself as a major leaguer.

His contract called for him to become a free agent in November—which he did. But the Orioles made it clear they wanted him back. In December, he signed a one-year contract for $2 million and went to spring training in February knowing he would be fighting for a starting spot in the outfield.

Which was all he could possibly ask for.

Montoyo

Four of the International League's fourteen managers made it to the big leagues at the conclusion of the 2012 season.

The least surprising promotion was Ryne Sandberg's move down the northeast corridor of the Pennsylvania Turnpike to Philadelphia, to become Charlie Manuel's bench coach with the Phillies. Manuel would be sixty-nine on opening day in 2013, and the general consensus was that he was likely to retire at the end of the season. Sandberg was clearly being groomed as his successor. That turned out to be true—but it happened before the 2013 season was over. With the Phillies struggling, Manuel was fired in August and Sandberg was hired to replace him.

The Cubs, who had opted not to hire Sandberg in 2012, went 61-101 under Dale Sveum. Sveum was brought back for 2013, but there was talk that if things didn't improve markedly, the Cubs would be looking for a new manager for 2014. Things didn't get a lot better in Chicago and Sveum was fired, but Sandberg was no longer an option—he already had a big-league managing job.

David Bell also returned to the majors—in Chicago, but not working for his dad on the South Side with the White Sox. Instead, he was hired by Sveum to be the Cubs' third-base coach. Logistically, the move was perfect for Bell, since the Cubs trained near his home in Arizona, meaning he wouldn't have to travel until the regular season started.

For Sandberg and Bell, given their playing careers and connections, moving up to the majors wasn't a big surprise. For Arnie Beyeler and Mike Sarbaugh—career minor leaguers as players and managers—their promotions were dream-come-true moments.

Beyeler had always wondered if his playing career, "the back of the bubble gum card," would keep him out of the majors. Apparently, his work on the field, leading Pawtucket to the Governors' Cup title in spite of all the turmoil going on in Boston, didn't go unnoticed. Shortly after John Farrell was named to replace Bobby Valentine as the Red Sox' manager, Beyeler was named to his staff as the first-base coach. After twenty-seven years of living the minor-league life, Beyeler would be staying in five-star hotels and riding on charter airplanes in 2013—and, in October, savoring a remarkable World Series win in Boston.

Mike Sarbaugh, also a minor-league lifer, got to live the major-league life too. Sarbaugh was considered a rising star in the managing world, so it wasn't a shock when Terry Francona asked him to join his new staff in Cleveland. Sarbaugh had moved steadily up the ladder in the Indians' organization, winning at each stop, so the move made sense.

One other manager left his job: after working for the Braves as their Triple-A manager for six seasons, Dave Brundage opted to accept Sandberg's job in Lehigh Valley, apparently deciding that playing in front of crowds of close to ten thousand each night was preferable to crowds of four thousand.

There was one other change, but it didn't involve a managing change. In fact, it involved changing an entire *team*. As often happens in the minor leagues, two franchises were swapped by their major-league teams. The New York Mets had feuded at different times with the locals who ran the Buffalo Bisons, and when the Toronto Blue Jays, looking to move their Triple-A affiliate closer to Toronto than Las Vegas, brought up the possibility of a swap, the Mets agreed.

And so, Wally Backman and all those who had worked for the Bisons in Buffalo—including Chris Schwinden—headed to Las Vegas (which, for the record, is *not* terribly close to New York, but this was the Mets, so logic wasn't terribly important), while those playing for Las Vegas—where Schwinden had pitched briefly in 2012—headed to Buffalo.

That would mean changes for everyone. The city of Buffalo would now have an American League affiliate in town with an entirely different roster of players and a new manager in Marty Brown. Those who had played in Las Vegas in the PCL a year earlier would be adapting to the International League, generally known more as a fastball league than a breaking-ball league. The opposite would be true for the former Bisons. "Definitely a different kind of pitching out there," Schwinden said. "The parks are different; I'm sure the umps are different. It will all be new—which isn't all bad."

The move of the Mets-Bisons out and the Blue Jays–Silver Stars in meant there would be six new managers in the IL for 2013, starting with Brown in Buffalo and Brundage in Lehigh Valley. The other four new faces would be Randy Ready, the former major-league infielder who left the Texas Rangers' organization to succeed Brundage in Gwinnett; Chris Tremie, who was promoted from Double-A Akron to take Sarbaugh's job in Columbus; Gary DiSarcina, an ex–Red Sox infielder who opted to leave a cushy front-office job in Anaheim to get back in uniform and ride the buses in Pawtucket; and Jim Riggleman, a former major-league manager in San Diego, Chicago, and Washington, who succeeded Bell in Louisville.

Riggleman had quit the Nationals abruptly during the 2011 season in a contract dispute and had gone all the way back to Double-A, managing the Pensacola Blue Wahoos in 2012. At the age of sixty he would be back in Triple-A. Players don't like to stop playing; managers don't like to stop managing.

The two longest-tenured managers in the league beginning 2013 were Dave Miley, who had been managing in Triple-A for the Yankees since 2006, and Charlie Montoyo, who had arrived in Durham a year later.

Miley would finally get off the road in 2013. Not only did his team have a newly renovated ballpark; it had a new name: the Scranton/Wilkes-Barre RailRiders, a name selected during an off-season name-the-team contest.

Montoyo had been through his worst season—in terms of wins and losses—as a Triple-A manager in 2012, but he came out of it feeling good about the experience.

"The losing wasn't any fun," he said. "We got buried early by that thirteen-game losing streak in April and never really had any chance to do more than try to get to .500. But when the season ended, I was pretty happy with how I dealt with it all. The pressures from the major-league club are always there, but this was even more than normal because of all the injuries they had.

"And I think I can honestly say that none of us [pitching coach Neil Allen and hitting coach Dave Myers] ever let up or complained about everything that was going on. That can happen to anyone at Triple-A, especially during a bad season, and it didn't happen to us. I was proud of that. I think we went out on September 3 with every bit as much enthusiasm as we did on April 5. We owe that to the players, regardless of whether they're the next superstar or someone just trying to squeeze one more year out of baseball."

That didn't mean Montoyo wasn't more than ready to go home and see his family after the final out on September 3.

The boys were both in school, and he was hoping that Alexander might somehow avoid a fourth round of open-heart surgery, which doctors had said was a possibility for the spring. It was the first time since he had arrived in Durham that there were no postseason games, so he was home a couple of weeks earlier than normal.

"It actually felt kind of funny to be home that soon," he said.

The Rays had never pressured him to join the team in September in past years because of his unique family situation. This time was a little different. One week after the season had ended—about the same time that previous seasons in Durham had ended or were about to end—Montoyo got a phone call from Mitch Lukevics, the Rays' farm director.

"The team's going to Baltimore and New York," he said. "We'd like you to go." He paused. "It would be good for you to be seen."

Montoyo understood. The Rays—with Evan Longoria back in the lineup—were making another late push for a playoff spot, and the six games in Baltimore and New York would be crucial. But that wasn't why Lukevics wanted Montoyo on the trip. He wanted Montoyo mixing with major leaguers—from the Rays and from other teams.

"I get it," Montoyo said. "He wants people to be aware of me. I knew he wasn't asking me to go because they needed another guy to throw BP or hit fungoes in pregame."

The trip didn't go terribly well for the Rays. They dropped five of six and, even though they ended up winning ninety games, came up short of the playoffs. Montoyo headed back to Arizona after the team's last game in New York and waited to see if his phone would ring during the off-season.

It didn't.

"Not a big deal," he said. "The minor leagues is what I know. To me the minor leagues *is* baseball. If that changes someday, great, I'd love the chance. I believe in my ability. But I'm not exactly old yet [forty-seven on opening day in 2013], so I feel if it's going to happen, there's still time."

The most disappointing news of the off-season was that the doctors felt that Alexander needed another round of surgery. It was scheduled for April 15, and Montoyo and the Rays made plans for him to be absent from the Bulls for as long as was needed.

"We've been through this enough times that we almost know just how to do it," he said. "I know that sounds strange, but it's true. We always schedule the surgery for a Monday because that means the surgeon will be in the hospital for at least the next four days after the surgery. In April, it means I can fly to Los Angeles [UCLA hospital] after a day game to meet the family.

"Last time I was prepared to be away for a month. After the fifth day, Alexander came home. I hope it goes as well this time."

Alexander would still be only five on the day of the surgery. "We hope this is the last one," Montoyo said. "The doctors say if this doesn't get it done, the next step is to consider a transplant." He paused for a long moment. "Obviously, we don't want that."

As always, Montoyo enjoyed spring training, the feeling of being around the major-league team and players and living the major-league life. In the back of his mind, though, he knew that opening day— April 4—wouldn't feel as much like a beginning as it normally did. It would be another day in the countdown to what he hoped and prayed would be his son's last surgery.

"He's done amazingly well considering everything he's been through," he said. "All I want for him is to be a normal, healthy little kid."

That, very clearly, was far more important than getting a job in the major leagues. Montoyo would sign up for Triple-A life forever in return for Alexander's good health.

The surgery was a success according to the doctors. After this, everyone just had to wait and see if the fourth time would be the charm. In September the Bulls won the Governors' Cup once again. Montoyo waited to see if his phone would finally ring.

LINDSEY AND SCHWINDEN

One of the off-season rituals for players is receiving a letter from the team they work for telling them when they are expected to report for spring training and, in some cases, *where* they are to report for spring training.

Those who have contracts guaranteeing them major-league pay know they will report to the major-league camp; they just don't know what day they are expected, because it changes from year to year.

In 2013, reporting dates were a little bit earlier than normal because the World Baseball Classic was going to interrupt spring training for some in March.

For others, the *where* is far more important than the *when*. Often, veterans sign minor-league contracts with a clause that guarantees they will be invited to major-league camp. Most teams will have anywhere from eight to fifteen "non-roster invitees" in their major-league camp. Scott Elarton and Scott Podsednik had both been non-roster invitees in the Phillies' camp in 2012.

Everyone else is at the mercy of the organization. "You hope they tell you to report to the major-league camp so you get a chance to show the major-league guys what you can do," John Lindsey said. "But if you don't, you just have to go and do the best you can."

Lindsey was pleased when the Tigers offered him a contract for 2013 shortly after the free-agent-signing period began. That told him he had made a good impression in Toledo and, clearly, Phil Nevin had said good things about him to the organization.

He wasn't shocked when the letter came in January telling him to report March 10 to the minor-league camp in Bradenton. It wasn't what he wanted, but it was what he had expected.

"Maybe I'll get some at-bats in exhibition games down there," he said. "But if I don't, I'll go back to Toledo and try to put up numbers like last year, and if they need someone, I'll be right there. It's not perfect, but it's a lot better than starting the season in Mexico."

While Lindsey wasn't surprised when his letter arrived, Chris Schwinden was. He had thought he had pitched well enough the last two months of the season in Buffalo to earn an invitation to the major-league camp. He'd been there in 2012 after finishing the season in New York and had hoped he would at least get a few weeks with the major leaguers. Like Lindsey, his hope was to make an impression.

He would have to do so from the minor-league camp. His report date was the first week of March, and it was to the Mets' minor-league camp in Port St. Lucie.

"To be honest, when I first opened the letter, I was pissed," he said. "It was a letdown. My thought had been if I got to the major-league camp—even if I didn't go north with the team—I could leave some good impressions with them that would put me high on the list to be called up when the season started. That's what happened in 2012—I was up before April was over.

"But I'm going to take the approach that I became a better pitcher last summer, especially with my changeup, and I have to keep working. I still haven't got the sinker where I want it, so maybe if I can get that going, I'll really be ready not just to make the majors but succeed in the majors. That's the goal now—to succeed up there."

Schwinden laughed. "After last year, I have to think this year is going to be calm and easy by comparison."

With the Mets moving their Triple-A team from Buffalo to Las Vegas, life in the minors would be different. "I liked Buffalo, felt very comfortable there," he said. "Never minded pitching in cold weather. The good thing about Vegas is that it's a lot closer to home and I should finally get to pitch in Fresno in front of all my friends and family. I never did make it there last year."

Schwinden, of course, had been scheduled to pitch in Fresno during his brief stint pitching in Las Vegas the previous June, but the Blue Jays had released him before that start. He had ended up making his next appearance in Columbus—as property of the Cleveland Indians.

Schwinden had two goals for 2013: make it back to the majors, and pitch well there and spend the entire season in one organization. Four organizations in thirty-five days was a little much.

TOMKO

Lindsey and Schwinden might have been a little disappointed when they received their letters telling them where and when to report, but chances were good that Brett Tomko would gladly have traded places with either one of them.

After the national championship game in Durham, Tomko flew home to San Diego and sat down to talk to his wife, Julia, about their future. Being part of a championship team had been enjoyable, and to some degree Tomko felt at peace with the idea that his career might be over.

For years, he had collected memorabilia from his baseball career. He had baseballs—thirty-eight of them—signed by every catcher he had ever thrown to in a major-league game. Some were from guys he had pitched to on more than one team. He had a signed bat from Rico Brogna—the first player ever to homer off him. And he had a signed bat from Mickey Morandini, the first player he had ever struck out.

"I'd always planned when my career was over to build a really nice case for the baseballs," he said. "When I got home in September, I told Julia I thought it was time I start building the case. I enjoyed the experience—I like doing things like that, and I'm pretty good at it. But as I was doing it, I almost had the sense that I was building my own baseball coffin. It unnerved me a little. Made me wonder if I really was ready to hang it up."

When the free-agency period began in November, Tomko started sending out e-mails and making some phone calls to people he knew in front offices. Most said the same thing: check back with us in the spring.

"I think they wanted to see who else they might be able to sign," he said. "Obviously, a forty-year-old pitcher was more of a back-burner, 'We'll call you if we need you' sort of guy."

There were nibbles as spring training drew closer. Colorado wanted to watch him throw at one point, and the Blue Jays did watch him throw. Still, as everyone was leaving for spring training, Tomko was at home, looking for work.

"This is the first time in nineteen years, other than when I was rehabbing from the shoulder surgery, I haven't been leaving for spring training right now," he said one afternoon in February. "It's an odd feeling. Most of my springs have been in Arizona, and I've just loaded up the car and driven there by myself to get ready. Now I'm sitting at home."

Home, but not necessarily home for good. Tomko was throwing regularly at a nearby high school and planned to face hitters in batting practice on a normal spring training schedule.

JOHN FEINSTEIN

"I'm acting as if I'm in a camp," he said. "I'm throwing side sessions as if I was getting my arm ready for exhibition season. I'm going to throw to live batters soon. That way if someone calls and says, 'Are you in shape to come right into camp?' my answer will be yes. Julia and I have talked, and she wants me to ride this through to the very end because she knows that's what I want to do.

"I'm not completely crazy. Every time I called a team this winter I said the same thing: 'Look, I want to play right now, but I know it won't be for much longer. Whenever I'm done, I'd like to coach or manage. If you're looking for a guy who has experienced *everything* from top to bottom in baseball, I'm you're guy. There probably isn't anything a player is going to come to me with that I haven't seen.'

" 'Hey, Brett, how do you deal with being unbelievably hot, throwing like you've never thrown before?' I can tell them I experienced a half season where I was as good as anyone in baseball. Then I can tell them that *same* season I was also the *worst* pitcher in baseball for a couple of months.

"I brought all that up just to get my line in the water down the road. Right now, though, I want to try to pitch one more time."

The plan was to wait for a call as spring training moved along. If no one called, Tomko had talked to independent league teams in York, Pennsylvania, and Camden, New Jersey, about pitching for one of them.

"Other guys have done it," he said. "I figure I have nothing to lose. It's going to be over soon one way or the other . . . why not go as far as I possibly can? Who knows, I could be one of those great comeback stories. It *does* happen."

And so, when April rolled around, he was off to York.

Stop No. 28.

LOLLO

For Mark Lollo, there was no chance to beat the odds. Umpiring was a zero-sum game: you were in or you were out.

For most of October, he heard nothing official from Major League

Baseball. He wondered—briefly—if perhaps Cris Jones had reconsidered or someone had stepped in and spoken up on his behalf.

"I never let myself think it for very long," he said. "I knew they had until November 1 to let me know one way or the other. I didn't want to be disappointed when the formal call came."

It finally came a couple of days before the deadline. Cris Jones and another supervisor called him together and thanked him for his years of service but told him he would not be renewed for 2013.

"I guess I'd have been shocked if it had been the other way around and they'd said I was coming back," Lollo said. "What bothered me, though, was the corporate-speak. I thought after twelve years I deserved more than something that felt like I was being read an HR letter from some company. I know baseball's a big business, but it still left me feeling pretty empty and sad."

Lollo was already looking for work outside baseball even before the formal call came. But he found himself stewing about the call, because there was one question he wanted answered and nothing in what Jones had said had answered that question for him. Finally, about a week after the phone call, he sent Jones an e-mail.

There was no anger in it, just a question: "Cris, I need to know the answer to this question: Can I go to my grave knowing I did absolutely everything possible to become a major-league umpire?"

Jones replied: "If you want to give me a call, I'd be happy to discuss."

"It occurred to me right then and there I didn't want to talk to him about it. I just knew whatever the answer was, I wasn't going to get what I needed—even if he said I'd done everything, I wasn't going to feel like I'd gotten a completely straight answer.

"So I decided to call Larry Young. He had been the supervisor who first brought me up to the majors in 2011, and I thought he'd tell me the truth—no matter what the truth happened to be. He called me right back, and I told him I had one question I needed answered. When I asked him, his answer was very direct: 'Don't even think about it ever again. You did everything you could. Timing is everything in life. You just didn't get lucky with timing.'

"That was the closure I needed. It doesn't mean it doesn't hurt and that I'm not still grieving over it to some extent. But I felt as if I had some closure after that."

Lollo began to interview extensively after the call. He was offered a job as a money manager after going through a lengthy interview process but decided at the last possible second he didn't want it. Everywhere he interviewed he did well.

"Five interviews, five offers," he said. "But I was holding back. I just wasn't ready."

Finally, in February, he was offered a job by a company called Uni-First, a uniform supply company. The office was forty-seven miles from his home in a suburb of Columbus, but the company told him he would be able to work from home a couple of days a week. Lollo accepted.

"I still haven't decided if I want to try to officiate again some-place," he said. "I've thought about applying to do Big Ten baseball or even to do high school football. I think I might enjoy that.

"The whole thing's a process for me. Right now, all my friends are leaving for spring training. A year ago I was in major-league spring training thinking I wasn't that far from being a big-league umpire. Now I'm driving to an office every day.

"It's better for my family; I know that. But I can't honestly say I'm completely over it."

There's an old saying: great athletes die twice.

Umpires too.

ELARTON

It took Scott Elarton a solid month to stop feeling sore, once he had made the two-day drive from Allentown to Lamar in early September. The hamstring that had caused him to miss a start in August still hurt, but beyond that he just felt, well, thirty-six.

"It had been a while since I'd gone through an entire baseball season, much less an entire season healthy," he said. "My last full season of pitching was 2007. Five years is a long break even if you're young—which, in baseball years, I'm not. So it took me a while. But gradually I began to feel better, and there was no doubt in my mind that I wanted to try to pitch again. I'd enjoyed myself too much to just walk away."

The question, like with Tomko, was whether he could find someone who would give him the chance. He spoke with Phillies general manager Rubén Amaro, who had been responsible for the chance he'd gotten in 2012, and Amaro was honest with him: "He said, 'Right now we haven't got anything for you,'" Elarton said. "They have some younger pitchers they feel are getting close, and a thirty-seven-year-old didn't exactly fit into that plan. He told me that could change as they got closer to spring, but I knew I'd better start looking around."

Elarton picked ten teams who he thought might be looking for insurance in the form of an experienced starting pitcher. If he knew someone with a team, he sent him an e-mail. Otherwise he just sent a note to the farm director. He figured that was the logical starting point.

Like Tomko, Elarton wrote his own notes and e-mails rather than relying on an agent to do it. If there was a deal to be made, then he would involve an agent. "At some point in your career, you can't ask your agent to do that kind of digging for you," he said. "Plus, I think it's harder to say no directly to a player than to his agent." He paused. "Of course it's not *that* hard.

"I got nine noes," he continued. "Just polite responses saying they weren't looking to sign anyone—as in me—at that time."

The tenth response came from Brad Steil, newly named as the Minnesota Twins' farm director. He said that he and general manager Terry Ryan would have interest in signing Elarton to a minor-league contract.

"I jumped at it," Elarton said. "It was a chance to pitch. I still believe I wasn't that far away from being major-league ready the first couple of months of last season, and with that year under my belt and another good off-season I can get back to the majors. I don't think I'd go back if they told me Triple-A was the ceiling. I need that competitive carrot, the belief I can pull something off people don't think I can pull off. I mean, think about it, how often do guys go five years between trips to the big leagues?"

The Twins' offer gave him hope, a chance at least to pull off the unlikely. His family was 100 percent for it. "As soon as I told them there was a team that wanted to sign me, everyone's reaction was, 'When do we leave for spring training?'" he said, laughing. "They were ready to jump in the car that day and go."

Elarton wasn't at all surprised when his reporting letter arrived telling him he was expected in the minor-league camp in Fort Myers, Florida, on March 7. Even the thought of an overcrowded minor-league spring training clubhouse didn't bother him.

"Last year it was a shock to my system because I'd been in the major-league camp for a month," he said. "I'd gotten spoiled living in the lap of that kind of luxury, so it was tough walking in there. This year, I'll be there from day one, so I don't think it will bother me.

"In fact I'm looking forward to it."

And so it was that on March 1, the Elarton family loaded up the car to make the cross-country trip to Florida. They had several days before Scott had to report, so they took their time, stopping often during the 1,794-mile journey. Their ultimate destination wasn't so much Fort Myers as it was Baseball World.

"I know I'm going to walk into the clubhouse and there will be a locker with my name on it and a uniform," Elarton said just before heading south and east once again. "I'm still a baseball player. Honestly, I can't think of anything much better than that."

In a very real sense, he spoke for everyone in the game: major leaguer, minor leaguer, independent leaguer. Player, manager, coach, scout, umpire, broadcaster, writer, or fan.

They all have one thing in common: they love the game.

Before they take off their uniforms for the final time, they find out a truth that was eloquently captured in the words of longtime pitcher Jim Bouton in the closing words of his seminal book, *Ball Four.*

"You see," Bouton wrote, "you spend a good piece of your life gripping a baseball and in the end it turns out that it was the other way around all the time."

Truer words were never written.

ACKNOWLEDGMENTS

The best thing about doing a book on life in Triple-A baseball is that your job every day is to go to a ballpark.

The second best thing is that when you walk into a clubhouse, people don't instantly look at you with narrowed "What are you doing here?" eyes, as often happens in the major leagues. For a reporter, being sent to the minors isn't all bad. In fact, it can be great fun. At least it was for me.

Almost without exception, the people I encountered during the 2012 season, beginning in spring training right through the Triple-A national championship game in September, were receptive and patient. When I had to go back for second or third interviews—or even postseason interviews—they were more than willing to sit and talk. Not one player complained about being asked to talk about life as a minor leaguer, even those who had spent a lot of time as major leaguers.

And so, as is always the case, I have a long list of people to thank. First, the fourteen managers in the International League: Arnie Beyeler, Joel Skinner, Dave Miley, Dean Treanor, Ryne Sandberg, Wally Backman, Gene Glynn, Tony Beasley, Ron Johnson, Dave Brundage, David Bell, Phil Nevin, and Mike Sarbaugh. Special thanks to Charlie Montoyo, who was one of my Triple-A tour guides beginning in February.

Thanks also to Randy Mobley and Chris Sprague in the IL office, who were both available for every ridiculous question I posed all season long. Thanks also to Mike Rizzo and major-league managers Tony La Russa, Buck Showalter, Joe Maddon, and Davey Johnson, who took time to talk to me about their minor-league experiences and some of their minor leaguers.

As you'll quickly figure out while reading this book, I spoke to a long list of people but chose a core group of nine to make the central focus of the book. Those nine were Charlie Montoyo, Ron Johnson, Scott Podsednik, Chris Schwinden, Nate McLouth, Brett Tomko, Scott Elarton, John Lindsey, and Mark Lollo. I thank them especially not only for dealing with me during the lengthy interviews I did with them at the outset, but for handling subsequent requests and phone calls with both patience and humor.

There were many, many others I spent time with. They include the great Dave Rosenfield and his general manager, Joe; radio play-by-play men Matt Swierad and Steve Hyder; Scott Strickland, the grounds crew/weather guru of Durham; and the following players in absolutely no order at all: Buddy Carlyle, J. C. Boscan, Evan Longoria, Sam Fuld, Brooks Conrad, Craig Albernaz, Pete Orr, Pat Misch, Tug Hulett, Chris Giménez, Steve Vogt, Jesús Feliciano, Rich Thompson, Chris Dickerson, John Maine, Doug Bernier, Corey Miller, Nick Evans, Danny Worth, Jeff Larish, Danny Dorn, Adam Loewen, Frank Herrmann, Dontrelle Willis, John Lannan, Zach Duke, Dan Johnson, Bryce Harper, and Conor Jackson.

On the publishing side I want to thank my new editors at Doubleday, Jason Kaufman and Bill Thomas, who have treated me like gold since our first meeting. Thanks also to Jason's assistant, Rob Bloom. I hope this will be our first of many projects together. As always, I couldn't possibly get a book done without my agent, Esther Newberg, who should love this book since a Red Sox farm team ended up as champions of the International League. Thanks also to her remarkably efficient assistant Zoe Sandler, and to Liz Farrell for putting up with me on the audio side. Thanks also at ICM to Kari Stuart, Lyle Morgan, and my legal protector John Delaney.

And, of course, friends and colleagues: Keith and Barbie Drum; Jackson Diehl and Jean Halperin; Ed and Lois Brennan; Rick Brewer; David and Linda Maraniss; Lexie Verdon and Steve Barr; Jill and Holland Mickle; Terry and Patti Hanson; Doug and Beth Doughty; Bob and Anne DeStefano; Bud Collins; Wes Seeley; Andy Dolich; Pete Alfano; David Teel; Stan Kasten; John Dever; Gary Cohen; Beth Shumway-Brown; Beth Sherry-Downes; Pete Van Poppel; Omar Nelson; Fran DaVinney; Billy Stone; Mike Werteen; Chris Knoche; Phil Hoffmann; Joe Speed; Jack Hecker; Gordon Austin; Eddie Tapscott; Steve "Moose" Stirling; Tiffany Cantelupe; Anthony and Kristen Noto; Pete Teeley; Bob Zurfluh; Vivian Thompson; Phil Hochberg; Al Hunt; Wayne Zell; Mike and David Sanders; Eddie Evans; Bob Whitmore; Tony and Karril Kornheiser; Mark Maske; Ken and Nancy Denlinger; Governor Harry Hughes; General Steve Sachs and Tim (no title) Maloney; Matt Rennie; Matt Vita; Matt Bonesteel (you cannot be an editor in the sports department at the *Washington Post* unless your name is Matt); Kathy Orton; Camille Powell; Chris Ryan; Harry Kantarian; Jim Rome; Travis Rodgers; Jason Stewart; Mike Purkey; Bob Edwards; Tom and Mary Jane Goldman; Mike Gastineau; Dick and Joanie (Hoops) Weiss; Jim O'Connell; Bob and Elaine Ryan; Frank Hannigan; Geoff Russell; Jerry Tarde; Mike O'Malley; Jaime Diaz; Larry Dorman; Jeff D'Alessio; Marsha Edwards; Jay and Natalie Edwards; Len and Gwyn Edwards-Dieterle; Chris Edwards and John Cutcher and, of course, Aunt Joan; Bill Leahey; Andy North; John Cook; Paul Goydos; Steve Bisciotti; Pam Lund; Kevin Byrne; Dick Cass; Mike Muehr; Martha Brendle; Joe Durant; Gary "Grits" Crandall; Drew Miceli; Bob Low; Steve Flesch; Brian Henninger; and Tom and Hilary Watson. Thanks again to Jake Pleet for the miracle we all witnessed on June 4 of 2012.

Thanks also to the folks who in the last couple of years have made me believe you can enjoy working on TV. At the Golf Channel: Tom Stathakes; Molly Solomon; Courtney Holt; Joe Riley; Dave Taylor; Kristi Setaro; Matt Hegarty; Eric Rutledge; David Gross; Ben Elisha; Alan Robison; Jon Steele; Brandon Ratay; Frank Nobilo; Brandel Chamblee; Rich Lerner; Whit Watson; Tim Rosaforte; Gary

Williams; Kelly Tilghman; Todd Lewis, and Kraig Kann—who is now with the LPGA. At Comcast: Joe Yasharoff, Rebecca Schulte; Frank Crisafulli; Larry Duvall; Chick Hernandez; Jill Sorenson; Julie Donaldson; Brian Mitchell; Tim McDonough; and Kim Foley, who attempts to achieve the impossible every week.

And my new colleagues and friends at CBS Sports Radio: Andrew Bogusch (Ranger boy); Max Herman; Peter Bellotti; Eric (the intern) Spitz; Chris Oliverio; Dan Mason, and Kaitlyn Richard. Thanks also to Steve Cohen, Steve Torre, Chris Russo, Bruce Murray, and Tom Kress, who took me in for eight months at SiriusXM.

Also, the usual suspects in different sports: At the USGA: David Fay (ex-exec director); Mike Davis; Mike Butz; Mary Lopuszynski; Pete Kowalski; Suzanne Colson; Amy Watters; and Craig Smith (still). Frank and Jaymie Bussey are unique and extraordinary. At the PGA Tour: Marty Caffey; Henry Hughes (sigh, still); Sid Wilson (same); Joe Schuchmann; Todd Budnik; Dave Senko; Doug Milne; Chris Reimer; Colin Murray; John Bush; Laura Hill; James Cramer; Joe Chemyz; and Phil Stambaugh. Special mention to Dave Lancer and Ward Clayton and, as always, to Denise Taylor and Guy Sheipers. At the PGA of America: Joe Steranka (emeritus); Julius Mason; and Bob Denney.

The rules guys—of course: Mark Russell (and my favorite Republicans, Laura and Alex Russell, without *ever* bringing up the election results); Jon Brendle, Steve Rintoul, Slugger White (to whom I *will* bring up the election results); Robbie Ware and Mike Shea. Special thanks to John Paramour, who always keeps me sober. (Sort of).

Basketball people: David Stern; Tim Frank; Brian McIntyre; Rick Barnes; Mike Brey; Jeff Jones; Lefty and Joyce Driesell; Seth and Brad Greenberg; Fran Dunphy; Jim Calhoun; Jim Boeheim; Brad Stevens; Shaka Smart; Billy Donovan; Larry Shyatt; Tom Brennan; Tommy Amaker; Dave and Lynne Odom; Jim Larranaga; Mack McCarthy; Pat Flannery; Ralph Willard; Jim Crews; Zach Spiker; Emmett Davis; Billy Lange; Fran O'Hanlon (still the last coach standing). Frank Sullivan was the best, is the best, and always will be the best.

I wish I didn't know so many doctors but glad I know the ones that I do: Eddie McDevitt; Dean Taylor (saved only by Ann); Bob Arciero and Gus Mazzocca, not to mention Tim Kelly; Steve Boyce; and Joe Vassallo.

The Damon Runyon of hoops—Howard Garfinkel; and the only honest man in the gym (now and always), Tom Konchalski.

The swimming knuckleheads with whom I hope to swim again someday soon: Jason Crist; Jeff Roddin; Mark Pugliese; Clay F. Britt; Wally (no one *has* a Wally) Dicks; Paul Doremus; Danny Pick; Erik Osborne; John Craig; Doug Chestnut; Peter Ward; Penny Bates; Carole Kammel; Mary Dowling; Margot Pettijohn; Tom Denes; A. J. Block; Pete Lawler; and (three-timer) Mike Fell.

The China Doll/Shanghai Village gang lives on, even though I am an infrequent visitor: Aubre Jones; Jack Kvancz; Chris Wallace; Arnie ("the Stud Horse") Heft; Stanley Copeland; Reid Collins; Harry Huang; George Solomon; Geoff Kaplan; Jeff Gemunder; and Murray Lieberman. Pete Dowling, Bob Campbell, Joe McKeown, Morgan Wootten; and Ric McPherson will always be members, even in absentia. Zang, Hymie, and, of course, Red remain absent friends always remembered fondly.

The Rio Gang continues to brawl constantly over politics and the quality of basketball being played at the alma mater: Tate Armstrong, Mark Alarie, Clay Buckley, and Terry Chili. For the record: they're right, I'm left, and they're wrong.

The Feinstein Advisory Board: Drummer Frank Mastrandrea, Wes Seeley, and Dave Kindred. I still hear Bill Brill's voice in my head every day.

Last, never least, my family: Bobby, Jennifer, Matthew, and Brian; Margaret, David, Ethan, and Ben. Marlynn, Cheryl, and Marcia. And, of course, Christine, who somehow puts up with me (I honestly don't know how); Danny, Brigid, and the world's smartest, prettiest, cutest toddler, Jane Blythe Feinstein.

INDEX